The Passionate Mind

by the same author

Concepts of Normality
The Autistic and Typical Spectrum
Wendy Lawson
Foreword by Lucy Clark
ISBN 978 1 84310 604 3

Life & Learning with Autistic Spectrum Diffability (DVD)
ISBN 978 1 84310 956 3

Understanding and Working with the Spectrum of Autism
An Insider's View
Wendy Lawson
ISBN 978 1 85302 971 4

Life Behind Glass
A Personal Account of Autism Spectrum Disorder
Foreword by Patricia Howlin
ISBN 978 1 85302 911 0

Build Your Own Life
A Self-Help Guide for Individuals with Asperger Syndrome
ISBN 978 1 84310 114 7

ASPoetry
Illustrated poems from an Aspie Life
Illustrated by Alice Blaes Calder
ISBN 978 1 84310 418 6

The Passionate Mind

HOW PEOPLE WITH AUTISM LEARN

WENDY LAWSON

Foreword by Rita Jordan

Illustrated by Lisa Simone

Jessica Kingsley *Publishers*
London and Philadelphia

First published in 2011
by Jessica Kingsley Publishers
116 Pentonville Road
London N1 9JB, UK
and
400 Market Street, Suite 400
Philadelphia, PA 19106, USA

www.jkp.com

Library of Congress Cataloging in Publication Data

Lawson, Wendy, 1952-
  The passionate mind : how people with autism learn / Wendy
Lawson ; foreword by Rita Jordan ; illustrated by Lisa Simone.
    p. ; cm.
  Includes bibliographical references and index.
  ISBN 978-1-84905-121-7 (alk. paper)
  1. Autism. 2. Cognitive styles. I. Title.
  [DNLM: 1. Autistic Disorder. 2. Attention. 3. Cognition.
  4. Learning. WM 203.5 L425p 2010]
  RC553.A88L3915 2010
  616.85'882--dc22
                              2010010040

British Library Cataloguing in Publication Data

A CIP catalogue record for this book is available from the British Library

ISBN 978 1 84905 121 7

Printed and bound in Great Britain by
MPG Books Group

Contents

ACKNOWLEDGEMENTS   9

FOREWORD *By Rita Jordan*   11

1.   Introduction   15
     The reasons for writing this book   16
          The power of words   17
          Brain configuration   17
     What to expect in the book   18
          The role of attention and interest   20

2.   The Autism Spectrum: Where We Are Now   29
     Introduction   29
     So what does the autism spectrum look like?   29
          Gender   34
          Autism spectrum strengths   34
          Learning style   35
     Sensory differences   36
     Summary   38

3.   Cognitive Theories of the Autism Spectrum   39
     Introduction   39
     Cognition and cognitive theory   39
     Considering theory in the autism spectrum   40
     Attention and interest   42
     Summary   43

4.   Cognitive Theory: Theory of Mind   44
     Introduction   44
          Definition   44
          Foundations for theory of mind   45
          Components of theory of mind   46
     Application to child development   48
          Development of theory of mind   50
          Difficulties with a rigid view of theory of mind development   52

The most noted test for theory of mind   55
Theory of mind research over time   56
Questions concerning theory of mind   57
Other potential questions   61
Summary   64

5.   Cognitive Theory: Executive Functioning   65
Introduction   65
Definition   65
Foundations for executive functioning theory   66
Components of executive functioning theory   67
Application to child development   68
Research over time   70
Executive functioning and theory of mind   71
Questions concerning executive functioning and the autism spectrum   71
Other questions and limitations   74
Summary   75

6.   Cognitive Theory: Weak Central Coherence   77
Introduction   77
Definition   77
Foundations for weak central coherence theory   78
Components of weak central coherence theory   81
Application in the neurotypical and autism spectrum populations   83
Research over time   84
Limitations of weak central coherence theory   85
Summary   90

7.   Cognitive Theory: Enhanced Perceptual Functioning   91
Introduction   91
Definition   91
Foundations for enhanced perceptual functioning theory   92
Components of enhanced perceptual functioning theory   94
Application in the neurotypical and autism spectrum populations   96
Research over time   96
Comparison with other cognitive theories   97
Limitations of enhanced perceptual functioning theory   98
Summary   98

8.   An Alternative Cognitive Theory: Single Attention
        and Associated Cognition in Autism   100
        Introduction   100
          Definitions   101
        Monotropism as a foundation for SAACA   101
          Attention   104
          Attention and brain configuration   107
          Monotropism and the sensory system   110
          Monotropism and interest   112
          Attention, motivation and interest   114
          Triad of impairments or product of SAACA?   116
          Processing style   117
          Monotropism and learning styles   119
          Complex cognitive skills coupled with interest and attention   120
        The cognitive components of SAACA   123
          Monotropism and literality   123
          Monotropism and thinking in closed concepts   125
          Monotropism: context and scale   128
          Monotropism: timing, sequencing and predicting   129
          Monotropism and non-social priorities   131
        Summary   132 •

9.   The Relevance of SAACA   133
        Introduction   133
        Everyday experiences for autism spectrum individuals   134
          When things change   135
          The concept of time   136
        SAACA's explanation of why autism spectrum and neurotypical
        perceptions are different   137
          Case studies   139
        Autism spectrum comprehension   148
          Problems with autism spectrum comprehension (if using a
          neurotypical lens)   150
          What might it mean when an expectation is not fulfilled?   152
          Problem-solving ideas using SAACA   153
        Tom's story – An extended case study   155
          Why does Tom have his difficulties?   160
          Can we help Tom cope with change?   160
          When and how do we execute an intervention for Tom?   160
          What about generalising Tom's learning?   161
          Reasoning behind using IT, visuals and structure   161
        Neurotypical parenting   162
        Summary   164

10. Looking to the Future   165
    Introduction   165
    A different learning style   165
        Completing tasks   167
        Normality   168
        It's in everyone's interest   171
    Experiments to refute or support SAACA   172
    Limitations of SAACA   174

LIST OF PUBLICATIONS   175

REFERENCES   177

APPENDIX A: A MODEL OF MIND PRESENTED AS A DYNAMICAL
    SYSTEM OF INTERESTS COMPETING FOR ATTENTION   197

APPENDIX B: PARAPHRASE OF CRITERIA FOR AUTISM SPECTRUM
    DISORDER   201

APPENDIX C: NON-COGNITIVE THEORIES OF AUTISM   204

APPENDIX D: PAINTINGS BY AN AUTISM SPECTRUM ADULT   213

APPENDIX E: SUMMARY OF COMMUNICATION 'OBSTACLES'   215

SUBJECT INDEX   217

AUTHOR INDEX   222

List of Figures

Figure 4.1 The development of theory of mind according to Baron-
    Cohen (1997), as adapted by Stagnitti (2004)   51
Figure 6.1 An alternative explanation to weak central coherence   88
Figure 8.1 Monotropic attention in autistic spectrum (AS) individuals
    and polytropic attention in neurologically typical (NT) individuals   105
Figure 8.2 Expected neurotypical development: Multiple connections
    between senses and interest states. Resulting from the ability to
    divide attention allowing for multi-tasking and social connectivity   121
Figure 8.3 Single Attention and Associated Cognition in Autism (SAACA) 122

Acknowledgements

The following text would not have been possible without the ongoing support of my partner Beatrice, whose encouragement and commitment to my best is unwavering. This text is brilliantly illustrated by my new friend and autie artist Lisa. Lisa, you bring to life so many of the issues and points in this text and this work is much the richer for your contribution, thank you!

To Professor Rita Jordan, who was with me in the very beginning of my journey as I sought to be one more voice in the crowd of autistic individuals speaking out against injustice and trying to earn the right to be heard, Rita, you are one of my heroes and someone whose life is making a difference, thank you.

To all my friends, but in particular to David Heyne, Judy Mason, Mary-Anne Fahey, Morris Gleitzman, Jamie Mcfaduen, Lucy Clark, Vicki Bitsika, Janet Pett, Glenys Jones, Elaine Hack and John Brown, huge thanks for your proof reading, support and ongoing encouragement to keep on keeping on. To my PhD supervisors, Dr David Hamilton and Associate Professor Karen Stagnitti, your belief in me and my work initially gave me the energy to keep going.

To Dr Dinah Murray, whose work provided a platform for my own and whose valued friendship, constant support and encouragement mean so much, thank you, Dinah.

To all the researchers and professionals whose interest in the topic of autism has allowed the development of this text, thank you; without your work and focus upon the need for understanding and intervention in autism there would be no arguments.

I wish to acknowledge all the individuals and families living with autism whose courage and commitment to getting through each day in a world that so often does not appreciate or tolerate 'difference', is remarkable. Positive attitudes towards autism and the belief in the right to exist as oneself is at the very heart of this work. We are each travellers in the journey of life. Having support and understanding along the way can make a positive difference to that journey, not only allowing the journey to impact us, but also giving back the opportunity for us to positively impact upon it too. This work is especially dedicated to Mr Don, 1957–2009.

Foreword

I am pleased and honoured to be asked to write a preface for this fascinating book by Wendy Lawson. Wendy first came to see me when she was attending a university in England as part of an exchange programme. I recognized that she was autistic (to keep to her preferred mode of description) by her manner, gait, posture, speech delivery, and so on; however, I was not aware of the effort it must have taken her to visit me and the determination and persistence needed to make the journey. I hope I am now more sensitive to at least some of the things that Wendy finds difficult but I am even more aware of her courage and determination through which she achieves so much, exemplified by her doctorate and writing this book. Wendy personifies the view of another of my autistic friends (Ros Blackburn) that in autism one must recognise and accept the differences (even difficulties) but not let them be an excuse for not trying and that success is often (if not always) possible, given an approach adapted to the individual. It is hardly ever true to say that people with autism *can't* do something, but rather that they may only be able to do it if the task is presented in a way they can access, or they may need some support to achieve.

This book is an indictment of the deficit model of autism that seeks to characterise a list of deficits in autism contrasted with the corresponding abilities of typical development. It does not deny difference and even admits that those differences may compromise functioning and development in typical situations in life. Yet, as Wendy points out, what is typical is not necessarily advantageous across cultures, and across time, for all people. Wendy points to the success most autistic people have operating in cyberworlds with technology-assisted modes of learning; computer environments seem to be a natural learning environment for those on the autism spectrum. The world is moving into an era where inability to engage in socially and linguistically mediated learning environments (which have been the norm to date) will no longer be such a barrier to education and it is my generation who are disadvantaged through their slow, painful access to technologically aided environments that now seem almost intuitive to the young. People on the autism spectrum fit more naturally into that IT environment and their differences from their equally technologically aided peers no longer appear salient or even of great importance. It is not that social interaction will no longer be important but that the forms of social interaction may become more 'monotropic' (to use a term explored in this book) and thus more accessible to all. I find it hard to adjust to the notion of a 'friend' as defined by Facebook, but perhaps I am bemoaning the loss of dominance of my social understanding of the world; listening to my technophile grandchildren, I recognise that I am now 'quaint' and am becoming 'untypical' (if not yet 'abnormal') in my interactions.

The critique of the dominant cognitive theories in autism in this book is well constructed and supported. The rationale for a new theory based on attention differences (in turn, related to structural brain differences) is also well thought out and logical, if not yet supported by empirical data. Wendy is at an advantage in being able to use introspection to assess the theory, and her insights form an important part of the book. However, she suggests more empirical ways of testing the theory and certainly gives sufficient bases for making such tests.

I would have liked to see a critique of social explanations for autism or at least to see how this new theory fits into such 'explanations'. Even cognitive theorists have recognised the crucial role that social facilitation plays in the young child's development of understanding of self, other and the wider world, whose meaning is largely socially negotiated with others. The SAACA theory opens up an old question of whether the differences in autistic development arise from a fundamental difference in responsiveness to social stimuli or whether (as one would assume from SAACA) social stimuli are affected simply because of their cognitive complexity (or in terms of SAACA, their requirement for polytropic processing).

I would also like to know how the theory relates to the different degrees and kinds of social responsiveness found in autism. It is a long time since Wing and Gould postulated different kinds and degrees of social engagement in autism (separate from universal autistic difficulties in social understanding), which might be characterised as different degrees of social interest. My experience is that these interest differences lead to different styles of engagement in autism and should lead to different kinds of teaching. But that too is an empirical issue that needs testing.

Finally, I should congratulate the author and the artist for making this book so accessible. It deals with complex, difficult issues but in a very engaging way. The illustrations aid understanding and are not just amusing 'extras'. The personal examples bring it to life and provide us theorists with a yardstick against which to judge the theories. It even manages to offer practical advice, in the midst of all this theoretical discussion. Such an eclectic book is hard to pigeonhole but, like the plea for the way we should treat people with autism, perhaps we do not need to do this at all.

Rita Jordan
Former Professor at Birmingham University

CHAPTER 1

Introduction

Emotion, either on or off!

THE REASONS FOR WRITING THIS BOOK

For the reasons outlined below this book could be the most important read you will ever encounter concerning the autism spectrum (AS). Certain difficulties, especially associated with the processing of language, social demand and societal expectation, are happening every day in my life and in the lives of others living with AS. This book, unlike any other, has been written to explain the enigma that is autism and to suggest ways of working positively with us to promote a future we all hope for.

With the above in mind, first I question traditional theories of autism, their implications, gaps and lacks; second I outline a newly developed theory – single attention and associated cognition in autism (SAACA) – with its implications and ways to address gaps in other approaches; and third, from the perspective of the new approach, I explore practical outcomes for individuals, families, places of education and employment.

As background to this book, and to my original PhD thesis, Murray's (1986) work on language and the interest system with its relationship to 'attention' forms the platform for the extension and consequential development of the newly developed theory of SAACA (outlined in Chapter 8). Murray (1992) introduced the idea of monotropic and polytropic attention and their connection to autism and the interest system. Murray, Lesser and Lawson (2005) refined this idea and associated monotropic tendency with only 'having a few interests highly aroused' (p.140), whereas a polytropic tendency was described as having 'many interests less highly aroused'.

Within the context above 'interests' refers to a system of connected awareness that presents quite differently, according to whether you are on the neurologically typical spectrum (sometimes referred to as 'NT' or 'normal') or whether you are on the autistic spectrum (AS). Typical interests, in this context, are a product of alignment of one's own interests with the interests of others, most often connected to presentation of self.

This system of typical interests will form a belief about social norms and society in general. For example, in social conversation when an NT person is asked 'How are you today?' (e.g. by the teller in the bank), one might answer 'Fine thank you', even if one was not feeling fine. Whereas, for those of us in the AS population, some might answer with a long, detailed monologue about their health or their special interest, or they might ignore the person asking the question because they cannot process an answer fast enough.

So you see, we experience social interaction quite differently because our interest systems are configured differently. This concept is explored in more detail later in this book.

The power of words

I believe words are very powerful and build into images that can either have a positive or a negative impact. Being diagnosed with an autism spectrum *disorder* doesn't inspire confidence in either the individual themselves or others around them. This is one reason why I prefer the term autism spectrum *diff-ability* to autism spectrum disorder. The other reason I prefer diff-ability is because I believe those of us on the autism spectrum learn differently, suggesting we are individuals who are differently abled to someone else more neurally typical (NT). Therefore, the term diff-ability sends a much less negative message than the word 'disorder', is much more accurate in its description of who I am and may mean I get a better shot at life because others are less defensive around me.

However, being differently abled poses problems in a typical world that does not allow for diff-ability. AS individuals miss lots of the usual bits of information that lead to good social understanding so we live with misunderstanding.

This book is the product of several years of thinking and study concerning these issues and, as such, it seeks to set out the reasons why AS exists, what it is and why it's an important part of being human.

Brain configuration

The most important discovery I have made is that attention and its partner, interest, operate differently according to the type of brain one has. By 'type' of brain I mean whether you are AS or NT. Murray's work on monotropism (tightly focused interest) and polytropism (diffused interests) (Murray 1986, 1992, 1995, 1996) is foundational to this thinking.

How one thinks and understands the world is very different, therefore, according to how one's brain is configured. Although difference and disability are not the same thing, they often are received by the population as 'not normal'. With this in mind I attempt to explain and explore the typical interests that help create the current understanding of either NT or autistic learning styles. Exploring this in some detail, I hope to connect readers to a broader concept of the term 'normal' and add to the wider range of human experience. For AS individuals, understanding typical descriptions of normal can be a huge task. For the typical population, the perception of the term *normal* can lead to unrealistic expectations of self and of others (Cigman 2007; Lawson 2008).

WHAT TO EXPECT IN THE BOOK

The information for this book is taken from my formal PhD thesis, but to make this book a less academic and more practically accessible read I have removed a number of references and all the associated tables that originally displayed the levels of evidence for my arguments. The full original thesis can be found on my web page: www.mugsy.org/wendy. Also, unlike the original work, I refer to myself and my own experiences as well as those of other autistic people. I do this in order to bring to life the reality of the issues I am writing about.

In a number of places I have used my poetry to help illustrate the points I am making. For me, poetry is a way of putting words on paper that reflect back to me a picture that helps to build an understanding. Lisa Simone also illustrates the text with her insightful drawings. Drawing for Lisa is like poetry for Wendy.

To help with the logical thinking of the issues expressed, the following format is outlined. Chapter 1 introduces the background and rationale as well as outlining the problems with current understanding of AS. It also suggests reasons for exploring traditional theories concerning AS. Chapter 2 summarises the current state of play with reference to AS and particular issues of incidence, gender ratio and the impact of the clinical picture seen in AS and experienced by AS individuals. Chapter 3 defines terms such as cognition and attention and lays out the foundation for exploring particular theories with relationship to these constructs. Chapter 4 explores theory of mind, based upon Baron-Cohen's concepts (i.e. the ability or the difficulty with reading intention and appreciating the mental states of self and of others as a rigid developmental process) with their relationship to NT development and to AS.

Chapters 5, 6 and 7 explore in more detail each of the other major cognitive theories, their gaps and limitations. Chapter 8 introduces and explores the idea of SAACA in a way that offers to address the gaps in other theories of AS. Chapter 9 demonstrates the relevancy of SAACA and expected outcomes of this understanding. Chapter 10 offers a number of positive and valuable expected outcomes from the newly developed theory and also some implications for the future.

Autism Is:

Autism is: being present in this world,
But not entirely of it.
I am one step removed and curled,
The switch just doesn't click.
I perform the role of my perception,
And play many parts so well.
But minus files for my redemption,
My part in life I cannot tell.
Life is like a video,
I watch but cannot partake.
My uneven skills are but an echo,
Of the frustrations which I hate!

However, my focused use of time and space,
I would not give away.
I know that I am especially placed,
For some developed career one day!

Using person first language (e.g. saying person *with* autism rather than autistic person) is thought of as being politically correct. I, and many others (see Jim Sinclair: Don't Mourn For Us: www.edmonds-institute. org/dontmour.html) however, prefer the term autistic person. This is because autism isn't some added-on appendage that I can take off. It's very much an integral part of who I am.

As you read this book you will notice that, sometimes, I refer to myself as 'Wendy' rather than as 'I'. When you think how often a person might refer to themselves as 'I', then I hope you will understand why I prefer to use my own name. For example: 'I really fancy a take out tonight,' says Jane. For some of us such a statement could be confusing. If you are 'I' who am 'I'? I am not Jane, I am Wendy. So, at times, referring to myself as 'Wendy' rather than as 'I' helps me to gain a wider understanding of things that pertain to me.

The role of attention and interest

As an autistic adult I remember well my thinking about autism as an assessment that was pronounced upon me. I remember wondering what it all meant and which bit of me this autism was in. Over time I came to realise and understand that autism is who I am; autism is the lens through which I learn, think, feel and relate to all of my experiences. Having said this, I am confident that my being autistic is an advantage when it comes to scientific discovery, research, study and much more.

Whenever I am reading, or researching the topics surrounding the autism spectrum, I am struck with the fact that AS appears to have no 'one' connecting thread or genetic pattern. For many of us sensory issues are uppermost (e.g. Kern *et al.* 2006, 2008; Lawson 2000) whilst others do not appear to suffer with sensory discord (e.g. Prince-Hughes 2002). Individuals live with obsessive and ritualistic needs that resist change (APA 2000; Kanner 1943) and social interaction is problematic for all AS people (Attwood 2000; Newson 2000). Some of us have lots of problems using language (e.g. Eisenmajer and Prior 1991), whilst others have good language but appear out of sync with the general population. But the one thing we all have in common is the ability to focus intensely upon an area of interest.

Could it be, then, that as human beings our sensory systems and associated cognitive processes (thinking, processing, problem solving, decision making and so on) are connected to a particular ability to focus? And could it be that this ability is different according to whether you are non-autistic or autistically developing? So, with this question in mind I invite you to travel with me on a journey to uncover the whys and wherefores of what autism is and what it is not.

Murray, Lesser and Lawson (2005) suggest the common features characterising AS can be attributed to a particular spread of attention. 'Attention' could be thought of as ability to focus, noticing or noting something of particular interest. In Murray *et al.* (2005) the term used to describe how NTs use attention (i.e. several interests are aroused at any given time) is polytropism and the term used to accommodate attention in AS is monotropism, or a particular ability to have single interests, rather than many at once.

Interest, in this book, is thought of as any aspect of awareness that is brought to our attention. This could be a special interest such as a particular TV programme we would like to watch, or it could be that we are hungry and need to eat. Therefore, interest is actually about more than just one thing and could be thought of as 'an interest system' or 'systems of interest'.

I know we all have times when we feel overwhelmed and wish that the demands upon us would stop. But, if you are polytropic as a typically developing individual you will be able to think, feel, notice and so on pretty much all at the same time (during the course of a usual day). Whilst if you are monotropic and autistically developing, such as I am, you will be good at either thinking, or feeling, or noticing, but in serial fashion, one at a time. I can multi-task, but only if I have available attention, am interested and have energy resources within my interest tunnel. This suggests that attention and interest are partnered differently according to whether you are NT or not.

Polytropic attention – several interests happening at one time.

By contrast, monotropic attention is focused attention allowing a tighter, smaller set of interests at any one time (Murray and Lesser 2006).

Monotropic attention – Zaffy loves everything to do with his Volkswagen and this occupies all of his attention!

The idea of being able to multi-task or connect to lots of interests raised at the same time (e.g. thinking, feeling, talking and eating) is, in layman's terms, often associated with being female, whilst males are often said to be good at tasks requiring single focus with one interest engaged at any one time. However, I am autistic and female, and I represent one in two of the autistic population so maybe we need to think beyond gender? Maybe the gender descriptions of males as 'systemisers' and females as 'multi-tasking socialites', who tend to be operating on more emotive terms, is too black-and-white a concept (Carter *et al.* 2007)?

I do not want to make the mistake of placing individuals into boxes, like we tend to do with issues regarding ones sexuality. For example, I was once told that only male's had the right equipment for proper sexual activity with females. Therfore, only heterosexuality is the norm.

If this is so, then nature itself has things all wrong. I love knowing that swordfish females can if required change their gender to become males. I love knowing that only male seahorses carry the eggs and nurse their young. I love knowing that some female and male monkeys increase the bond between them by same-sex relations, and that generally within the animal and bird kingdoms sexuality is not something that folk get hung up over. So, with regard to the autism spectrum, come travel with me and make up your own minds.

I believe monotropism describes much of the autistic disposition, but it cannot be solely responsible for the full picture. If monotropism alone was responsible for AS, it would mean autistic behaviour might be evinced whenever any individual was focused upon one thing at any given time. However, this does not seem to be the case. Frequently NTs focus their attention but do not exhibit behaviours that qualify as a diagnosis of AS. Therefore, finding an explanation of AS that fits with the clinical picture described by the diagnostic criteria (see Appendix B) and experienced by us as autistic people might have a monotropic foundation, but it needs to have other flow-on applications.

This is why the ideas associated with traditional theories of AS are being questioned in this book and the newly developed theory of AS concerning the concepts associated with the use of single attention and associated cognition in autism (SAACA) are suggested. SAACA is argued to be responsible for the pattern of characteristics seen in AS and experienced by us as the AS population. SAACA, which was developed from the idea of monotropism, explains the autistic learning style unlike any other. Current traditional theories of AS have too many gaps and fail to accommodate the clinical picture seen in AS. Within this new approach a particular learning style is said to be responsible for the current criteria for an AS assessment and the AS individual's experience.

SAACA suggests the autism spectrum should be considered not as a terrible tragedy that needs to be cured or redeemed, but as an important learning style. As we will see in later chapters SAACA provides ways to accommodate, work with and develop an individual's fullest potential.

Since Kanner (1943) first documented his ideas of autism, currently considered by some as autism spectrum condition (ASC) (Jordan 2008), research by cognitive psychologists and others has sought to explore the way we live. Although AS is present from infancy, is thought to be neurological in origin and has varied impact upon us and our families, it is not defined as one thing in the diagnostic manual. Rather, each aspect of AS has its own entry, albeit under the global umbrella term of Pervasive Developmental Disorder; for example, autistic disorder and Asperger's disorder have specific criteria in the diagnostic manual(s) (e.g. DSM IV-TR: APA 2000). The new DSM-5, expected to be released in 2012, will review current diagnostic criteria and might draw assessment into a tighter circle, losing the term *Asperger's* and bringing this previous diagnostic category back under the wing of 'high-functioning autism'.

From the early 1980s and through to the present time, psychological theory concerning AS has been based upon what is commonly known as 'the triad of impairments'. This is because the following three areas (triad) of an individual's life appear to be impaired: social understanding, communication and imagination. The concept of 'the triad' provided diagnostic criteria for AS and offered direction for intervention and potential therapies for those of us living as autistic people. However, it seems 'the triad' is no longer enough.

So, ever since we came to appreciate AS as a neurological disposition, many cognitive theories for the clinical picture shown by us have been put forward. However, Happé and Ronald (2008) concluded that no cognitive theory currently could explain AS because they say our condition is too complex and relates to more than just the properties of cognition. When one considers the clinical picture we present (this is presented further in Chapter 2), Happé and Ronald's argument appears to be a reasonable one. However, in this book I will show that there is a cognitive theory that accommodates the complexities of who we are.

The approach, later espoused, considers connections between sensory-motor systems, the interest system and that of attention; it is thus known as a sensory-motor, interest and attention loop. I suggest the latter two systems are the areas that are often overlooked in much of the current thinking on AS. In naturalistic settings the cognitive qualities of interest and attention might seem difficult to measure. What we do know, however, is that blood flow to the brain is increased in times of vigilance, which can be measured by Doppler sonography. Thus, by this method we can measure attention and interest. Even though such tests are not readily available at this time, the constructs of interest and attention are nonetheless very important.

It is a fact that interest could be applied to any moment in time when one's awareness is brought to the forefront of one's attention, whether, for example, by virtue of necessity, excitement or fear and so on. The concept of attention, in this capacity, would indicate the brain's ability to allow the appropriate bodily facilities to notice or bring 'online' that which one might need.

Dewey (1913, 1938, 1956), a respected authority on the rights of individuals and education, among other things, stressed the importance of maintaining and utilising interest. Without interest, Dewey stated, attention and connections to learning not only are less available, but individuals lack the needed perceptions to stay motivated, and their needs, as well as their relationships and values, cannot develop to their fullest potential.

Dewey's comments about interest and connection may be thought of as intuitive appeal, especially, as some might argue, since it is difficult to measure interest and attention. However, it is important to acknowledge that common experience (inclusive of attended and motivated interest) and science show that learning goes hand in hand with sensory-motor development and cognition.

Neuropsychologists agree that a way to hold attention in young adolescents is through sensory-motor experience (e.g. action learning) but many fail to connect this to concepts of interest and attention. In addition, we know that the distinct interest systems in the NT population and in the AS population are relying upon different brain configurations (e.g. Dawson *et al.* 2005; Mottron *et al.* 2006).

Teachers have long known that interest builds awareness, and awareness leads to concepts and connections (e.g. Kluth and Chandler-Olcott 2008; Marshall 2008). With these concepts in mind, all cognitive theory concerning AS should note the developmental attributes of the sensory-motor, attention and interest systems, because these systems work together in a sensory-motor interest loop.

This is because the interest system is an array of neuronal activity sparked by any factor or variable allowing the brain to connect it to awareness. For example, when one's attention is focused during states of fear, desire or need, the brain makes us aware of what we feel, think, need or want. These emotions and thoughts are as much a part of our interest system as any specific hobby or interest. Therefore consideration of sensory-motor processing and interest is necessary for NT and AS developing individuals to form connections and understanding of academic, emotive or social awareness.

Parents sometimes say to me that they can't tell what their AS son or daughter is interested in. It can be difficult to 'see' what an individual is interested in, but this doesn't mean that we can't measure interest or that what we can't see doesn't exist. If the constructs of interest and attention are difficult to see, how does one know if someone is interested, especially if their behaviour is not giving signs that can be easily interpreted as interest?

First, the Lesser and Murray (1997) model of 'Mind' as a dynamic system of interests suggests that interest is a consumer of attention (whether 'see-able' or not) and that it can be 'seen' in the form of an equation (see Appendix A).

Second, research by Belmonte *et al.* (2004) and Gomot *et al.* (2008), who used functional magnetic resonance imaging (fMRI), shows that in AS, individuals are using single focus (thus explaining our insistence upon sameness, obsessive interests, resistance to change and so on) resulting in or from specific brain configuration, and are doing so differently to that of the NT population. One must conclude, therefore, that interest and attention are measurable in at least these two ways.

And third, if you are unsure what an AS individual is interested in try giving them a digital camera and see what they take pictures of. I suggest they will only take pictures of things that interest them.

So, with reference to sensory-motor processing, the interest system and attention, I will paint a picture of those traditional cognitive theories associated with AS. In the same way I will also explore the approach that SAACA takes, outlined later in Chapters 7, 8 and 9. This approach concerns the interest system, AS, attention and the role of a sensory-motor awareness loop. Essentially this means exploring how attention, the interest system, the senses and the ability to think and/or act are connected in both the NT and AS populations. To continue looking at theory and assessment of autism I acknowledge that the diagnosis of AS is often puzzling for professionals, researchers, families and individuals alike. So, to assist in understanding AS, cognitive theories of autism such as 'theory of mind' (e.g. Baron-Cohen, Leslie and Frith 1986; Baron-Cohen *et al.* 1994) have been relied upon to explain the enigma that is AS. Currently there are four primary cognitive theories of AS. These are: poor theory of mind (ToM), executive (dys-)functioning (EF), weak central coherence (WCC) and enhanced perceptual functioning (EPF).

To explore the above in more detail we will look at the experiences we have as AS people and also those that non-AS people share to see how they compare.

I use falsification as a methodology to demonstrate whether or not cognitive theories of AS can be considered as full explanations.

Falsification is a research term implying that statements claimed to be true may be false if proved to have exceptions (e.g. 'all swans are white' is true until we find a black swan). This is important because to date such theories are often universally accepted as accounting for the clinical picture seen in AS, whereas falsification shows up the weaknesses.

For example, ToM theorists claim that poor theory of mind explains AS. If this is true, then it will stand up to the falsification test. If it does not then it cannot be used as a universal statement about AS.

Current thinking on AS is being challenged by some professionals and others; for example Jordan (2008) suggested that we consider autism not as a disorder but as a specific 'spectrum condition' that enables individuals to learn via particular learning styles. She states that it is only when such learning styles are not accommodated or when autism impacts on an individual's life to the extreme that the label 'autism spectrum disorder' (ASD) be considered rather than 'autism spectrum condition' (ASC).

To date, the traditional cognitive theories of AS have tried to offer reasonable attempts to show why AS exists, and a variety of interventions have ensued that attempt to offer therapy and educational models to address the issues faced by us, as the AS population. However, many of these are based upon a deficit model suggesting AS is a triad of impairments. In some minds this implies AS is a disease and, therefore, AS individuals could be thought of as 'sick' and needing to be cured or contained. 'I don't want to be "cured" says Josh Muggleton. 'If I was "cured" of my autism then I wouldn't be who I am. I am happy being me and my diff-ability allows me to do things I couldn't otherwise do' (Muggleton 2008).

Although there is currently wide support showing that AS is a biological condition genetically disposed (e.g. Bailey *et al.* 1995; Björne 2007), this does not necessarily mean AS is a 'disorder'. It would be fair to say that genetics define much of whom we each are and that personality, environment and the interaction of these also have a contribution. So, although it is not yet known what 'triggers' NT, or AS development, some researchers suggest AS is triggered by a number of external factors (e.g. Shattock *et al.* 1990) (see Appendix C), whilst others note development, AS or NT, is diverse and different for us all (Björne 2007). It is the latter approach that I am adhering to. So, some of the biology associated with typical and AS development will be outlined further on; however, the exploration of environmental factors is summarised in Appendix C.

Our senses are our first port of call for all information and sensory modalities (e.g. visual, auditory, tactile channels and so on) and usually work harmoniously with one another in NT development. However, for many AS individuals, sensory discomfort and dyspraxia are not uncommon. This may be due to a lack of connectivity associated with the different use of the sensory system, processing, attention and resources.

Although I'm suggesting development in AS is different to NT development one should not assume that all difference is deviant, in the sense that even if difference is outside the bell-shaped curve (usually considered as the template for normal), it could still be seen as relevant to neural diversity, rather than deviant or dysfunctional.

CHAPTER 2

The Autism Spectrum: Where We Are Now

INTRODUCTION

Current cognitive theories variously suggest that the autism spectrum (AS) results from brain insult, genetics and brain configuration, through to AS being the result of higher evolutionary development. Some theories still focus upon the triad of impairments based upon a lack of theory of mind (e.g. Baron-Cohen, Ring *et al.* 2000); others argue AS behaviour comes from the inability to see the big picture (e.g. Brosnan *et al.* 2004; Happé and Frith 2006); whilst others see issues with executive functioning as the heart of the matter (e.g. Frith 2004; Gillberg 2003) or that AS is due to the types of deficits in cognition, behaviour and social understanding associated with all of the above. However we get there, I believe AS is about brain configuration leading to a specific cognitive style. Of course, personality and an amalgam of other things (e.g. culture, upbringing, IQ, education) add to this picture.

SO WHAT DOES THE AUTISM SPECTRUM LOOK LIKE?

Transition

Autism is: 'I like it here, please do let me stay'.

Autism is: 'I know it here, please don't take me away'.
If and when I leave this place to travel to another space,

I need to know it right away. I need to know that I'm OK.
Transition is so fleeting, it leaves not time to stay.
Will I have time to settle, or will I be whisked away?

I know that change can happen.
I know it can take time.
But how can I know what this will mean?
What this will mean for mine.

Transition is about moving,
'to where or what' one asks?
This is my very question,
from present or the past.
Time for me is all the same, (I'll say that again)
Time for me is all the same,
I know not of its future.
I only know I trust in 'now'
Tomorrow can come, I just need to know how.

Traditionally, autism is seen as a spectrum of characteristics that differ
in intensity and severity across the developmental paradigm, hence the
term *autism spectrum* (AS). To view a condensed interpretation of these
see Appendix B which has relevant information taken from comparative
DSM-III to DSM-IV-TR (APA 1980, 1987, 1994, 2000) for autistic
disorder and for Asperger's disorder.

AS is not a disease but a developmental disposition (e.g. Baron-Cohen
2001; Björne 2007; Dworzynski *et al.* 2007, 2008) or a neurobiological
condition of the brain that impacts upon development (e.g. Gillberg and
Coleman 2000; Minshew and Williams 2007, 2008). Because AS is a
developmental disposition, its impact varies across the lifespan, and the
same individual may demonstrate fluctuating capacity on a daily basis.
For example, we may demonstrate interesting responses (e.g. resistance
to change, peculiar interests and attachments to both objects and people)
that may vary.

According to where an individual 'fits' on the autistic continuum,
difficulties with a number of everyday issues will also vary. Thus,
assessment currently includes a number of diagnostic categories with
their own entry in the diagnostic manual but each with a variation
traditionally associated with degree of impact upon daily life.

Some of us are echolalic and use idiosyncratic language such as pronominal reversal (reversal of personal pronouns, e.g. I and you), but we may not always do this. At other times we have unusual responses to sensory stimuli. Again, however, this may vary from individual to individual and even vary immensely for the same individual. It is this pattern of uneven skill and variation of skills that is so complementary to an assessment of AS.

However, the idea of autism as a spectrum of diff-ability is only a recent concept. Before this, classic autism was once thought of as a rare condition (Kanner 1943). Figures being proposed today, however, include a wider spectrum with broader diagnostic criteria and suggest from 1 in 58 to 1 in 160 children being diagnosed in the Western world with AS (Chakrabarti and Frombonne 2005; Martin 2007). Many might argue that if AS is on the increase then genetically we must be bringing something of great value in order for the human race to keep it going. I agree!

It's interesting that agreement on what constitutes 'autism' is still being debated. Wing (1998a) regarded 'social impairment' (difficulty) as the core characteristic of AS. Mesibov, Shea and Schopler (2000) agreed with this, but they added 'the inability to organise oneself' to the array of difficulties experienced by us as the AS population. I certainly have huge difficulty getting, being and staying organised and yet I need obsessively to organise things my way!

AS is usually associated with delayed development in some areas and the current literature also suggests that between 60 and 70 per cent of us will have an intellectual disability (e.g. La Malfa *et al.* 2004). Some of us have concurrent difficulties, and possibly multiple areas of concern (e.g. epilepsy, learning disabilities, attention deficit disorder and/or mental health issues: Brereton, Tonge and Einfeld 2006; Curran 2008). Then again, these issues occur amongst the NT population as well. It amazes me how often this is forgotten.

AS is a very 'changeable' disposition and most of us move through the continuum at different stages in our lives. That is, for example, a child of four with a diagnosis of classic autism may appear closer to that of a child with Asperger's autism at 14 years of age. Some might argue this is one reason for moving Asperger's autism into the category of high-functioning autism. However, this will create a multitude of discontent amongst the current Asperger population whose very identity and existence is in being an 'Aspie' and not an 'autie'.

For me, the distinctions are unimportant because it still comes back to understanding us as members of the AS population, wherever we are on the spectrum. I am concerned if we get caught up in the debate over labels that issues of deeper significance will be missed and we could lose sight of the wood for the trees. So often in AS we are more different than we are alike!

Narrative stories of individual lives demonstrate that the continuum has always existed (Blackman 2006; Gerland 1997; Grandin 1996, 2000; Grandin and Scariano 1986; Holliday Willey 1999; Jackson 2002; Lawson 1998; Shore 2002, 2004; Williams 1992, 1994). Even Kanner (1971) (whose work in the 1940s is still used to base current AS diagnostic criteria upon) noted that children from his original study, on a follow-up study nearly 30 years later, were markedly different in that they had developed many abilities not seen initially. Hence, evidence for a continuum in AS has existed since this condition was first noted as 'autism'.

It is because AS is viewed as a condition with many possible characteristic variants, that the criteria for an assessment of AS is now streamlined and the addition of Rett's disorder, childhood disintegrative disorder and Asperger's disorder to DSM-IV (1994) have been added. It was hoped that this would enable individuals diagnosed with AS to be seen as a more homogeneous group. It also aids and assists research to determine the aetiology, prognosis and appropriate support for us as AS individuals, wherever we appear on the spectrum; of course, the literature and theoretical basis for AS do not mean this automatically translates to appropriate and practical support within any given society.

The conditions considered as autism spectrum outlined above share many common denominators. However, from this point forward, wherever AS appears it will refer to the group as a whole, excluding Rett's disorder and childhood disintegrative disorder.

The ongoing debate concerning Asperger's autism and its impact upon individuals is of interest because there are many schools of thought ranging from Asperger's being a milder form of autism (Attwood 2007) to it being a totally disabling condition (Robison 2008). I believe it can be either, according to the situation an AS individual with Asperger's finds themselves in. Ability, or difficulty, is connected to interest. In a social setting an AS individual's ability can fluctuate depending on sensory stimuli, expectations, interest and available attention and energy resources.

Within the debate many wonder what the difference between classic autism and Asperger's autism is. An Australian television programme accessed on the internet (Holland 2008) depicted the recent research by Rinehart et al. (2008) that suggested the two conditions could best be differentiated according to the individual's particular gait or walking style. The Asperger population were said to have a less stable gait from the pelvic region than exhibited by individuals with classic autism. But, overall, individuals with classic or Kanner-type autism showed a higher level of gait disturbance (Rinehart et al. 2006; Rinehart et al. 2008).

Although the studies found there was a lack of motor coordination in gait for both classic autism and Asperger's autism, they suggested gait disturbances were more obvious in classic autism. They highlight this as an area of further research that may help in assessment. So, if we lose the Asperger's title as a sub group of AS, I wonder if appreciation of different styles in gait could be helpful? Is it important that we know about people and their differences in motor coordination? I think it could be.

An interesting observation I made concerning the gait studies mentioned above is that in video footage taken during earlier studies when a child was asked to walk along a straight line (indicated on the floor in white) whilst holding an object of interest to them, they walked without the previously noted clumsiness. This factor was not mentioned in the studies' research outcomes or discussion, but is relevant to the ideas concerning interest and attention depicted in this book.

The ability to share in joint attention is taken for granted. Most people simply expect that when they point out something of interest to them, others will join in. In the above scenario motor coordination and joint attention was taking place for the lad as he walked and played his game. But his attention was only shared between his ability to walk and his ability to focus upon something of interest to him.

Carpenter, Pennington and Rogers (2002) noted that when comparisons were made between NT developing children and those with autism, the AS children did at times engage with others on joint attention tasks. Why did these children choose to share attention, and was interest a common denominator? Gernsbacher et al. (2008) offer clues from their research which, they argue, shows joint attention is happening, but just happening differently to that in typically developing children.

Gender

When it comes to issues of gender it was once believed AS was predominantly a male condition. However, AS occurs in both males and females, and it seems that whatever our gender if an individual is somewhere on the spectrum of autism our thinking and problem-solving abilities differ from that of the NT world. For example, many of our skills and strengths only show up under certain conditions. This is why some studies show that though we may pass a variety of cognitive tests, we do so differently from the NT population.

Interestingly, there are very few studies addressing the cognitive profiles of autism from a gender perspective. But, what is seen in AS is a picture of uneven skills right across the lifespan, even though this uneven ability may change from day to day. I think that so often this skill ability is maximised when acquainted with our specific area of interest (e.g. working with numbers but not so good with words; mapping and geographic skills but nonverbal; able to use technology above age expectation but not able to cope with being part of a group). Baron-Cohen would say these abilities are associated with systemising, but I suggest they are more connected with the use of interest and available attention whatever our gender disposition.

Autism spectrum strengths

When reading various biographical accounts by AS individuals it becomes apparent that many of us have a variety of strengths and not only difficulties. It is also noted that strengths in AS can enable us to thrive and build the type of competence needed to exist successfully in areas of education, employment and family life (e.g. Attwood 2007; Gernsbacher and Frymiare 2005; Grandin 1996; Lawson 2008). At times such strengths even offer an advantage to the AS population over and above that seemingly found in the typical population. For examples of this see Baron-Cohen *et al.* (1998). Also, there seems to be more of us these days than previously noted. I believe the reality is that because AS is on the increase it must be genetically viable and of value to humankind.

Learning style

With the appreciation of different learning styles in mind and the understanding that schools operate on the basis of team work, it is apparent that many of us, as the autistic population, will find school difficult to navigate, unless our particular 'style' is accommodated. For being part of a team requires specific skills that many of us will lack, unless our interest and attention are brought online. I believe that coordination skills, organisational ability and an appreciation of 'Other' can occur and are available skills, but, for those of us as autistic people, only within the area of our interest and attention tunnel.

For some of us, the traditional school setting only serves to hinder our educational potential rather than enhancing it. If bullying and social difficulties are interfering with academic and social learning, Attwood (1998) suggests exploring different educational means, such as home school and special school, as viable alternatives. Although these might be real alternatives at this present time, I envisage a time when the broader community recognises the AS learning style and it is fostered in our traditional settings, making true inclusion a reality for many.

Inclusion
I seem to be standing alone,
I'm the odd one,
The one on my own.
Steve chose Andrew, Shane and Will.
I'm left standing; standing here still.

Teacher points in my direction,
'Wendy, you can join Paul and Tony'.
I start to walk and think 'if only'.
'If only I were more like them,
If only I could, if only they would…'

But they don't hear my unspoken words,
They don't know just how much it hurts.
To be included, wanted and welcome,
What a treasure that would be.
Instead I stand waiting, thinking 'please come…'
Please choose me, choose me, choose me.

SENSORY DIFFERENCES

Sensory differences occur for many of us. There is the paradoxical phenomenon of hyper- and hyposensitivity to sound, light, taste and touch. I look forward to a time when sensory needs in AS children and adults are accommodated and included in any educational, vocational and family setting. It does appear, at the time of writing, that the DSM (currently being reviewed) will not consider sensory difficulties and differences, even though it was postulated earlier on in the discussion concerning the next version of the DSM (which will be the DSM-5) that because there are striking differences in sensory perceptions and subsequent information processing in AS these should be considered in any AS criteria (Chamak *et al.* 2008).

A vacuum cleaner sounds like a jet plane to Zaffy. The pain is like a dentist's drill. Even though Zaffy knows it's only a vacuum cleaner, it doesn't make it less painful or reduce the fear and anxiety.

For some of us, it might be that visual differences can account for a variety of what some see as bizarre behaviours (e.g. looking out of the corners of our eyes, rubbing our eyes vigorously, looking at parts of objects side on and so on). Being tactile defensive and experiencing 'skin crawling' sensations; experiencing discomfort when skin is in contact with particular materials; needing to be without clothing; removing shoes; and even the compulsion to stroke smooth china objects, are all quite common experiences in AS.

I suggest that most of us have preferred senses for taking in information (touch, smell, taste and so on are experienced as sensory channels for all communication). For example, for some of us, the only way to work out where we are in time and space is by touch. For others, everything goes into the mouth; and for others still, understanding the world via smell or auditory input is not unusual.

Hermelin and O'Connor (1970) noted that AS children do not seem to associate and integrate sensory modalities, thus making it difficult for them to form a whole picture. For example, incorporating many senses, one might know a dog is a dog, no matter what the breed is, because of how it looks, feels, smells and sounds. Grandin (1996) learnt to recognise dogs in general when she realised all dogs, no matter their size, had the same kind of nose.

In AS, therefore, we appear to use one sensory mode at a time. This allows us to access parts of the picture in detail, but unless interested we do not pay attention to the whole story. However, once we find some way to link things together, as Grandin has, we may recognise that some things belong to a wider generalised concept (see Gardner 2008).

Talay-Ongan and Wood (2000) have also shown support for sensory differences in AS through a questionnaire that explored sensory profiles in AS across differing domains. They concluded that sensory differences in AS could be responsible for interfering with the mechanics of observing and interpreting the mental states of others because the ability to attend via joint attention would be impoverished.

I understand the conclusions by Talay-Ongan and Wood (2000) above but I also believe that single focus and single interest present different explanations of the reasons for our AS responses. These responses are based in our ability to form mono connections between interests rather than multiple connections to multiple interests. This means joint attention can be achieved, but it needs to happen as we join the dominant interest of the AS individual and move on out from there.

With reference in particular to sensory perceptions, all of us, AS or otherwise, know the influences that our senses have upon our perceptions. If we think we smell dinner cooking it can spark an interest in food or it can close us down to the idea of eating. It depends upon how we feel about food (e.g. hungry or full), what type of food we fancy (e.g. savoury or sweet) and even whether we are on our own or with someone else. Sense, perception and action are all inter-related. If you are neurotypically developing, because you can integrate your sensory information, label it, decipher it, utilise it and so on, your sensory perceptions tend to be self-limiting and an end in themselves.

For us, however, sensory perception is experienced as a separate entity and it may not have a natural boundary or border (not be self-limiting). This can mean sensory information keeps coming and can easily overload us. For example, I can experience my clothing as a heavy weight upon my body rather than as a garment that looks good and serves a useful purpose, such as keeping me warm or protected from the weather. If this is the case, I may feel an overwhelming need to take off the garment and remove the heavy 'feeling' upon me.

This may be the same for footwear, an affectionate embrace or the sound of someone's voice. All too often, however, my responses to sensory overload are interpreted as challenging or difficult behaviour rather than understood as a sensory issue which is easily rectified (e.g. use a different fabric or garment design; give firmer but shorter hugs; lower voice volume during conversation or speak to me side on rather than face on).

All of the above show us that AS has various effects, some difficult, some useful and some simply different.

SUMMARY

For such a long time AS has been thought of as a neurological disorder with only negative connotations and implications. Over the past couple of years, it's as if we have woken up to the idea that AS is a particular learning style associated with deep focus. As such, gender, motor and sensory differences are now making their way into the picture. Alongside these is the understanding that strengths and positive abilities are part of the AS lifestyle and, as such, we must question earlier theories that only considered that AS was deviant and devastating. Individuals and families need to be supported in their quest to develop their fullest potential. This must come from a position of value and not one of deficit or impairment.

CHAPTER 3

Cognitive Theories of the Autism Spectrum

INTRODUCTION

In this chapter the reasoning behind the idea of 'theory' with regard to AS and cognition will be the main focus. I will briefly mention non-cognitive theories of AS (a summary of these can be found in Appendix C), but as I am only concerned with cognitive theories at this time, only these will be explored in detail.

Cognition
I think, therefore I am.
I feel, therefore I exist.
I notice, but only the things that I 'see'.
I need you to notice, yes to notice me.

COGNITION AND COGNITIVE THEORY

Thinking and feeling states represent different entities. However, feelings are a direct result of our thoughts or cognitive processes. Cognition can be thought of as mental operations such as thinking, conceiving, reasoning, symbolising, insight, expectancy, complex rule use, imagery, belief, intentionality and problem solving. Klin *et al.* (2003) emphasise that cognition is embodied (cognition includes the perceptual system, the intuitions that underlie the ability to move, activities and interactions with our environment and the naive understanding of the world that is built into the body and the brain) defining it as 'bodily experiences accrued as a result of an organism's adaptive actions upon salient aspects of the surrounding environment' (p.345).

In all of us, as developing individuals, cognition is informed via our senses. This necessitates the integration of a number of 'channels' from which information is gleaned to enable the brain to process the information and allow us to make practical use of that information. For example, we all receive information from these channels (our senses, such as sight, hearing, touch, smell, taste and proprioception) and then the information is sorted and processed according to interest (i.e. usefulness, priority, need, desire and so on).

The concept of cognition with the consideration that there are many routes to understanding and developing will be explained in relation to the four cognitive theories of AS that were mentioned earlier on. To reiterate from Chapter 1, the cognitive theories that were explored in the work related to this book are: theory of mind (ToM) (Baron-Cohen *et al.* 1985, 1994); executive functioning (EF) (e.g. Hill 2004; Russell 1997); weak central coherence (WCC) (e.g. Happé *et al.* 2006); and enhanced perceptual functioning (EPF) (e.g. Mottron *et al.* 2006). All of the theories mentioned will have their own chapter, devoted to summarising aspects of the particular theory in more detail.

Looking at cognitive theory in AS is appropriate because AS is currently thought of as a developmental disorder which leads to difficulties in social understanding, communication and imagination (or having rigid thinking). These are all components or aspects of cognition. In AS, the difficulties of these particular aspects of cognition are referred to (as mentioned earlier) as 'a triad of impairments'. Of course, Wendy and others are now saying that this picture is incomplete and not appropriate as a real description of our abilities and difficulties.

CONSIDERING THEORY IN THE AUTISM SPECTRUM

First, a 'theory' has to have certain properties. For example, according to Happé (1994b), for an idea to qualify as a reasonable theory that explains AS, it needs certain components: it must fit with what we know about normal development; it must explain the specific patterns of deficits and abilities in autism; it must give a causal account of why we see specific behaviours and social difficulties in individuals with autism; and it must generate ways of testing the theory.

There are a number of theories concerning the development and the diagnosis of AS. Non-cognitive theories of AS (Appendix C) are based on the belief that AS is triggered by environmental factors. New and different non-cognitive theories about the causes of AS appear regularly. It is suggested in the non-cognitive theories of AS that AS may relate to food-stuffs a child eats (e.g. dairy products wheat and other cereal products), metals the child has inhaled or absorbed from the environment (e.g. lead, mercury) or the problems associated with being vaccinated against common childhood diseases (live viruses and/or bacteria passing into the blood stream and not being expelled by the body defences).

So, moving on from non-cognitive theories of AS, as I summarise the current cognitive theories of AS, it becomes apparent that they are inadequate. Rather, as I consider the research, the current literature, the case studies, myself, my friends and humanity at large I come to the conclusion that AS should be thought of as a cognitive difference or style. This being so, it must be concluded that AS is not a mental disorder, but rather a distinctive way of thinking which affects behaviour.

However, this does not mean that AS can be taken out of the realm of disability. To date, unfortunately, AS is still not readily understood or accommodated by society in general. This leaves individuals living with a condition that is disabling by the nature of the society in which it exists, rather than by the condition itself. This can be said with confidence because many of us, against the odds, are learning and developing into capable adults, when we are given the right support, structure, access and conditions (Kluth and Chandler-Olcott 2008).

With respect to general expectation Clark (2008) noted that:

> Society tends to follow without questioning a model of interacting and supporting AS individuals based upon the medical model of interpreting behaviour. This model assumes individuals are disabled because of their deficits and difficulties. Therefore, focus should be upon fixing, curing or correcting these to enable the individual to exist in normal society.
>
> If society was, however, to follow the social model of disability (which suggests that the society is equally responsible for enabling individuals with disabilities to

live and exist within the society as disabled people) then curing or fixing the person might not be paramount. The social model of disability affirms that we should not attempt to change the individual so much as accommodate that person and support them in ways that enable them to live positively as themselves. This would mean structuring services and support to give disabled individuals access to health, education and employment services in ways that suit their needs rather than trying to get them to fit into existing generic models that suit the typical population.

Thus, only as a society gains understanding of an individual and their cognitive difference ('diff-ability') and also uses the understanding to inform appropriate interventions, will that individual's 'disability' be less disabling.

ATTENTION AND INTEREST

When I use the term 'attention' I'm referring to a facility that enables focus and builds awareness. *Distribution of attention* relates to the idea of an interest system within which attention is a limited processing resource. For example, the more interested one is in X, the more attention one devotes to X – and the less attention is available to spend elsewhere.

When you read about 'interest' in this book it is taken to mean neuronal activity that is sparked by the act of attention that connects to meaning and holds awareness in a capacity that builds into thought, words and/or action. Examples of such 'interest(s)' include hobbies and special interests, but interest can also be part of a system (of interest) that is inherently connected to need, desire, emotion, want, thought, words, deeds, dreams and any other activity that captures one's attention.

At times, in the typical population, individuals will put their own interests on hold to accommodate the interests of others (e.g. stop to say 'hello' when they really want to go). In NT development dividing one's attention between 'Self' and 'Other' seems a very natural process, whereas, in the AS population, we seem to find dividing our attention very difficult, unless it is clearly connected to our own interests. This difference in how one uses attention and interest is not a matter of choice in AS but I believe it to be our default setting, or the way our brains are configured.

The concept that individual brains are not just a collection of cells (white and grey matter) but of systems and individualised sections that work in harmony with each other, is not new. The human 'interest system' encompasses any and all neuronal activity that the human brain needs to notice either consciously or unconsciously (i.e. hunger, pain, sound, desire and so on). Appendix A summarises this concept and depicts interest as a mathematical equation. Of course, maths is just one format that clearly illustrates the equation of interest and attention. Within our daily lives we each live out this equation as we interact with our environment and with one another. Whether we align our interests with each other's or whether we fail to note them might simply be a matter of how our brain is configured.

SUMMARY

The above chapter has explored the issue of theory and cognition in AS. It has opened a door to debate on these concepts and leads us into consideration of the impact that interest and attention have upon our learning and appreciation of 'Self' and 'Other'.

CHAPTER 4

Cognitive Theory: Theory of Mind

INTRODUCTION

This chapter explores the idea that, as humans, we use the ability to comprehend concepts of 'Self' and of 'Other' in relationship to self; and that understanding our own mind and the signals given out by others as to what is on their mind happens in a particular way. This is called having a 'theory of mind' (ToM), possibly via certain brain architecture or a theory of mind mechanism (ToMM). ToM is a widely acclaimed traditional theory applied to cognitive development. It was developed from an idea based on Wimmer and Perner's (1983) model of how typical children develop belief.

Definition

ToM is said to offer an explanation for understanding, appreciating and accommodating the mental and emotional states of self and others. Others see ToM as *the cognitive mechanism in a part of the brain architecture* that enables the appreciation and representation of mental states of either oneself or others.

Tests for imagination, creativity and appreciation of 'false belief' are all used in ToM assessments. This is because such tests aim to show how well or how poorly ToM is working for an individual. Some of these tests are explored in more detail later in this chapter. ToM will be discussed in relationship to cognitive development, which includes social and emotional attributes, attention and interest. In particular, ToM in AS experiences will be compared to ToM in NT development.

Foundations for theory of mind

Although 'theory of mind' was a term used initially in 1978 by Premack and Woodruff to address the ability to attribute independent mental states to self and others in order to predict and explain actions, the theory has grown and developed over time from studies on how the normally developing child gathers, appreciates and uses social understanding. It is now a pervasive theory that, as well as being used commonly to refer to 'mind reading' (Happé et al. 2006; Vogeley et al. 2001, 2004), is also applied to other areas of 'mind', such as mind structures, mind processes, individual minds, cognition and philosophy of mind. Hence, with respect to earlier descriptions of AS behaviour, Baron-Cohen et al. (1985) hypothesised that individuals with autism lacked a 'theory of mind'.

Happé (1994b) suggested that Baron-Cohen's hypothesis was based upon Leslie's (1987) work where the usual understanding of NT two-year-olds with regard to pretend play and imagination was being studied. It seemed that these 'qualities' were expressed and experienced differently by AS children. For example, it appeared that AS children lacked imagination and, therefore, the cognitive mechanism for appreciating and representing the mental states of either themselves or others. It was said that they failed to 'mentalise' (Frith and Frith 2003; Happé 1994b). Mentalising, therefore, is said to be the product of being able to 'put oneself into another's shoes' or to see things from another's perspective.

False belief is a term used to appreciate the apparent hidden or unconscious process(es) that an individual might experience during interaction with others. It concerns the assumed 'knowing' of what actually is happening and what you might think someone else thinks about an event, happening, emotion and so on. I vividly remember, as a child of four years old, believing that my mother was being mean because she had failed to provide me with a drink of orange juice that I wanted. The fact that I hadn't asked her for the drink (I was not using spoken language at the time; I didn't speak until after my fourth birthday) was irrelevant because I had thought it, therefore she must know it. This was my thinking at that time. In fact, I believed that if I thought something then everyone else must think it too!

However, in typical dynamics there are first-, second-, third-, fourth- and fifth-order false belief concepts. For example, Shakespeare's play *Othello* creates a story that builds upon the characters' interpretations of reality. The wife of Othello, Desdemona, is made to appear to Othello as a woman who has deceived him and who is plotting his downfall (first-order belief). These beliefs have been planted by enemies of Othello who Othello believes are his friends (second- and third-order beliefs). The audience watching the play know the truth and the plot of the friends (enemies) of Othello and can 'see' the mindset of Othello's conspirators (fourth- and fifth-order beliefs). Second-order beliefs and beyond involve understanding a character's thoughts about another character's thoughts, about another character's thoughts and so on, and tasks to test for ability to understand false beliefs are usually passed by NT children aged between five and seven years (e.g. Hughes and Leekam 2004).

The Baron-Cohen, Joliffe *et al.* (1997) and Baron-Cohen, Wheelwright *et al.* (1997) ToM explanation of autism offers an account that stresses representation of mental states is vital in order to understand and predict other people's behaviour. Importantly, it assumes this is the *only* basis of all social interaction (Baron-Cohen *et al.* 1985, 1996, 1997, 2008). It is this thinking, plus the concepts that ToM claims to represent, that I am challenging.

Components of theory of mind

ToM is said to be constructed from various components that provide ability to attribute mental states such as belief, intent, desire, pretending and knowledge to oneself and others and to understand that others have beliefs, desires and intentions that are different from one's own. Although such components have not been identified physically, it is thought by some researchers that such ability is physically located within the structures or architecture of the brain (e.g. Leslie 1994, 2000; Vogeley *et al.* 2001).

For example, Leslie (1994) has suggested that this cognitive mechanism may be innate and discrete, and he called this the 'theory of mind (mechanism) module' (ToMM). Leslie originally suggested that ToMM was formed from three components and operated in children as young as 18 months. As a mechanism it enabled the developing individual to tell the difference between pretend and belief, for example, to know when a banana was being used in play as a telephone, or to know what another individual would believe about a marble and where it might be placed. This explanation is important because belief reasoning is assumed to play a central role in making inferences about other people's mental states.

According to Leslie the three components in ToMM enable it to be used by individuals as a computational tool. This allows the child to appreciate mechanical agency, actional agency and attitudinal agency with regard to what is real and what is pretend, or what the agent believes and what the child believes. This tool facilitates the mechanism for separating belief from pretend. Its first component is the 'expression raiser' (a cognitive state involving attention, interest and recognition). Second, this idea is passed on to the 'manipulator' (the cognitive controller) that allows the child to comprehend the idea in action as either pretence or belief, theirs or the agent's. Third, it suggests the child already has a pre-supplied primitive template, and working together the expression raiser and the manipulator lead into the formulation by age four of agent, attitude and proposition (truth, pretence and belief). This third attribute is referred to as the 'anchor' in Leslie's ToMM which allows the child to attribute the difference between truth (reality), pretence (falsehood) and belief (your mind and mine).

Earlier versions of ToMM did not account for the discrepancy in age between 18 months and four years (Leslie 1987). That is, children failed false belief tests at 18 months but passed them when older at four years. So Leslie introduced the idea of the selection processor. This, according to Leslie, was the missing link that was more developed in the older child, allowing the child to select out pretend from belief.

Doherty (2001), however, argues that Leslie's ToMM explanation of how children separate pretence, belief and other emotive states is redundant as a theory because it simply echoes other theories such as Robinson and Mitchell's 'reality-masking' theory of propositional attitudes in children (Mitchell and Lacohee 1991). In Mitchell's work the idea is that children's early insight into the representational character of mind is masked in traditional prediction tests of false belief because such tests are based on backwards prediction of what might be rather than on forward thinking associated with false belief. For example, backwards prediction can be shown in the following story. Peter has put his watch in the drawer in his bedroom. Joan, Peter's young niece, sees Pat, the housekeeper, move Peter's watch when she puts the clean washing into Peter's drawer. When asked 'where will Peter look for his watch?' Joan will answer in the drawer. This is thought of as 'backwards prediction'. If Joan thinks that Peter knows his watch has been moved, she will predict that he will look for his watch in its new place. This is the forward thinking, or forward prediction explanation... even if Peter is not in the room when the watch is moved. However, there are substantial arguments on both sides of the fence.

In later research Vogeley *et al.* (2001, 2004) demonstrated that one can see particular activity in certain areas of the brain during tasks concerning ToM and 'Self', reflected on MRI (magnetic resonance imaging) scans. They have concluded that this shows there is an associated brain architecture or area associated with ToM. Those who might not agree with this concept argue that MRI images only highlight the activity, not the process of its origin, and that evidence of the activity is not the same as the architecture responsible for it (e.g. Gerrans 2008; Gerrans and Stone 2008).

Non-modular theorists (i.e. those who do not believe that behaviour is located in specific brain regions) would argue that virtually all behaviour is influenced by genes but virtually no behaviour is determined by genes. Björne's (2007) research reinforced the idea that genes and experience interact to inform learning. Non-modular theorists of ToM argue that understanding oneself and others can be developed over time as a child learns from experience (Gerrans 2008). They suggest this type of learning is interactive and is an outcome of an organism's whole interaction with its environment, not just one aspect of it. Even so, many such theorists accept that ToM exists but that it cannot be precisely located in the brain since it is a generalised facility made up of a variety of learnings and perceptions (Gerrans 2002).

APPLICATION TO CHILD DEVELOPMENT

Often ToM is applied to AS and typical spectrum individuals alike; it appears to explain either the ability or difficulty with cognitively representing mental states in order to be better or worse equipped to predict other people's behaviour. Although this, in turn, appears to account for the development of an understanding of 'Self' and 'Other' (or the failure to do so), I wonder if the above is the only explanation for our appreciation of self and of another's mind?

ToM or lack of ToM is said to be responsible for the patterns of deficits and strengths seen in AS, and the causes of specific behaviours and social difficulties experienced by us as autistic individuals. Again, I question these assumptions and will put forward a different point of view.

Knowing that someone other than self has feelings, desires, hopes and dreams, some might argue, is what makes human beings different from other animals (Hobson 2008). The ability to be able to 'read' another person is said to be limited or non-existent in AS individuals (e.g. Baron-Cohen 1997, 2000, 2002; Happé 1996). With the above concepts some have implied that to be an AS individual could mean being less than human. For example (as cited in Dawson *et al.* 2008, p.71): 'Scientists in various fields have proposed that autistics teach us about what is fundamentally and uniquely human – because it is this essence of humanity that autistics lack.' This just goes to show how little imagination the neurologically typical (NT) population have if this statement is truly representational of the group as a whole, but I tend to think it is not.

In addition, being 'mind blind' (Happé 1994b) if one is an AS individual implies that NT individuals are 'mind sighted'. By implication, therefore, NT development is meant to result in a higher social conscience and understanding of 'Other' which should lead to, for example, more successful marital relationships. Yet, currently, statistics in Western society, for divorce rates among married couples (apparently typical in development), are estimated to be 50 per cent (Stanley 2007). This suggests that even the non-autistic typical population, with apparent 'normal' development in areas of imagination and ToM ability, still have problems relating to one another and communicating effectively.

This means that ToM proposals can be misleading if they promote and equate normal development with success in understanding 'Self' and 'Other'. When it comes to the AS population most of the research on ToM has considered those of us with an intellectual disability or with language delay (e.g. Charman and Swettenham 2001; Howlin, Mawhood and Rutter 2000). But other research shows that it is not only a problem for AS individuals with an intellectual disability (Dahlgren and Trillingsgaard 1996), nor is it confined to the AS population in general.

According to Dahlgren, Sandberg and Hjelmquist (2003) and others (e.g. Peterson, Peterson and Webb 2000), poor theory of mind exists in other populations. It can be found among the deaf, the blind, many with schizophrenia, those with intellectual disability, those with deficits in attention (e.g. Goldstein and Schwebach 2004), motor control and perception (e.g. Gillberg and Coleman 2000) and those with language impairment (Tager-Flusberg 2001).

One of the difficulties for ToM theorists is that some of us as AS individuals pass the tests for ToM (e.g. Baron-Cohen 2002; Bowler 2001). Baron-Cohen, who so clearly postulated his theory of ToM as being the explanation for AS, has since found AS individuals pass tests for ToM, be it for reason of maturation or a matter of language skills. If individuals pass the tests but are autistic ToM cannot be claimed as fully explaining the AS condition. This suggests that problems with ToM might be the product of other difficulties rather than the cause of them.

Consider that NT three-year-olds fail ToM tests concerning false belief, yet such children obviously can join in pretend play with others and are able to 'read' intentions of others (sometimes showing understanding of very complex themes: Stagnitti 2004), albeit in an immature and simplistic way. With regard to this, Bloom and German (2000) suggest that although typical three-year-olds are too young to have the more sophisticated ToM, usually associated with being four years old, they obviously communicate and talk to others in appropriate speech, implying linguistic skills needed for the ability to pretend and understand the pretence of others. Within the scientific community, even with this knowledge and understanding, three-year-old children and AS children are placed in the same group as children who 'lack' theory of mind. This argument presents a problem for ToM theorists.

Development of theory of mind

Within the typical population, infants display actions and awareness that imply a growing understanding of concepts such as pretence, false belief, intention and other cognitive processes leading to the understanding of 'Self' and 'Other'. That this development occurs is not in question here,; what is in question is how it occurs and whether this development follows the same pattern in all individuals or whether it can be acquired via different processes. It is in the answer to these questions that the theory behind the AS condition and our subsequent behaviours can be better understood.

Stagnitti (2004) shows clearly, as evidenced through ability to join in with pretend play, that AS children can and do acquire an imagination. Many autobiographical accounts written by AS individuals also demonstrate that the experiences of imagination may not be

0–9 months

A child can tell if your intention toward him/her is friendly or unfriendly by:

*Touch – rough touch = upset, cry

soft touch = calming, happy

* Auditory – 'harsh' noises = cry 'soft' noises = happy

* Vision – if you walk to toward the door, you are going to leave me…

Eye to Eye contact shares information about intention

10–18 months

Shared – Activating – Mechanism

Children start to understand that you could have the same belief as me, for example, I like red buses, and you could like them too.

18+ months

Theory of mind develops where children understand belief, false-belief, and representational thinking. Children understand people can think different things to each other.

('Learn to play' unpublished workshop handouts. Diagram based on Baron-Cohen's book, *Mindblindness*, 1997. Used with permission from Stagnitti)

Figure 4.1: The development of theory of mind according to Baron-Cohen (1997), as adapted by Stagnitti (2004)

directly associated with social skill or social understanding, but are more connected to verbal expression or to personal perception and experience (e.g. Holliday Willey 1999, 2002; Jackson 2002).

Figure 4.1 shows Baron-Cohen's view of a rigid development for ToM; there may be others. It is a worry that so many professionals take typical development to be such a rigid deployment of assumptions and consequences and that if you do not follow this time line then you are considered to be deviant or disordered, even when many families report that their children were late talkers, just like their father was. Or that their child seemed to miss the stage of crawling and went straight into standing up and then walking, and many other such stories. There are so many different family stories of genetic dispositions and environmental interactions. Did the child learn to respond because Daddy noticed her or did Daddy notice the child because she smiled? Does it really matter who prompted whom, where and under which circumstances, or should we all be recognising that we each learn differently and what works for one might not work for another?

Although I didn't talk until after my fourth birthday and I wasn't good at team sports at school, I did well at individual sports (swimming and running) and I did well within the academic areas of my interest. In fact, I learnt and built connections to understanding once things that were of interest to me were put into the picture. I didn't develop typically, although I did develop connections and understanding both of myself and of others, although I did so albeit through different means.

Why do we so easily appreciate that we all like different things (e.g. rock music versus classical music, reading books or only reading the newspaper, science fiction on the TV versus the 'soaps', hot spicy foods compared to 'plain' food, living in the city compared to living in the countryside and so on and so on), but we fail to appreciate that we might develop differently when it comes to ways of understanding 'Self 'or 'Other'?

There are many questions concerning ToM; some argue, therefore, that the number of questions raised cast doubt on its appropriateness as a legitimate theory for typical cognitive development. It is far too black and white and serves to reinforce the myth that there is only 'one normality' and all else outside of this developmental paradigm is disordered and deviant.

Difficulties with a rigid view of theory of mind development

ToM experiments by Baron-Cohen and colleagues rest upon the premise of development shown in Figure 4.1. It is obvious that many problems arise from these presumed attributes because some individuals clearly do not follow the time lines or the expectations outlined in Figure 4.1. Some are not on the autism spectrum, whilst some others, who do fit such criteria, go on to be diagnosed with AS. Thus ToM, as a theory of development, cannot be taken as a given for the acquisition of understanding of 'Self' and 'Other', either in typical development or in AS development (Minshew and Williams 2007, 2008; Minshew and Hobson 2008).

In typical development there are individuals without an AS diagnosis who apparently negotiate the expected milestones (shown in Figure 4.1) and still develop deviant behaviour (Blair 2005; Kennett 2002). In AS development many AS individuals show they do understand the concepts of 'Self' and 'Other', pass tests that show an understanding of false belief, have a strong commitment to 'doing the right thing' (Grandin 2000) and, against the odds, form successful relationships (Shore 2002).

These disparities highlight the shortcomings of Baron-Cohen's explanation of ToM for AS individuals. It should also be noted that children from families with more children, rather than fewer, develop ToM at a different rate, i.e. the more older siblings in a family the more likely the younger ones are to develop a stronger sense of 'Self' and 'Other' at an earlier age (McAlister and Peterson 2007). This is not noted in the rigid development of ToM shown in Figure 4.1.

In Figure 4.1 the typically developing child aged 0–9 months is said to be discovering their world, via their senses, in relationship to 'Other'. For example, touch, sound and sight are postulated as being the means to cognitive connection concerning the child's perception of intention by another. Rough touch indicates the possibility of potential harm or unfriendliness whilst soft touch portrays caring and calming attributes as intended by another. This is of interest because in AS soft or light touch may be felt as pain (Gerland 1997; Grandin 1996; Lawson 1998). Could this mean, therefore, that we might be building a sense of harm anticipated by being around individuals who commonly use soft touch?

Also in Figure 4.1, the idea that visual contact as an individual leaves a room is interpreted as meaning 'I am being left...or abandoned' in typical infants of this age, but may not be noticed by infants who later gain a diagnosis of autism, is also of interest. Many of us report that we are often so taken up with what we are focused upon that we fail to notice that others are looking at us, leaving us or even waving to us (e.g. Gardner 2008; Grandin 1996; Hoy 2007; Jackson 2002; Purkis 2006). However, once awareness occurs, we may be able to connect more readily (Gardner 2008; Hoy 2007; Jackson 2002; Purkis 2006). Could, therefore, the process of developing awareness of 'Self' and 'Other' be occurring differently for those of us within the AS population from those in the typical population (e.g. Kampe, Frith and Frith 2003)?

The assumptions of Figure 4.1 appear to preclude the possibility that understanding of 'Self' and 'Other' could develop in any other way. So, although it is not disputed that many of us pass ToM tests (e.g. Baron-Cohen *et al.* 1997; Bowler 2001, 2007; Bowler *et al.* 2005; Bowler, Gaigg and Gardiner 2008), we should be asking why we do (i.e. if the possibility of developing ToM or understanding via other pathways is happening in AS, it should be explored). It does appear that understanding, of 'Self' and 'Other', can be built in non-typical ways. It is a fact that many of us acquire a ToM in spite of our difficulties and therefore may be doing so by using other processes that are not typical (Björne 2007; Minshew and Williams 2007; Murray, Lesser and Lawson 2005).

It is suggested (e.g. Castelli *et al.* 2002; Happé *et al.* 2006) that selective and repetitive behaviours may be the result not of poor ToM but actually of a different way of thinking. In their studies they noted that several students had particular skills that seemed to be due to a particular ability to attend to detail rather than global information. Their theory has since been talked about as a *cognitive style*.

To support this idea some cite AS individuals such as Stephen Wiltshire, who can draw in precise detail 3D images after only seeing them, for example, from above in a helicopter. Stephen displays a grasp of precision and detail way beyond the scope of most artists (see Wiltshire 1989). Pring, Hermelin and Heavey (1995) have studied the development of Stephen's gift, and argue that his capacity to 'filter out' global impressions of his surroundings fosters his talent for producing perfect perspective drawings from memory. Although Stephen enjoys familiarity and structure, he is able to cope well with surprises when they are connected to his area of interest. It should be noted also that Stephen can engage in appropriate conversation, especially once his attention and interest are aroused. So, we should be exploring the role that attention and interest are playing in Stephen's life, and in our lives generally.

Good 'ToM suggests that an individual is good at recognising the emotive and cognitive state of themselves and of others. Sometimes this is referred to as "mind reading"' (Happé 1994b, p.48). It is suggested that ToM enables one to appreciate various beliefs. However, in Stephen's case this might happen only once he is made aware or becomes aware, via his interest.

If ToM has a physical location within the brain (Vogeley *et al.* 2001, 2004) and ToM is the only way of enabling individuals to 'mind read' and anticipate behaviour of both 'Self' and 'Other', then individuals with AS would consistently fail ToM tests right across the autistic spectrum. With appropriate experimentation where individuals are given particular tests exploring belief (such as first-hand belief tasks through to fourth-hand belief about what one thinks others believe about an event or emotive state) the evidence should be consistent, but it is not. For example, Baron-Cohen (1987) and Baron-Cohen *et al.* (1985) disagree with Baron-Cohen *et al.* (1997) and Baron-Cohen *et al.* (2003) over the issue of AS individuals passing tests for ToM, and, therefore, over the conclusion that all AS individuals lack a ToM.

Kanner (1971) demonstrated that AS individuals improved over time, in particular, their social skills, even without specific intervention. If ToM is responsible for AS then such AS individuals could not improve over time and still be autistic.

The most noted test for theory of mind

To test for ToM, researchers have used what is called a first-order false-belief task. In this task, the individual needs to understand that another person can hold a wrong belief about the world. Most NT developing children pass such tests by the time they are four years old.

However, in 1985, Baron-Cohen *et al.* tested 20 children with autism on a 'theory of mind' task called 'The Sally-Ann task'. In the Sally-Ann task, two dolls named Sally and Ann were used to represent two characters. The doll called Sally puts an object in box X (her box) and then leaves the room. Whilst Sally is absent the doll called Ann moves the object to box Y (her box). When Sally returns, the child is asked: 'Where will Sally search for the object, in box X or in box Y?' Most four-year-olds say box X.

Typical children younger than four years say box Y because there is a developmental transition as children move from age three to age four. This implies only children of four years and older have the ability to have a theory of mind. Baron-Cohen *et al.* found that this task, which they claimed implied an understanding of false beliefs, demonstrated the apparent inability of AS children to comprehend the mental states of others because 16 AS children (80 per cent) in his study failed the first-order false-belief test and four children (20 per cent) passed.

Theory of mind research over time

Over the years, many conventional 'theory of mind' tasks appear to have supported findings that poor ToM plays a role in the clinical picture in AS. However, in some studies researchers have refuted the idea that only ToM is responsible for the AS condition. In addition to these studies, AS individuals who write about their lives also challenge concepts concerning ToM (e.g. Hesmondhalgh 2006; Purkis 2006).

Happé's (1995) research showed that five AS participants passed first-order beliefs and six passed second-order beliefs. She suggested AS individuals passed the tests and seemed to display an understanding of both 'Self' and of 'Other', but still failed to connect to learning in ways that NT individuals did. Happé found people who passed ToM tests failed to separate distinct meanings to written words in varied contexts such as 'tear in her eye' or 'tear in her dress'. Happé argued this is not a ToM problem but one of failing to read context, or failing to connect to the bigger picture.

For reasons such as these, Bloom and German (2000) argued that passing tests on false belief requires other abilities, not just a theory of mind, and they also state that such tests can be passed without an understanding of false belief (see Baddeley and Wilson 1988, 1995).

Leslie's ToMM (Leslie 1994; Leslie and Roth 1993) aimed to demonstrate the concept of acquiring an understanding of emotions and pretend play as well as understanding false belief. Leslie argues that children understand the concept of 'pretend' by the age of two years (they can pretend a banana is a telephone). But, although at 18 months old children can imitate a telephone with a banana they do not understand 'belief' (the banana is still a banana and only represents a telephone) until they are four years old.

In contrast, Perner's (1996) explanation suggests children of 18 months can use pretence in their play but only in a primitive way, possibly because by 18 months they can use an object that looks similar to the intended object (Stagnitti 1998). Perner suggests children younger than four years understand neither the full concept of pretend nor that of belief but rather, prompted by the exaggerated and emotive play of others (e.g. mother) come to understand that this is a game (pretence) rather than a reality. This ability enables young children to separate 'reality appropriate' and 'reality inappropriate' action from one another.

Thus, pretence and belief are more fully understood through the process of maturation and are emulated via action as copied behaviour from others in children younger than four years (Clift, Stagnitti and DeMello 1998, 2000).

Questions concerning theory of mind

Although ToM is accepted and respected as a reputable theory that offers an account for typical cognitive development there are those who question the validity of ToM as a theory of relevance. For example, Björne (2007) asks whether ToM is a correct theory or approach to be exploring the development of how individuals make sense of others' behaviour and remarks that tests of false belief are not tests for ToM. She suggests that ToM does not fully account for social understanding, social development and the appreciation of 'Self' and 'Other' in the form of mental states. Her work clearly demonstrates that even in chickens many responses once considered innate and instinctive may not be so. For example, she quotes the research by Moore (2001), who mentions earlier work demonstrating that chickens cannot dig for worms if they cannot see their own toes. Experiments that covered chickens' toes with taffeta stockings showed that this behaviour is not instinctive but needed other variables that might not be immediately apparent to onlookers. Despite being hungry, the fact is the chickens stared at the worms rather than ate them. If the socks were left on for longer than two days the chickens failed to develop normal eating habits.

The experiments above show that behaviours thought of as innate might actually need other environmental triggers or variables that are not even generally appreciated. So, thinking outside the square in AS, the dominant interest needs to partner attention and motivation to help us build connections to understanding.

This is another reason why, according to Björne (2007): 'Researchers in the field of autism must be bold and creative, and not be content with the claim that some behaviors are innate, but start the search for non obvious variables involved in the development of autism' (p. 30).

Björne (2007), whilst stating that ToM has had a huge impact upon traditional understanding of human development, points out that it can no longer be accepted as sufficiently explaining the enigma which is autism. Thus, Kaland, Mortensen and Smith (2007), Minshew and

Williams (2007), Björne (2007) and Baird (2008), like so many others, are suggesting that AS individuals use other mechanisms to make sense of the world we all live in. This makes perfect sense to me.

Also, like Björne and the increasing number of other researchers (e.g. Dziobek *et al.* 2006; Grant *et al.* 2005; Hale and Tager-Flusberg 2005), Bowler (2001) suggests we look at why AS individuals pass ToM tests and not only at why we don't.

With this in mind maybe there is a hint in the work by Kennett (2002), who shows how three lines of evidence support the idea that moral judgement is not impaired in autism. Kennett cites the studies by Blair (1996), who found that autistic children were just as likely to show good moral judgement as NT children of the same age and tested with the same tests (e.g. the moral/conventional distinction test). Similar findings occurred in research by Grant *et al.* (2005). Blair's (1995, 1996, 1999) studies even demonstrated that the children who failed false-belief tasks for ToM still showed good moral judgement.

Yet, in much of the literature (e.g. Baron-Cohen 2005) ToM is seen as synonymous with reasoning and empathic judgements, such as those that might impact upon the issues of morality (e.g. Vignemont and Frith 2007).

There would obviously be many reasons for the difficulties that we experience as AS individuals. ToM is only one aspect of that debate. Williams, Goldstein and Minshew (2006) suggest the primary precursor to an impaired ToM and other social difficulties exhibited in AS is the failure to imitate; they do not mention the role of interest as having any part in such difficulties.

Yet Kennett's work clearly demonstrates that although imitation might not be the route taken to access an understanding either of moral judgement or of the usual expectations in the social world, such values and concepts do govern many AS individuals' lives (Kennett 2002). Kennett cites autobiographical accounts (e.g. Temple Grandin and Jim Sinclair) where authors who are autistic suggest they hold high moral standards due to logically and methodically working things out as rules and the right thing to do, rather than being founded upon an emotive feeling state. Kennett, like Bacon *et al.* (1998), also notes that autistic children are responsive to the distress of others, for example:

> In summary, the emerging picture is that individuals with autism are meaningfully responsive to distress in others, and they are capable of moral judgement and reasoning.

> The exception to this would be in cases in which the ability to recognise and judge a moral situation depends upon theory of mind or social knowledge beyond the capabilities of an individual with autism (e.g. lying and manipulation). (Kennett 2002, p.5)

Diehl *et al.* (2003) found that AS adolescents did as well as or better than NT children with certain theory of mind tests, when they were given both social inferencing of psychological states as well as logical inferencing of physical states. They concluded that task type, variations in vocabulary ability and the provision of support influenced performance on the false-belief tasks.

Therefore if ToM abilities can be prompted, this means that ToM as a way of understanding 'Self' and 'Other' can exist in AS individuals even though such abilities may not typically be noted. Also, if ToM can be nurtured in AS individuals, then ToM issues cannot explain the complete clinical picture seen and experienced in autism. This is in agreement with Blair (1999), who has suggested that the moral perception of AS individuals may be based upon an understanding of value that exists because it does, rather than it only being of value if it is 'like-me'. I totally understand this thinking and can only echo that this is true of my own experiences also. Does it matter if the route to my arrival at a destination is different from the way someone else gets there? Surely the issue is that I arrive!

This argument is supported by others (e.g. Bowler 2007), who dispute that false belief is a useful way of measuring ToM. Murray (1992, 1996) and Lesser and Murray (1997), with particular concerns to interest and attention and their role in human interaction, have debated that individual development is based more upon the interest system than upon ToM (which states there is only one way of appreciating concepts of 'Self' and 'Other'). This reasoning makes sense to me and fits in with much of the nature and interaction between us all as people. Whether we align our interests with others as in polytropism or follow the dictation of our dominant interest, as in monotropism, it's all about 'interest'.

When considering 'the triad of impairments' as the basis for AS individuals' experience, the ideas of rigid thinking and being imaginative seem contradictory. Yet so many of us exhibit imagination and are creative in ways that have enabled the typical population to sit back and wonder with awe, whether this is in the realm of engineering, science, computing technology or the mapping of some geographical location. These abilities may be the product of a distinct focus and interest, which is at the very heart of the arguments presented in this book.

With regard to its connection to imagination and creativity Murray (2006) has pointed out that the foam rubber shapes used in the 'Torrance Test' (a test developed in 1964, 1974, by Torrance commonly used to explore creativity) to explore issues of imagination and creativity in AS individuals (Craig and Baron-Cohen 1999) might not be measuring autistic creativity so much as on the one hand reflecting the restricted range of actions and interests by which the study participants must have been selected in accordance with the diagnostic criteria, and on the other hand measuring typical willingness to suspend interest in the truth (i.e. no it is not an airplane, it is a foam rubber shape). This would imply such a test is null and void when used with AS individuals who demonstrate creativity and imagination but possibly by different means. As Minshew and Williams (2007, 2008) and Minshew and Hobson (2008) have concluded, AS individuals may be using different parts of our brains from the NT developing population and this will mean we perceive life and learning quite differently.

Minshew and Williams (2007) and Behrmann, Thomas and Humphreys (2006) suggest we demonstrate a really remarkable ability to use the visual parts of the right side of the brain. Goodale and Milner (1992) found that there are separate visual pathways allowing the brain to decide between perception and action in typical development. This is important and something we often take for granted when we consider cognitive development.

With this in mind, Minshew and Hobson (2008) showed that AS individuals process information differently from NT individuals. For example, they suggest we may use other abilities as a way of compensating for some of the language problems we may have. Minshew and Williams (2007) also suggest the visual parts of the brain might be responsible for a preference that we have for processing details, which, they conclude, may sometimes be a decided advantage.

This type of advantage might even show itself differently from within the NT population. For example, imagination and creativity are often linked, but might not be seen by the typical eye as such. Steve Silberman (2008) suggests that many musicians, scientists, mathematicians, artists and others were/are very creative and imaginative in their work, despite their autism or despite similar difficulties. A research project exploring whether poetry (for example) by AS individuals is as valid or as valuable as poetry by NT individuals found that the works by AS individuals were as poetic and as imaginative as any other work (Lawson 2006; Roth 2007). See Appendix D for examples of creative art works by an AS individual.

Having said this, of course, terms such as creativity and imagination do not describe the same attributes. Many individuals report being able to imagine what someone else might be feeling or going through, but the same individuals might not consider themselves to be creative or good at activities requiring creativity.

For reasons related to the above, many suggest that ToM is inadequate as a theory for how children develop cognitively, and that it might even lack any real scientific evidence (Björne 2007; Bloom and German 2000; Bowler 2001; Bowler *et al.* 2005). For example, as Bowler *et al.* (2007) point out:

> Children with autism have been shown to be delayed in their development of an understanding of the representational nature of mental states (Baron-Cohen *et al.* 1985) and, even though older and higher-functioning individuals with autism and Asperger's syndrome often pass false belief tasks (Bowler 1992), this may happen because they bring different underlying processes to the tasks (Bowler 1992, 1997; Happé 1995). As Bowler *et al.* (2000) argue, if the apparent lack of difficulty on 'theory of mind' tasks seen in higher-functioning individuals with autism results from the operation of different mechanisms, then we would predict impaired performance on tasks. (p.126)

Therefore, ToM might not be the issue with difficulty in the performance of typical ToM tasks, rather an individual might be using different brain mechanisms connected more to, for example, sensory perception, remembering and a host of different implications from these, rather than to belief. If this is the case, the idea of ToM as an appropriate theory to describe the difficulties we have (as AS individuals) with social perception, for example, would not be applicable.

Other potential questions

Those who support the idea of ToM suggest it could be represented in one of two different ways: modular or non-modular. Modular theorists suggest there is a specific part of the brain where ToM can be located (e.g.

Fodor 1983; Leslie 2000) and non-modular theorists, such as proponents of general learning theory (e.g. Baron-Cohen *et al.* 1994; see also Donovan and Bransford 2005; Hobson 2008) suggest ToM is a product of interaction with one's environment. So, even some ToM theorists may be unsure of ToM as a 'general' theory for cognitive development.

AS individuals can and do pass a variety of tests for ToM. Could, therefore, the cognitive differences between NT developing individuals and those of us on the autism spectrum be attributed to the way that access to perception occurs to enable learning (e.g. Casanova *et al.* 2007; Gallese and Goldman 1998)? Could our cognitive architecture differ? If so, it might be that understanding issues related to 'mentalising' can occur, but by differing means.

Even if ToM did explain some of our difficulties, Hill (2004) and Sally and Hill (2006) suggest it doesn't account for many of the 'non-social' difficulties we encounter. These are referred to as any behaviour that is not associated with social interaction (e.g. sensory dysphoria). If AS individuals can be shown to have imagination (i.e. we are able to think of something that is there even when it isn't), and if we do pass typical tests for ToM, then the issues might be more concerned with learning differently, rather than learning typically. This has all sorts of implications for education, relationships and employment.

In their longitudinal studies (2007), Rutherford *et al.* concluded that the autistic respondents lacked imagination. I think this should be given another look with the ideas of interest and attention as added variables. I believe that executive function, inter-subjectivity, imitation or general development (the areas of task testing in the study) might not be the main contributors to AS development, as they seem to be in NT development. Rutherford *et al.* (2007) point out that it is the qualities of joint attention that are uppermost in the ability to join in with pretend play. Therefore, attention and the interest system (which were not explored in Rutherford *et al.*'s study) require more research.

If learning differences (styles) differ in the AS population, and if interest and single attention guide an individual's learning, then the faculty of 'imagination' itself might develop differently in AS and NT populations. If this is the case then typical theories of ToM and how they traditionally relate to imagination might be redundant or irrelevant.

Debate between researchers who suggest that ToM in AS individuals is formed from attributes associated with 'Theory theory', rather than simulation theory continues (please see original thesis for explanations

In conversation, Zaffy has to access a library of existing visual files in order to extrapolate meaning

of these terms). For example, Kennett (2002) noted that some AS individuals, like Temple Grandin, talk about accessing information by referring to the 'libraries' or storage systems they have in their minds. They can reach into various archives and retrieve the right 'strategy' or 'conversational piece' that appears to belong to a particular occasion.

Grandin (2000) is said to be working and living from videos that she can replay in her head and thus she can, by approximation, learn the stages, methodically and in a calculated fashion, of the mental states of others. This process, although seen as simulation, is quite academic. It suggests that high-functioning autistic individuals are theory theorists, rather than simulationists (Kennett 2002).

This idea simply means that ToM might be learnt or achieved by AS individuals differently from NT individuals.

The ideas outlined above question the concept that ToM is formed only from an understanding of 'like me' or of 'feeling' from the other person's perspective. Appreciating value in and of itself may also be a route to constructing an understanding of 'Self' and 'Other'. In some ways the words of the song by Don Francisco: 'Love is not a feeling, it's an act of your will' (1991) indicate that choosing to act, even without an emotive precursor, must take some form of understanding of other persons.

Many AS individuals live lives ethically and morally with character and personality profiles that demonstrate that high moral standards are uppermost in all of our chosen activities (Gardner 2008; Gernsbacher and Frymiare 2005; Lawson 1998). Those who do not demonstrate these qualities invite the questions: Would they be this person if we took AS out of the picture? And has this individual been hoodwinked by others into performing immoral actions or actions leading to criminal activity? If the answer to questions like these is 'most likely', then lack of ToM in the AS individual is not the issue here.

SUMMARY

Many queries and questions have been raised in this chapter concerning ToM theories, for example: what are they measuring, and are false-belief tasks the right way, or the only way, to assess imagination, creativity and/ or how individuals come to make sense of either their own worlds or the worlds of others? There is much evidence to support the view that AS individuals are capable of acquiring awareness of other minds, though this may happen later than in an NT developing child. Also, other aspects of AS may interfere with the development of a good understanding of other people, who tend to be non-literal and hard to predict.

This chapter summarises some of the current debate around evidence for ToM as a theory that explains all the characteristics seen in clinical assessments of AS individuals. Clearly the evidence is weighted towards ToM not explaining enough of the AS experience. The next chapter will explore the cognitive theory of executive functions (EF) and the idea that EF is dysfunctional in AS. Whether this can account for the total picture seen in AS, or even for some aspects of it, is still under debate.

CHAPTER 5

Cognitive Theory: Executive Functioning

INTRODUCTION

This chapter will summarise the cognitive theory of AS, known as executive functioning theory, often closely linked with ToM. I suggest that even though it is apparent that we (AS individuals) have difficulties in the area of executive functioning (e.g. planning, prioritising, organising and so on), the close relationship that ToM and EF appear to share in the typical population does not account for why these difficulties exist for AS individuals, so much as it simply informs us that they do.

Definition

Executive functioning (EF) theory is a term used to describe the ability to plan, prioritise, organise and implement the functions an organism needs to think and do in an appropriate order and fashion (e.g. Ozonoff 1995). These include cognitive control mechanisms, such as attentional flexibility, inhibition of prepotent information, updating information in working memory and the ability to delay instant gratification (e.g. Miyake *et al.* 2000). Others have defined EF in a similar way; for example Hill (2004) suggests EF can be thought of as an umbrella term for functions such as planning, working memory, impulse control and inhibition, as well as for the initiation and monitoring of action.

Foundations for executive functioning theory

Unlike ToM, the theory of EF did not eventuate from the study of typical development but from the research associated with symptomology found in individuals with brain injury (e.g. Decety and Lamm 2007). Many of the characteristics and daily difficulties we (AS individuals) have (e.g. difficulties with planning, thinking ahead, prioritising and self-regulation) can also be seen in individuals with brain injury who live with dysexecutive syndrome (Burgess and Simons 2005). Dysexecutive syndrome usually means affected individuals have damage to the frontal lobes (e.g. Chiavarino, Apperly and Humphreys 2008).

Initially this prompted the idea that EF might explain the characteristics seen in AS. However, studies of prefrontal cortex activity in typical and atypical cognitive development (Zelazo and Muller 2002) concluded that EF is not always impaired in individuals with prefrontal cortex damage.

Also, EF is found not only in humans but in many other animals too (Grandin and Deesing 2003). This implies that EF is not confined to the human species and that it operates on a variety of levels. Vohs and Baumeister (2004) explain that EF refers to the brain circuits that help individuals to prioritise, integrate, regulate and take charge of other cognitive functions. These manage the brain's cognitive activity and enable individuals to practise self-control and self-regulation across a number of domains. Such functions are often impaired in some brain-injured individuals (Shallice and Burgess 1991). For example, members of the Country Women's Association knitted squares and sewed them together to make blankets that could cover the laps of brain-injured men whilst seated or in a wheelchair. They did this so the men were given a measure of privacy if they could not resist the urge to masturbate whilst in public. Usually this act is only meant to be performed in private and NT individuals are aware of this when their EF is intact.

At times many of us (the AS population) have difficulty separating private from public and many other areas commonly associated with EF. I suggest that how the brain manages matters of 'attention' and 'interest' could account for many behaviours often thought of as impulsive, inappropriate or out of sync, just like those resulting from brain injury. You can read more about this in Chapters 8, 9 and 10.

Components of executive functioning theory

The three principal components of EF are working memory, inhibitory control and attentional flexibility. Duncan (1986) suggested executive functions are the various processes that underlie purposeful behaviour, as in planning, focusing of attention and memory. Therefore, according to Duncan, EF enables the mind to exist in the present but also to plan ahead and let go of the immediate situation, if necessary. This makes it easier to change ideas, change plans and follow the interests of 'Self' or 'Other' because there exists a mental model or internal representation to guide the individual to appropriate actions.

Ideas about the components of EF have grown and developed over time; for example, Royall *et al.* (2002) suggest the concept of executive functions has developed into two separate themes. They define the terms generally to mean functions that give executive control over other functions but imply they are separate. One theme considers the cognitive functions associated with the frontal lobes of the brain; these can be acquired as skills giving rise to insight, choice and judgement. They are all skills that can be measured, which means it is easier to appreciate impairment and loss of these skills in brain-injured people.

The other theme suggests that EF controls complex activities and their execution almost independently of will or choice. More explicitly this refers to the non-executive processes that underlie the executive functions. It is in these domains that evidence is seen of dysfunctional EF, for example the inability to organise or plan ahead as well as loss of memory and of abilities to prioritise or regulate self-expression and behaviour.

Recently, components behind these abilities have been located, suggesting they build into the theory of executive functions as brain architecture that allows the brain to promote and designate particular circuitry for prioritising, integrating and regulating other cognitive functions. This means that EF then 'manages' the brain's cognitive functions and provides the right mechanisms for self-regulation (Vohs and Baumeister 2004).

The brain's neural networks are created differently for different tasks. Some networks manage other networks so there is a hierarchy. Particular networks located in the prefrontal cortex, the limbic region and the cerebellum, for example, assist with coordinating and integrating quite

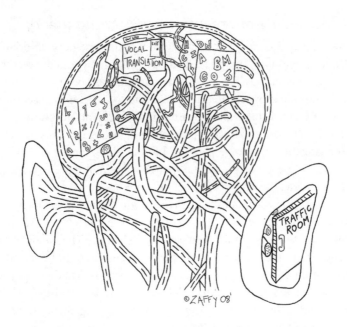

specific cognitive functions 'as a conductor might manage the differing aspects needed for an orchestral piece of music' (Brown 2006).

The idea of the brain using different networks for different tasks is not new but is very important when we consider the issues related to autistic behaviour. The brain is an amazing organ and its plasticity to adapt and take on board different ways or routes to achieving particular outcomes via such networks is well known (Minshew and Williams 2007).

APPLICATION TO CHILD DEVELOPMENT

Blair, Zelazo and Greenberg (2005) suggest that EF is essential in the developing child so that the child can grow in confidence and competence. They also stress the importance of being able to shift attention and take charge of self, when necessary, to inhibit self-expression and delay gratification. These are important abilities that allow individuals to relate in social situations with more consistency of success. These are also the very areas that many of us (AS individuals) have difficulty with (Hoy 2007; Jackson 2002).

The operations of the (pre)frontal cortex in· the brain includes EF functions and in AS this area of the brain is less active during executive function tasks than in the typical brain (Lathe 2006). However, executive dysfunction is not only specific to AS but is found in a variety of individual experience including attention deficit disorder, obsessive compulsive disorder, Tourette's syndrome, phenylketonuria and schizophrenia (e.g. Geurts *et al.* 2004).

Whilst basic prefrontal and executive functioning develop during early infancy (Hughes 1998), it seems that these functions work in tandem with lower processing brain functions and appropriate sensory connections that enable awareness and perception to be coordinated into appropriate action (e.g. Björne 2007; Blair *et al.* 2005).

As already suggested, sensory profiles, perceptions, awareness of 'Self' and 'Other' could be experienced quite differently in AS than in the typical population. This might not be an EF issue or a relationship to ToM, but it might be related to a totally different system or perception loop that has more to do with the interest and attention systems of the individual.

In NT development, adults point to an object to share something of interest and the child demonstrates joint attention by joining that adult in attending to what they are declaring. However, if an NT adult points to something of interest to them, and possibly not of interest to the AS individual, usually we fail to follow the direction of that declarative pointing (Newson 2000). However, Robins *et al.* (2004) found that we passed EF tests when interest was engaged from our perspective. This appears to be direct evidence that executive functions are active in the AS individuals in their study, but that they may be working differently.

Hill (2004) noted in her review that there are many factors leading to EF problems and these occur across other populations and disability areas, including language disorder and learning disability. She concluded that it may be more informative to focus on the influence of learning disability.

To date, the literature on EF and its connection to the characteristics typical of AS show that AS individuals have many EF difficulties. However, the same literature fails to give a consistent causal account of why. It also fails to show consistency across studies that the difficulties evidenced in AS are uniform and apply to all AS individuals.

EF problems are common among other disability groups and groups of individuals with learning disability; this means EF difficulties are not peculiar to AS. This is not to understate the importance of EF as a common factor in daily life difficulties for so many of us (AS individuals). It is, however, not enough, as a theory, to explain the particular pattern of difficulties, strengths and sensory differences experienced by AS individuals.

Research over time

To test how well EF is working for individuals, tests such as the Wisconsin Card Sorting task were developed by Grant and Berg (1948). This test and others like it (the Tower of Hanoi/London) are identified in the neuropsychological literature. Again, however, Hill (2004) in her review states that the emerging picture for EF difficulties as a core deficit in AS is unclear possibly due to inconsistencies in the studies performed associated with IQ discrepancies and learning disability differences across participants.

Many studies have tried to explore what comes first. Is it EF dysfunction that causes difficulties seen in AS and some disruptive behavioural disorders such as attention deficit with hyperactivity disorder (ADHD), or is EF in normal working order but negatively influenced due to other issues (e.g. Shallice *et al.* 2002)?

If neural networks are wired up differently in AS from that which is encountered in typical development, it might account for why so many of us pass tests but seem to get there via different routes. For example, to explore if EF dysfunctioning was the cause of such difficulties as ADHD, Willcutt *et al.* (2005) provided a meta-analysis of 83 studies that administered executive function measures, such as the Stop-Signal Task, Porteus Mazes, Tower of Hanoi and Wisconsin Card Sorting Task, to groups of children and adolescents with ($N = 3374$) and without ($N = 2969$) ADHD.

Their analysis indicated that groups with ADHD exhibited significant impairment in neuropsychological measures of response inhibition, vigilance, working memory and planning. However, they also suggested that difficulties with EF were not the cause of ADHD but clearly a side effect.

EXECUTIVE FUNCTIONING AND THEORY OF MIND

The assumption by some is that EF and ToM need to work together to appropriately inform one another. They are considered as close relations because they are both cognitive theories concerning how individuals think and process information, but also because they appear to share some of the same brain circuitry. For example, Bull, Phillips and Conway (2008) point out that MRI studies show in the normal population the prefrontal cortex is active in both EF and ToM activities. This, they say, suggests a shared or interactive neuro-anatomical system. However, they also note that the same studies have failed to separate belief and reasoning, the cognitive processes supporting other EF functions, so this sheds doubt upon a domain-specific brain architecture for ToM.

Philosophically one would argue that belief and reasoning are crucial to the operation of executive functions. To date, however, we have not found any brain architecture that relates specifically to these concepts. Rather, belief and reasoning are aspects of deeper concepts associated with wider ideology, incorporating a variety of systems all working together, rather than being the outcome of brain architecture working independently.

Questions concerning executive functioning and the autism spectrum

The issues cited above raise two questions. One concerns the earlier discussion about connections between belief and ToM; that is, the issue describing individuals who pass ToM tests on false belief but still have other issues commonly related to ToM and EF (e.g. social and communication problems). The other concerns issues about specific architecture in the brain for connections between EF and ToM.

Therefore, although EF theory could be argued as a theory that accounts for AS, especially when combined with ToM, it does not account for why some of us pass both ToM and EF assessments. For example, Joseph and Tager-Flusberg (2004) found when they compared 31 verbal school-aged AS children on three tests of ToM and EF that although children had a variety of differing scores on these tests their autistic difficulties with social interaction seemed more to do with linguistic competence and social reciprocity. The AS children in Joseph and Helen Tager-Flusberg's (2004) study also displayed the need for repetitive routines and showed signs of sensory issues not accounted for by either ToM or EF theories of AS.

Apparently, some of us, at times, fail to utilise our senses, skills and abilities because we experience disconnection between the will to do (intention) and the ability to act (action) (Baggs 2008; Wing and Shah 2000). This means I may feel or have a sensation but not recognise what it is connected to or where it comes from, so the moment incapacitates me. This is not a theory of mind issue, nor is it to do with executive functions. If this is happening, then neither ToM nor EF fully explains some basic and core issues in AS that many of us battle with on a daily basis.

Difficulties with patterns of sensory dysphoria are often associated with AS and are described as being one of the main reasons we suffer with sensory issues that NT individuals don't notice or can filter out from their attention (e.g. continuing to listen whilst other possible distracters are operating in the background, such as traffic noises and so on). I suggest such sensory difficulties could be the reason why some of us fail to self-regulate or seem impulsive, disorganised and unable to wait or to delay self-gratification.

So, although it appears that there is no doubt that executive functions in AS individuals are often impaired, the reasons why this is so are still being debated. Whether ToM is working alone or in tandem with EF, it still does not account for the full clinical presentation of AS or the various experiences we (AS individuals) have.

It is clear that to date many believe ToM and EF are both impaired in AS and that the two theories collectively account for many of the characteristics of AS. However, those supporting these arguments do not explore the role of interest and attention working alongside these theories. Thus, although I am not questioning whether or not these difficulties exist for AS individuals, I am querying the reasons why.

In accounts written by us (AS individuals) mention is made of the need to stay with what is familiar and to resist change (e.g. Hoy 2007). Many of us say that we have difficulty shifting attention and prefer structure and routine rather than variety and surprise (e.g. Dern 2008; Grandin 1996; Jackson 2002; Williams 1994). These difficulties can be explained by other reasoning, later explored in Chapters 7 and 8. Impulse control and the ability to appreciate and monitor 'Self' with regard to 'Other' is also difficult, but this is not only peculiar to AS (Sergeant, Geurts and Oosterlaan 2002).

So, although it might be tempting to think of these difficulties as only EF problems, related to issues with inhibition or self-regulation, Minshew and Williams (2007) clearly demonstrate that brain configuration is different in AS. They suggest that using different brain processes implies slower processing and this time-related factor would impact upon issues such as 'self-regulation'. This important concept suggests many of the difficulties we experience might not be related to ToM or EF but simply to the using of different processing attributes from those used in the NT population (O'Connor and Kirk 2008).

Therefore, although Gerrans and Stone (2008) suggest ToM might be implicated in AS, it does not account for the fuller clinical picture (even when working in tandem with EF) that we present with, such as completing a puzzle upside down (Happé 1994a) or superior results on block design tests compared to typical controls (non-autistic individuals paired for the study) (Mottron *et al.* 2006). Gerrans and Stone (2008) also suggest the difficulties seen in AS on ToM and EF tasks may result from what they call low-level social input systems, such as failure to share in joint attention.

That Gerrans and Stone mention 'systems' such as those that refer to joint attention, is very interesting. In Chapter 7 concepts about attention and interest as inter-relating systems informing learning are put forward and this inter-relating system is suggested to be different in AS compared to the NT population.

There is no doubt that EF is influenced by working memory, inhibitory control and attentional flexibility, enabling individuals to function with appropriate executive properties, but as Welsh, Pennington and Groisser (1991), amongst others, suggest, the latter (attributes of attention) have not been given enough credence.

In their earlier research Frith, Morton and Leslie (1991) have argued that the meta-cognitive skills necessary for understanding mental states (theory of mind) are necessary for adequate executive functioning. Consequently, if understanding mental states is impaired, then EF will also be impaired. Although this might be the case, I am challenging the traditional explanations for why this is so. For example, more recent research shows that EF is not always impaired in individuals where associated difficulties (e.g. brain injury) are apparent (e.g. Blair 2005; Hill 2004; Yerys *et al.* 2007).

In the study by Yerys *et al.* (2007) two experiments were conducted; the first experiment to see if EF difficulties were present in the AS group and the second experiment to see if EF was a secondary deficit to AS. In both experiments 18 AS children were compared to 18 children of mixed aetiology and 18 typically developing children on specific EF tasks. These children (mean age was 2.9 years) were matched for mental age (MA) and all completed a battery of EF tests that consisted of the three measures: Windows, Spatial Reversal and A-Not-B.

It was found that EF difficulties were not present in the AS children but that they could develop as a secondary difficulty from AS. Thus, even though research has shown a relationship between EF and ToM and has found that these are two areas highly correlated in autism (e.g. very young children who gain a diagnosis of AS fail to show joint attention: Dawson *et al.* 2004), it is not enough to state that because they coexist in a condition they are causative of related issues.

I can only echo again that attention and interest may be part of the equation not given enough consideration. So, despite poor EF being named as responsible for difficulties behind so many tasks (e.g. turn taking; following instructions; shifting attention and so on), attention and interest could be the missing common denominators.

Other questions and limitations

As suggested throughout the above, weak EF occurs for a variety of reasons. Although EF in autism is weak and difficult to track, this does not mean it is the explanation of the characteristics seen in AS. Another explanation is the lack of connection (or exceptional connection) between various brain structures (Minshew and Williams 2007, 2008; Minshew and Hobson 2008).

Whether over-convergence, lack of connection or only connecting via certain channels, it can be argued that being focused on detail and not so aware of the bigger picture could be a useful tool in some situations. Under certain circumstances (for example, when we are allowed to focus upon activities of our own choice), the brain structuring described by Minshew could bring about some benefits in allowing us to focus better upon the task in hand.

This suggests when AS individuals are interested and focused, we display executive function similar to NT individuals. For example, Griffith *et al.* (1999) found in their study of 18 AS children compared to 17 typically developing children as matched controls, all with a mean age of 4.3 years, that the AS children showed equal attention to EF tasks when their interest was used: '...the tasks were arranged in a fixed sequence...

To make sure the child's interest was used...keep motivation...the object searched for was determined by what most interested the child...' (Griffith *et al.* 1999, p.820).

For many of us, this ability to focus upon areas of interest does seem to take precedence (e.g. Holliday Wiley 2002; Murray 1992; Murray *et al.* 2005).

Sullivan (2002) emphasises the word 'notice' several times and talks about 'bringing online' her knowledge and ability to form connections and then act upon these. This is a phenomenon shared by others with learning styles directed by dyslexia and similar learning differences (Vidyasagar and Pammer 1999). It also implies the different use of attention and its cognitive dimensions. If this is so, EF would not be enough to act alone as a cognitive theory for AS.

Goldstein, Johnson and Minshew's (2001) research into attentional style in autism showed that dysfunctions in attention (failure to attend to aspects of allusions that typicals attend to) could be regarded as a core area of deficit among AS individuals. This type of evidence begs the question: Are apparent deficits in attention influencing weaknesses in executive functioning or vice versa? However, in 2010 it seems that the causal relationship between EF and attention still needs more research. There are hints in the literature that there is a relationship but this is not yet fully explained (Happé and Ronald 2008).

Difficulty with executive functioning is common amongst the AS population. However, this is quite different from suggesting that poor EF causes AS. Due to our particular ability to stay focused upon areas of interest, we (AS individuals) can demonstrate high levels of EF in connection with our interests. This shows that when interest and attention are positively interacting EF difficulties that are apparent at other times in an individual's life may disappear (e.g. Purkis 2000).

The next chapter will explore the theory of central coherence in autism as a core component and an explanation of the autistic spectrum.

SUMMARY

This chapter described the cognitive theory of executive functions deficit or dysfunction as a possible explanation for AS. It demonstrated ways EF and ToM might act in tandem and be related to a variety of behavioural outcomes. Some of the behaviours correlate to clinical descriptions of difficulties seen in AS, whilst other behaviours were related to acquired brain injury. However, it also highlighted the gaps in the theory and noted the types of situations and circumstance in which AS individuals demonstrate high levels of EF. Some other aspects of EF difficulty that seemed more related to attentional properties seen in other situations, such as ADHD, dyslexia and various learning difficulties, and which are not exclusive to autism, were noted.

CHAPTER 6

Cognitive Theory: Weak Central Coherence

INTRODUCTION

This chapter will define the term *weak central coherence* (WCC) and explore it as a cognitive theory of AS. It will outline the assumptions of WCC and show how they translate to behaviour commonly associated with AS. It will also summarise the strengths and weaknesses of WCC as debated in the original text this work is taken from. The background to the development of WCC theory, its core basis, foundation and subsequent claims and issues are outlined below.

Definition

A weak central coherence is defined as difficulties with drawing experiences, details and other such pieces of information together to access 'the whole picture' (gestalt). Some cognitive views concerning autism, especially those of Frith (1989) and Happé (1994a), suggest the attribution of a weak central coherence in autism (Happé, Briskman and Frith 2001). Happé suggested the clinical picture, presented by Kanner and Asperger, such as restricted interests, resistance to change, spikes of ability, savant abilities, excellent rote memory and preoccupation with parts of objects, are not accounted for by the triad of impairments said to be associated with ToM and EF.

Foundations for weak central coherence theory

Although Happé (1999a, 1999b) concedes that EF deficits might explain certain behaviours seen in AS, such as resistance to change, difficulties with forward thinking, impulsiveness and failure to appreciate consequences, she suggests that other behaviours experienced by some of us are not explained by poor EF.

Such phenomena as having an amazing memory for facts (Attwood 2007); having a memory for and using word strings rather than conversational sentences; having a memory for things that seem unrelated; using echolalia of particular phrases and seeming senseless terminology; having an unusual fascination with patterns, colours and objects (Dakin and Firth 2005); completing jigsaw puzzles by shape, rather than by following a sequence or viewing the completed picture; sorting faces by accessories such as nose, eyebrows or lips (Webb *et al.* 2006); recognising faces upside-down; and much more are not accounted for by theories such as ToM or EF. All the above behaviours associated with AS are well documented and supported by appropriate research (Riby and Hancock 2008).

> **My big picture**
> I stared at your picture for ever today,
> I hoped this would mean you weren't far away.
> Although oceans and skies separate each from our home,
> Your picture is present so you can't be gone.
>
> If I think for a moment that you are not here,
> I start to panic and become full of fear.
> If you are not here, do you still exist?
> Will I ever see you? Can this be fixed?

The poem above relates to a time when I had to leave my family and travel abroad to another country. Because I couldn't see my family it felt like they no longer existed; even the country where my home was seemed like a distant dream. I found it really difficult to connect to the reality that they still existed, and this caused me lots of fear and anxiety. It's as if only the present, the now and what I was in at the time were the only reality and everything else had gone. Some might argue that this was Wendy not connecting to 'The Big Picture' or only able to connect to the details of what was immediately present or available. Once I was able to look at the family photograph in my wallet, however, I could 'feel' them again.

Some might say this kind of experience is more to do with a processing phenomenon allowing AS individuals to access only local information rather than the global picture; or by contrast allowing typical individuals to get the gist of a story whilst discounting the details.

Happé noted during many different experiments (supported by the original thesis linked to this text) that we (AS individuals), even those of us with normal IQ, fail to read for meaning but read with ease the information that is given to us. This meant that at times AS individuals noticed the details but not the fuller picture. Some of us completed drawings by moving from minor details outwards towards the whole (e.g. starting with one window then filling in the other details of the house around it).

Various studies exploring and assessing abilities in AS have searched for keys to understanding and supporting AS individuals. Some tests (e.g. the block design task, below) showed that we do better on these tasks than other non-autistic people, and this finding led to further ideas on what might happen if tests were presented differently.

The block design task (BDT) (a subtest of the Wechsler Intelligence Scales: Wechsler 1997) uses coloured cards depicting various patterns and designs made from red and white coloured cubes. The participant is asked to look at the card and recreate the design with the blocks given to them. This test is timed for performance quality. However, Shah and Frith (1993) challenged the good performance results typically found in the AS population.

They found superiority of the autistic group on the BDT vanished when the figure to be reproduced was segmented. Shah and Frith concluded that BDT superiority in autistic individuals was due to locally oriented processing, or weak central coherence (WCC).

However, several others have compared the level of performance on the block design task with other verbal and nonverbal subtests, and have still found that AS individuals usually do better on the block design task than those in a control group (Van Lang 2003).

Riby and Hancock (2009a, 2009b) noted that we only looked at information we were interested in, or failed to note socially implicated information that we were not interested in. This suggests that systems concerning an attention, an interest and a sensory-motor loop could be part of the equation as to why we tend to do better on tests such as block design.

Frith (1989) believed that the spiky profile of strengths and weaknesses seen in assessments of AS children come from a single cognitive disposition. Frith argued that autism was a product of information-processing difficulties where the individual could not access or draw together diverse information to construct higher-level meaning in context, or gain a central cohesive picture of it. However, others have found that global information can be accommodated under certain circumstances (e.g. Bertone *et al.* 2005). This would make sense of why I could connect to home once I looked at the family photograph.

According to WCC, AS individuals lack the ability to form coherence over as wide a range of stimuli as is possible for us. For example, we may be so focused upon a particular detail or set of details that we fail to see beyond them towards the larger picture or broader meaning. Frith (2004) and Happé (1999a, 1999b) suggest that this explains the phenomenon seen in AS, which is not explained by ToM or EF theory.

Fascination with patterns, textures and colours

They argued that because AS individuals experience the world in fragments and are not able to see parts in relation to the whole, this accounts for the clinical picture seen in AS. This clinical picture includes behaviours such as insistence upon 'sameness' (e.g. the need for routine); difficulties putting ourselves in 'another's shoes'; problems with communication; and difficulties often associated with poor imagination or rigid thinking.

However, as demonstrated earlier in this text, imagination and creativity may not be impaired in AS so much as they may present differently. Some have suggested that being detail-focused is not so much a general disposition but more an ability to focus upon details only of interest to that individual (Murray *et al.* 2005).

Components of weak central coherence theory

Although it has been suggested that the brain is 'hard wired' to enable ToM and EF to function successfully, it is difficult to pinpoint the same for the theory of WCC. However, Happé (1999a, 1999b) suggested that the very nature of AS, described by her as 'mind blindness', points to difficulties resulting from poor central coherence even if no specific brain architecture can be located.

Happé states that neither ToM nor EF accounts for the full picture of AS, rather it is suggested that there may be two other 'cognitive characteristics' that are active in AS. One cognitive characteristic may be an evolutionary outcome of brain insult leading to weak central coherence and the other a positive ability allowing focus on detail, which forms the basis for a cognitive style, rather than disorder (Happé and Ronald 2008).

This latter characteristic is of interest because it suggests that we show that we can gain access to understanding of 'Self' and of 'Other', but that the processes we might need to use are not typical, and typical testing using traditional cognitive theory is failing to note this. It also suggests both the weakness in central coherence and the gains in local processing, which Happé identifies as cognitive style, could follow from the same fundamental difference in attention distribution and connection to the interest system.

I once was quite upset when some friends changed their mind about going out with me. They explained that some other things required their attention and this meant they were not free to be with me. I was really angry and I remember thinking, 'Just when you think you can trust someone who says they are your friend, they fail to act friendly. They let you down! It's better not to have friends rather than be lied to.'

When I shared this thought with one of my lecturers he explained that sometimes people changed their minds; that they were in fact allowed to. I knew people 'changed their minds' but I had not realised that this was allowed. Learning this and coming to understand this wider concept completely changed the way I viewed my friendships. Rather than thinking my friends were lying to me, I began to appreciate that it was possible for other things to happen that then led my friends to change plans to adapt to changed circumstances; this was allowed.

The fact that I could learn this once it was explained to me, once the wider picture was filled in, means I could grasp an understanding and connect the bits together. I suggest this happens more readily once I, and other AS individuals, utilise interest and attention in a manner that makes sense to us. So, is this poor central coherence or a matter of attention?

The WCC theory and EF deficit theory are tributaries of the 'cognitive development stream'. These theories suggest that autism allows typical information processing, but prevents or interferes with integration of diverse information (i.e. information acquired in relation to different interests, especially those that are different from or appear separate to one's own).

In accordance with the WCC theory, Happé (1999a, 1999b) suggests that we tend to process local rather than global information, and that this means we fail to process information in context. Initially, Happé supported the WCC theory with experimental evidence. For example, she found 88 per cent of AS individuals failed to 'succumb' to the Müller-Lyer illusion and 8 per cent to the Kanizsa triangle, when compared to the typical population (Happé 1996) The Müller-Lyer illusion shows arrow lines arranged in a form. The horizontal line segment on the far left looks longer than the other one, even though both segments are of the same length.

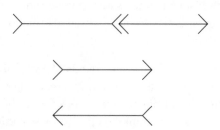

The Kanizsa triangle is a floating white triangle, which does not exist, but is seen. The brain has a need to see familiar simple objects and has a tendency to create a 'whole' image from individual elements (Gestalt means 'form' or 'shape' in German).

These results suggest that the second illusion requires a perception of gestalt (bringing information together or filling in the gaps) that might be greater than in the first illusion.

Hence, Happé argued that showing poor susceptibility to illusion was evidence of difficulty with gestalt or bringing together the different parts of a picture or understanding. Happé (1996) used six common visual illusions demonstrating poor susceptibility to illusion in AS individuals. According to her, failure to recognise illusions translated into poor central cohesion because one needed to process both local and global information, gaining access to context, in order to be deluded by the illusions. Therefore in this theory of AS, central coherence is lacking. Although this may be an attribute noted in AS I question the reasons for why this is so.

APPLICATION IN THE NEUROTYPICAL AND AUTISM SPECTRUM POPULATIONS

All of the mentioned cognitive theories, such as ToM, EF and WCC, have implications for both the NT and the AS populations. For example, Garner and Hamilton's (2001) research, which replicated that by Happé (1996) but with some minor adjustments (they used a computer rather than paper and pencil), demonstrated that the Kanizsa triangle was experienced as an illusion even more so by the AS group than by the typical group acting as a control group. This study consisted of 120 primary school children aged between four and seven years. AS children were included in this study only if their IQ was greater than 70 and learning disability was ruled out. All central coherence tests were taken on a computer, and results showed that the AS children performed better than the NT children.

Although Garner and Hamilton's (2001) initial trials needed human verbal instruction, the actual tests from which the results were derived were completed by the children using a computer without further human intervention. It could be argued that these tests taken on a computer ruled out interference from distractions that would otherwise be present – verbal instructions and all the body language of the assessors, plus white noise and other environmental factors. Therefore, the delivery of the tests conducted by Happé (1996) might have contained variables unaccounted for in their results and the computerised tests might have unwittingly eliminated such variables leading to a purer or less contaminated result. For example, in AS the verbal instructions take away the attention towards listening, the decoding and so on. Reading instructions from a computer screen means one less step (listening) to negotiate. Therefore is one less thing we need to attend to or accommodate. These results not only question whether WCC theory is relevant to AS individuals but also demonstrate that if children can identify global as well as local information in a given format (that is, the computerised testing might have been easier to concentrate on and allow for purer results) then WCC theory cannot be used to explain the AS condition. It is interesting that many of us find the use of technology enabling and helpful in connecting us to understanding in ways that allow us to build meaning; whereas, in typical daily social communication, the connection to meaning may fail to occur (Dern and Schuster 2007; Keay-Bright 2007).

Research over time

If WCC theory is the reason for the characteristics experienced in AS, then, according to Dakin and Frith (2005), this results in informational complexity preventing us from moving to an allocentric state of understanding (seeing the bigger picture) from an egocentric state of understanding (only seeing the elements of interest attended to by self). Or, the way that I interpret such implications is that AS individuals may fail to see the picture beyond that of the aspects of the world they connect to and may not generalise (or connect to) the bigger world outside of interest(s) noted or connected to.

The latter is evidenced in autobiographical and biographical accounts by AS individuals, or others that have shown AS individuals do accommodate the interests of others when we are able to attend to them. This might be initiated by using the AS individual's attention via their interest and moving outwards from this (e.g. Dern 2008; Gardner 2008; Gernsbacher et al. 2008; Riby and Hancock 2009a, 2009b).

Limitations of weak central coherence theory

Fletcher-Watson et al. (2006) suggest:

> Recent studies have shown that, contrary to the claims of weak central coherence, contextual processing is intact in autism, at least in the visual domain (Kourkoulou, Findlay and Leekam, 2005; López et al. 2003). If people with autism have weak central coherence they will not show differential responding according to inappropriate or appropriate context, whereas if people with autism can take account of context, they will respond in the same way as typical comparison participants. (p.546)

Fletcher-Watson et al. (2006) looked at the effects of context on attention. They found that both AS and NT participants integrated context and attention equally well.

In their study there were AS individuals aged from 17 years to 26 years (mean = 19.95 years) and all were of normal IQ. These individuals were matched with a typically developing control group aged 17 years to 32 years (mean = 18.21 years). The basic difference between the AS individuals and typically developing individuals on the task was one of timing; it was found that AS participants did equally well at attending to stimuli they were instructed to look at but that they failed to shift attention to a different object as quickly as controls. The researchers concluded 'that people with autism are able to identify context in a complex scene and then use that context as a selection tool when deciding which items upon which to focus their attention' (p.550).

In later studies Fletcher-Watson et al. (2008) showed that AS individuals used normal eye gaze in particular situations. These situations included noting changes to a picture that they looked at before and after changes had occurred. The AS individuals in their study showed normal attention. Again it is interesting that the format used in the study was a computer. Therefore, as well as demonstrating global attention, these individuals might have attended due to the medium used in the experiments, which captured their interest as well as their attention. Kourkoulou, Findlay and Leekam (2008) support the above studies in that they found visual orienting was normal in AS individuals.

The conclusions stated above question the WCC theory in AS because they show that we could identify context and draw conclusions from what we were being shown in the same way that typical participants did. The fact that we did so more slowly at times only supported the reality that AS individuals have EF difficulties (i.e. shifting attention) and will often take longer to process information. Again this implies the use of differing processes and not the lack of ability.

Garner and Hamilton (2001) have also questioned the proposition of universal weak central coherence in autistic people. They concluded that 'the idea that weak central coherence dominates all perceptual experience of autistic individuals is incorrect' (p.84).

Ozonoff et al. (1994) have also questioned the conclusion of weak central coherence in autism. They revealed that the autistic group in their study demonstrated no particular difficulty processing global features of a stimulus relative to two matched control groups (Tourette's syndrome and developmentally normal), aged 8 to16 years. One of the tasks they used was the H & S task, which examined local and global processing (e.g. seeing smaller numbers within bigger numbers or seeing the detail versus the bigger picture).

Hill (2004) suggested that AS children could be passing central coherence tests and EF tests because difficulties might only show up in learning-disabled AS individuals and not in AS individuals with normal IQ. Van Lang (2003) added support to this and suggested AS may not, of itself, account for the results (i.e. other factors, such as intellectual functioning, must also be considered).

Where ToM, EF and central coherence are concerned, Blakemore and Choudhury (2006) found that the typical developing brain 'grew' into these attributes; thus individuals were able or not able to pass particular tests according to age, developmental stage of life and other external and personal factors. This is not stressed in the literature concerning typical cognitive development but rather a rigid timetable of expectations is placed upon typical and autistic cognitive development without allowing for these other factors. Even anxiety, stress and fear will contribute to poor test results, but these are often not accommodated as variables in the test results outcome (e.g. Kassim, Hanafi and Hancock 2007).

Blakemore and Choudhury note (2006, p.308) that so many things depend upon 'interactions between genetics, brain structure, physiology and chemistry and the environment'. Thus AS individuals tested on central coherence tasks might not perform well between ages 7 and 11 years or before age 14 to 16 years, and then again might do better as young adults. Such findings are likely to be the result of the developing brain (e.g. changing in adolescence) due to typical life changes and hormonal surges. Very often these are not considerations in AS research.

Another way of reinterpreting the literature is to consider the idea that weak coherence is not the difficulty but rather the opposite, that a strong drive for coherence exists in AS. According to autobiographical accounts, and to some researchers, the need to order, orchestrate and achieve coherence is very high in AS, but the connecting information might not be available (e.g. Flavell 1988; Lawson 1998, 2001, 2008; Minshew and Hobson 2008; Mishew and Williams 2008; Murray 1992, 1995). It is interesting that such a phenomenon often occurs in other communities, such as in populations where children have been blind from birth (e.g. Green, Pring and Swettenham 2004) are deaf or have an intellectual disability or acquired brain injury (Griffin *et al.* 2006).

I suggest that problems in AS, such as building connections to concepts, are founded in monotropism, which leads to fewer connections between attention, interest and sensory and motor dynamics. NT individuals who can multi-task and draw aspects together from working memory, experience, long-term memory and a variety of other contexts do not necessarily get the picture right but they do have the advantage in a multi-tasking world where they are the majority.

Typical 'normality' is a paradigm that depends upon which lens one uses and what any given society depicts and dictates at any given time. Maybe psychology and typical understanding is informed by the Baron-Cohen example of rigid cognitive development and theory of mind understanding; or the EF theory of core deficits in planning and so on; or the failure to see the whole picture, as in WCC theory. Or maybe cognitive development can be different for other reasons. Remaining open to other possibilities is an important position for psychology to take. Figure 6.1 depicts an alternative picture to WCC and suggests the very opposite to WCC could be happening for AS individuals.

- Central coherence = ability to draw connections together from the 'big picture'. This can only occur with least effort, when one has access to the big picture via many differing channels (polytropism).
- The need for coherence is extreme in monotropism where all of the attention is gathered into one place. However, this type of coherence excludes information from outside the attention tunnel.

- Some executive functions (thinking, organising and ordering) are also extreme in AS. Sometimes this leads to obsessive ordering rituals, repetitive behaviour and/or lack of organisational ability outside the attention tunnel; but there is potential for positive outcomes from focused attention and interest.

Therefore:

- Polytropism and monotropism refer to attention distribution; these are more accurate terms than 'lack of central coherence'.

Figure 6.1: An alternative explanation to weak central coherence.

Garner and Hamilton (1999) claimed that earlier research on illusions was based upon an 'all or nothing' model, suggesting visual illusions were either being seen or not being seen. Their own experiments aimed to establish more accuracy and demonstrated how much or how little a visual illusion was experienced by AS individuals. Using a computerised measure for the visual illusion they could show when the illusion was being experienced. They used two illusions: the Müller-Lyer figure and the Kanizsa triangle. As mentioned earlier in this chapter these two illusions were chosen because they represented the extremes of the illusions used by Happé (1996).

The Garner and Hamilton (2001) study demonstrated that AS individuals could draw all the bits together when extraneous material was removed; that is, there was only a computer screen to look at. The computer screen also factored in that attentional activity was confined to the screen and that the social pressures of people, choice and social demand were eliminated as confounding factors. Their research showed that we could process global information and, in fact, did so better than the non-autistic groups. Results such as this refute weak central coherence as an explanation of AS because AS individuals perform in line with mental age on a variety of tasks that involve integrating information (forming a cohesive picture) (e.g. Scott and Baron-Cohen 1996; Scott, Baron-Cohen and Leslie 1994).

Ropar and Mitchell (1999, 2001) also query the WCC theory in AS. In contrast to Happé (1996), they found participants with autism were just as susceptible to visual illusions as controls. In their study Ropar and Mitchell presented a variety of visual illusions to individuals with autism using a computer screen. They then asked participants if target elements were the same size or different. If they were not of equal size participants were asked to use computer keys to adjust them so they would be the same size. This experiment highlighted the participants' susceptibility to the illusions by measuring how much they attempted to change what they saw so as to make the objects being viewed the same size. Their findings showed AS participants were as likely to be deluded as typical participants were.

The interesting development from these studies is that global processing might be under attentional control in autism (Charman *et al.* 1997; Milne *et al.* 2002; Milne *et al.* 2006). If this is so, then it is not a difficulty with poor or weak central cohesion that is at issue but what we are able to attend to (i.e. at any given moment) that could be a factor in the clinical picture we present.

Utilising typical cognitive processes implies the integration of a number of channels from which information is gleaned. For example, typical individuals receive information from their senses (i.e. sight, hearing, touch, smell, taste and proprioception) and then the information is sorted and processed according to usefulness, priority, need, desire and so on. Each of the cognitive theories of autism has grappled with a cognitive explanation of why individuals with AS function as we do. Each theory has limitations and each theory appears to fail to take into account the fact that typical individuals integrate several channels of information simultaneously, whilst we attend to information often from just one sense or channel at any one time. This implies the use of a different spread of attention in AS from that found within the NT population. This will have implications for the occupation of an interest system by both populations leading to particular characteristics as demonstrated in Figure 6.1.

Finally, Plaisted *et al.* (2006) note that there are two ways of looking at the cognitive theory of weak central coherence in AS. One is that

AS individuals have a preference for local processing rather than global processing. The other way of thinking of this is that we are better at discriminating between unique factors rather than common ones.

SUMMARY

Central coherence theory presupposes that global processing of a variety of information along with processing local information enables an individual to form an overall cohesive picture. It suggests that because AS individuals draw upon local information above global information, and fail to be deluded by visual illusions, we will have problems understanding the intentions and actions of others, or we have weak central coherence.

Some, especially looking at AS through the window of NT development, have interpreted AS behaviour as a lack of gestalt detail (difficulties seeing the whole and not just the detail) or as a lack of global processing ability in general terms. It might, however, be more concerned with an attention, interest and sensory-motor processing loop that is facilitated by other brain processes than those used by NT individuals.

This chapter has explored the WCC theory and its association with AS. It has also highlighted the many difficulties this theory has in explaining why so many of us process global information especially when it is within our attention and interest system.

In the next chapter Mottron *et al.* (2006) offer an alternative theory to WCC in autism, which they call 'enhanced perceptual functioning'.

CHAPTER 7

Cognitive Theory: Enhanced Perceptual Functioning

INTRODUCTION

This chapter outlines a cognitive theory of AS that is relatively recent and is yet another challenge to the traditional cognitive theories of AS. The background to the developing of enhanced perceptual functioning (EPF), its core basis, foundation and subsequent claims and issues are outlined below. Due to this being a fairly recent theory the research is limited. However, this chapter aims to show both the supportive ideology for EPF and also the areas that fail to accommodate EPF and AS.

Definition

EPF is a term used to describe the over-processing by the brain of various sensory and motor information in ways that make it easier to 'see' certain elements and miss others. For AS individuals, according to Mottron *et al.* (2006), this means: 'The over functioning of brain regions typically involved in primary perceptual functions may explain the autistic perceptual endophenotype' (p.27).

Foundations for enhanced perceptual functioning theory

Just as ToM, EF and WCC are offered as explanations for AS characteristics, EPF makes claims to do the same. As outlined in the previous chapter, WCC appears to offer clear suggestions as to why autistic individuals perform in a superior manner when compared to NTs on specific visual tasks. Some examples are block design, finding embedded figures and the Ebbinghaus illusion task (Wozniak 1999). Many of us perform equally well on some of these tests as typical individuals under certain circumstances, and many of us show little difficulty with issues of central coherence. For those who do have central coherence difficulties, sensory and other AS issues are not accounted for by this theory.

Mottron *et al.* (2007) and others have suggested EPF might explain why AS individuals show specific abilities in some areas that seem outstanding; in particular, when tested we tend to show superior processing of local details compared to typical non-autistic people.

The cognitive theories concerning ToM, EF and WCC follow a deficit model to explain the various characteristics seen in AS. EPF, however, suggests that rather than a deficit of connectivity within the brain there exists an over-functioning and enhanced perception leading to ability (in particular areas) that allows us to outperform typical individuals on some tests. These may be on the types of tests used to show gestalt activity via illusory tests such as those used by Happé, or tests like block design that also show abilities to see pattern, shape and gestalt.

During earlier work by Mottron, Pertz and Ménard (2000), results showed particular musical ability with perfect pitch in individuals tested. They began to consider that this didn't fit with the ideas expressed in WCC. Hermelin (2001) also noted that some of us had skills way above an everyday level of functioning. Mottron *et al.* (2001) demonstrated that the AS individuals in their research were able to achieve superior performance on visual and auditory modalities when subjected to low-level cognitive tasks compared to non-autistic people. It also appeared that the AS individuals in their research were able to accomplish complex cognitive tasks within those modalities and that these were related to the AS individuals' perceptions of everyday encounters, emotions, events, expectations and so on. They therefore concluded that enhanced perception with certain domain-specific tasks explained much of the

AS condition. Indeed, EPF could be a way to explain superior local processing.

Support for this concept was offered by Cascio *et al.* (2008), whose work with sensation and tactile appreciation of differences between light touch, warm and cool sensory detections and differences in a variety of textures demonstrated that we experience these differently from NT individuals. They found that although both groups appreciated pleasantness, the AS group showed increased sensitivity to vibration on the forearm as well as increased sensitivity to thermal pain on the forearm and palm. Their findings indicated normal perception along with enhanced perception in AS.

Such studies appear to support the claims of enhanced perceptual functioning in autism through research using rigid experiments with touch. However, if an AS individual is using one sense at a given time connected to single focus and this information is being filtered via an interest system governed by that sense, it could be argued that attention and interest used in that way might lead to the same conclusions about enhanced perceptual functioning.

When Hughes and Russell (1993) showed that AS children found it difficult to disengage from an object and shift attention to another required task, proponents of EPF suggested that this is evidence of EPF rather than difficulties with WCC. Wendy suggests that this shows single attention occupied by interest and little or no available attention to enable the shifting of focus.

What does seem clear, however, is that EPF implies we are using lower-level processes to make sense of seemingly high-level skills at local levels. By implication, this means engaging in a different way with social concepts from the typical population and being more prone to sensory dysphoria (over-sensitive or under-sensitive in tactile situations, for example). It does not mean autistic individuals fail to note global information, but it might mean a tendency towards noting stimuli differently.

Mottron *et al.* (2006) suggest that EPF operates outside the mode of attention (i.e. is a perceptual dimension often not even noticed by the individual). For example, they noted that participants in their studies seemed to complete tasks competently even when seemingly not attending to them (e.g. using peripheral vision). However, I suggest that attention and interest include the properties of perception and this isn't always noticeable or consciously appreciated.

Components of enhanced perceptual functioning theory

EPF in autism suggests that processing of sensory stimuli is facilitated by a different brain configuration that allows us to perceive stimuli in a more pronounced way. This will mean noticing particular and peculiar aspects of perception more quickly and more precisely than NT people will in similar situations. This has, for example, been demonstrated on tests of block design (Bonnel *et al.* 2003; Plaisted *et al.* 1998). Rather than seeing the processes being utilised to make sense of the world as split off or only focused on details, as suggested by the WCC theory, they are seen as enhanced perception (Mottron *et al.* 2003). In contrast to WCC, EPF does not assume that there is a failure of global processing. With regard to visual representation, the most recent update of the EPF theory specifically proposes

> that the automatic progression from local to global visual representation that occurs in normal vision is compromised but that, as a consequence, people with ASD retain access to local structure (which is lost in the course of normal visual processing). (Cascio *et al.* 2008, p.134)

Mottron *et al.* (2006) proposed EPF in autism means all aspects of perceptual function are hyper-developed. Hyper-development means heightened and connected deeply. If perception levels could be rated Mottron *et al.* (2007) suggest that perceptions that are performed by the earliest or most basic visual areas are the most superior. For example, the earliest and most basic visual areas pertain to what is seen and noticed first, in the way a child might see parts of an object before the whole thing. They propose this as the primary cause of autistic deficits (or strengths, depending on whether you follow the deficit model of AS or see this in the light of a different processing system, i.e. cognitive style). This implies that for us there will be a tendency towards conflict or imbalance between filtering out static information compared to sensory 'movement' of information facilitating potential overload. It also suggests lower-order processes (e.g. reading individual letters or words) might be more accessible than higher-order processes (grammar and reading for meaning). However, this should perhaps be thought of as the outcome of connection to interest and attention; I don't think that local versus global information is the core issue so much as the competition for primacy between available attention and the cooperation of the interest system.

So, although Mottron *et al.* (2006) suggest EPF means using higher-order processes in the brain with intervention from lower-order operations or outcomes, and that this is the reason why there is so much variability between AS individuals, similar outcomes may be attributed to monotropism and its products, as mentioned in Chapter 1. This will be explained in the next chapter.

Caron *et al.* (2006) propose that the components needed for EPF exist in the brain, and there is much physical evidence for this idea (e.g. Casanova 2008; Gazzola, Aziz-Zadeh and Keysers 2006; Koshino *et al.* 2008). In the experiments Caron *et al.* (2006) conducted with eight high-functioning autistic individuals (HFA) they found a visual/spatial (visualising and mentally manipulating objects) peak. They used the term HFA-P for these individuals. They compared performance on the block design task (BDT) at various levels of perceptual cohesiveness, as well as tasks tapping visual/motor speed, global perception, visual memory, visual search and speed of visual encoding. Performance of these individuals was compared with that of eight AS individuals without a visual/spatial peak (HFA-NP), ten typically developing individuals and eight gifted comparison participants with a visual/spatial peak. Both HFA-P and HFA-NP groups presented with 'diminished detrimental influence of increasing perceptual coherence' or, in other words, this group showed a spiky profile of weaknesses and strengths that compared with their matched comparison groups.

The outcome of this research was that neither of the autistic groups showed a deficit in construction of global representations: 'The HFA-P group showed no differences in performance level or profile in comparison with the gifted BDT-matched [i.e. higher full-scale IQ (FSIQ)] group, apart from locally oriented perception' (Caron *et al.* 2006, p.1789).

Interpretation by Caron *et al.* (2006) of the results of this experiment implied the primary visual cortex plays a role in EPF. They also suggest AS individuals who perform above expectation, even of typical individuals, on tasks requiring global processing is inconsistent with the weak central coherence theory. For example, Caron *et al.* (2006) found there seemed to be a difference in the posterior central occipital brain regions in AS individuals on tasks of low-level visual perception. They noted similar findings by other researchers such as Bonnel *et al.* (2003) and Sanders *et al.* (2007), who suggested perception in AS may actually be understood and identified differently from how it is organised and mapped in the NT population.

APPLICATION IN THE NEUROTYPICAL AND AUTISM SPECTRUM POPULATIONS

Research over time

Happé and Frith (2006) in their update of the WCC theory support the idea of priority for local processing and concede that this is not always a deficit. They state that global abilities are probably intact in autism and possibly low-level abilities are enhanced, rather than their earlier conception of impaired global abilities. They also suggest that instead of an obligatory reliance on local processing, autistic individuals have access to both but prefer local processing in open-ended tasks (Happé, Ronald *et al.* 2006).

Therefore, when tasks demand specific focused attention, rather than divided attention, AS individuals, like their typical counterparts, do better when they are sure of what to focus upon. And when individuals are guided to attend to one area or single stimulus it becomes apparent that AS individuals excel (e.g. Caron *et al.* 2006).

However, it would be premature to state that this is evidence for EPF because there have been findings of global advantage in autism (e.g. Mottron *et al.* 1999) and of no global advantage (Plaisted, Swettenham and Rees 1999).

For example, in Plaisted *et al.* (1999) studies were conducted to assess local and global properties in AS children compared to controls. A large global shape was used which was made up of smaller images. The first task used a selective attention procedure and the second task used a divided attention procedure. Participants were cued to attend to either the global images or local images making up the global image. Their studies found that AS individuals showed typical global/local perception by responding more quickly and accurately to the global than the local shape.

Interestingly, when divided attention procedures were used, where participants were asked to attend to both local and global levels to find a particular shape, AS individuals showed enhanced local processing. So, although participants did as well as controls, the AS individuals needed prompting to look for the global shape rather than focus upon the distinct shapes that made up the global object.

These inconsistent findings of global advantage in AS participants (advantage in Mottron *et al.* 1999, while no advantage in Plaisted *et al.* 1999) hint at differences connected to attention and interest but fail to explore these.

Comparison with other cognitive theories

According to Heaton *et al.* (2008), who compared and contrasted the theories of WCC and EPF, it seemed that a foundation for exploring AS differently was taking form. On the one hand EPF showed a current theoretical context or framework for enhanced perception, whilst WCC proposed that perception in AS is locally biased. Perhaps the only difference that comes to mind between the two theories is that EPF does not suggest a weak top-down central processing so much as a strong relationship between intact high-level processes alongside superior developed low-level perceptual processing abilities.

So, although Mottron *et al.* (2006) appear to suggest that EPF operates outside the mode of attention and is a perceptive dimension often not even noticed by the individual, the concept of attention used in this text is of a processing resource that is not always within awareness. Therefore, attention is the resource being utilised, but this may be outside of the AS individual's awareness or, in other words, 'subliminal attention' (i.e. attention below the awareness threshold) is in operation.

ToM suggests the clinical picture presented in AS is due to individuals not having the ability to 'put themselves into the shoes of others'. It states AS is a deficit disorder, whereas EPF argues that AS implies having a different perceptual ability that leads to autistic individuals having superior developed perception in some areas. This makes it difficult to work out what AS individuals should attend to, hence the difficulties highlighted in many social situations that are outside an individual's available script (e.g. difficulties in knowing how to respond when things don't go according to plan or expectation or in times of social demand).

Wendy suggests AS individuals are homing in according to attentional and systemic areas of interest; therefore in certain situations we seem able to attend exceptionally well. This ability might be what is enabling us to connect more readily to the demands of certain tasks (such as the block design test). It might be a reason why we become so focused upon our particular area of interest and, in spite of difficulties with social interaction and social situations, can do so well with other things.

Limitations of enhanced perceptual functioning theory

To date, EPF is a relatively new theory with regard to autism, and the empirical evidence to support or refute this theory is fairly limited. Much more research needs to be conducted in this promising area.

EPF offers a concise explanation for much of the clinical picture seen in AS when one considers the role of perception; however, it fails to explain the thought processes behind perception, that is, the concepts supplied by the ideas of an inherent system of interests. As initially posited by Murray (1992), the interest system of the NT population consists of multiple diffuse interests rather than single focused interests as seen in AS.

SUMMARY

Dawson, Mottron and Gernsbacher (2008) suggest that learning in AS is spontaneous and implicit to the AS individual concerned. They also suggest that such learning may be happening differently in AS than in the typical population. They describe the way that NT brains map and connect learning and suggest that such mapping of connections occurs differently in AS.

Wendy does not debate the claims that EPF makes concerning the idea that AS individuals learn implicitly and quite differently from that of typical individuals. I also agree that, rather than exploring AS through a window of 'typicality', researchers need to reassess how, what and why they only expect to see deficits in AS: 'An understanding of autistic learning, of how and why autistics learn well and learn poorly, may therefore require a non-normocentric approach' (Dawson *et al.* 2008, p.14). But, I suggest there may be other reasons why this is happening, and I question the lack of study or exploration of the role of attention and that of the interest system, which could provide an alternative explanation for similar outcomes.

Although there does seem to be sound evidence for perception differences in autism (Chawarka, Klin and Volkmar 2003), the issues appear to be connected to whether these are solely negative or whether there might also be a positive aspect to this. Interestingly, although Mottron, Mineau *et al.* (2007) argue that EPF is independent of attention, because it is a consequence of low-level processing, they also suggest that if the child is using attentional strategies, such as glancing out of the corners of their eyes or looking at the world via gaps in between their fingers, then to stop or prevent them from doing this would only increase their discomfort and would imply a questionable practice not supportive of the child's wellbeing.

I do not disagree with this idea, but I interpret the reason behind such an action quite differently, applying the idea of interest and connection to attention rather than low-level processes acting alone.

EPF is a viable theory that offers an account for why so many AS individuals do exceptionally well on tasks like block design. It demonstrates a testable hypothesis connecting attention or focus to perception, but it fails to note the connection of interest to this concept. Therefore, it only partially accounts for the picture presented by AS individuals.

The next chapter offers a newly developed theory about the reasons for the clinical picture seen in AS. It aims to explain the theory succinctly and concisely to demonstrate how it might be seen as a viable alternative to the theories already espoused in the previous chapters.

CHAPTER 8

An Alternative Cognitive Theory: Single Attention and Associated Cognition in Autism

INTRODUCTION

Four cognitive theories were outlined in the previous chapters. An alternative approach is Single Attention and Associated Cognition in Autism (SAACA). SAACA might explain why some individuals pass tests for ToM, such as those by Joliffe and Baron-Cohen (1999); show enhanced attributes outlined in Dawson *et al.* (2007); exhibit superior visual abilities shown in Plaisted *et al.* (2001) and respond empathically to objects, animals and people when they are attached or interested (Lawson 2001).

The sensory system, being the first port of call for any information that the brain takes note of, is also linked to attention and interest. I believe the linkage of attention, interest and the sensory system is different according to whether you are on the AS or the NT spectrum. In AS single attention works with a focused interest system and connects via a sensory system often monopolised by a single sense; whereas in typical development brain configurations consist of diffuse interests via divided attention and a well-connected sensory system. Therefore differing learning styles would result from these differing brain configurations (see Baron-Cohen *et al.* 2009).

This chapter explores the foundations for SAACA, which include attention, sensory systems, brain configuration, motivation and interest, and compares and contrasts them with the idea of a triad of impairments, which originates from a deficit model of autism rather than a social/biological model of autism.

Definitions

The term *monotropic* describes single attention and single channels for accessing and processing information (mono: single; tropism: direction/channel). NT developing individuals, although able to be single-minded at times, can respond to another interest or situation and shift their attention whether interested or not. This means they can use *polytropic* attention, which necessitates dividing their attention between a number of differing concerns simultaneously (poly: many) and accommodating many channels of information at any one time. Polytropism in typical individuals is argued to be their default learning style. This concept will be explored in more detail in this chapter.

I know that for many of us, shifting attention from an aspect of interest to one that we are not interested or invested in is very difficult. However, in AS this is often the reason we prefer sameness and routine, and why we may even appear to have one sense that dominates another. I suggest we use single attention connecting with and processing information one step at a time, which is the monotropic disposition, as our default setting. Therefore, attention and the interest system will work hand in hand to create an attention, interest, sensory-motor loop leading to a cognitive style.

MONOTROPISM AS A FOUNDATION FOR SAACA

Monotropism, or having the ability to home in on one aspect of communication or on one interest at one time, can happen to NT and AS individuals. However, rigid monotropism often occurs in an AS individual's world, and we are said to have 'tunnel vision' (Attwood 2007) or, as parents often say, 'my child seems only to be interested in his or her

Zaffy has to focus on one thing at any one time, and his interest is the connecting feature.

interests'. Monotropism will mean, for most of us, difficulties coping with change because we are single-minded. For many, this is demonstrated in our difficulties with change in routine, expectation, instruction, daily schedule, movement of attention or incorporating another set of demands into the present scenario. For example, coping with change can involve listening and then being required to participate in decision making without due time to process information; thus, being forced to move from one channel to another (Kluth and Chandler-Olcott 2008).

For many of us the discomfort at encountering change is one consequence of being attention-tunnelled or monotropic (e.g. Bogdashina 2006; Greenaway and Plaisted 2005; Murray *et al.* 2005). Evidence for this is apparent in AS individuals' daily lives. As Murray states:

> It is a lurch for AS individuals to be precipitated into a new attention tunnel from the one they were engaged in. It makes the individual feel bad. Therefore, engaging with an

AS individual on the basis of their own interests is making it much more comfortable for that individual than bringing other pressing interests to bear. (D.K.C. Murray, personal communication, 16 April 2007)

In AS a monotropism foundation is also evident within the process of interpreting language. For example, when as an AS child I was told that I was going to Grandmother's house, I remember being quite upset if I then had to wait. To me, the action statement (going) meant immediately. For me and for other AS individuals, especially children who have not had a chance to learn over time, 'going' (a verb or 'doing' word) *implies immediate action*. It seemed totally illogical to be 'going' later or 'going' soon (Hoy 2007; Lawson 2008; Sainsbury 2000). This example shows literality in language, a product of monotropism.

The relative concepts of 'in a while', 'later', 'when we are ready' and so on may not seem logical or may not seem to apply to the immediate moment if the present tense verb 'going' is used. Typical individuals may appreciate the fact that one can prepare to go because they can usually simultaneously hold in their minds the two concepts of now and the future. When concepts like those highlighted above are learnt by us, understanding can be amassed. However, this is very tiring and, at times, we either give up trying or resort to a behaviour that seems to fit with our valued outcome (i.e. keeping things the same or stopping change) (Bitsika 2003, 2005; Bitsika, Sharpley and Orapeleng 2008; Lawson 2008).

It appears usual for typical individuals to have diffuse interests connected to a number of differing concepts from *family* to *work* to *shopping* to *animals* and so on. NT individuals can cognitively and physically move from one concept to another, share interests common to each other and even take an interest in something they perhaps don't care about particularly. They seem able to put their own interests on hold to accommodate the interests of another, especially if they are governed by social priorities.

We (AS individuals), by contrast, would find this very difficult, choosing rather to stay where our own interest and attention are focused on things that are familiar and stable. Shifting attention from one subject or object of interest to another is something we would find very difficult, if not impossible, unless our own interest was engaged as part of the exchange (e.g. Kluth and Chandler-Olcott 2008; Vismara and Lyons 2007).

With regard to interest, Murray suggested AS individuals might have an interest system that functions according to the stable structures they have furnished themselves or to those in their surroundings. In a monotropic interest system connectivity is more streamlined but less diffuse than that of the typical population. This might be due to an interest system that is more 'pure' in the sense that it hasn't been modified or contaminated by other people's expectations (D.K.C. Murray, personal communication, 10 March 2005).

Mann and Walker (2003) agree and note that there is a fundamental difference between an AS individual's cognitive states of interest and attention. They suggest that typical interests confer with the social elements around and within the environment, which attracts and enables social interaction; whilst AS individuals operate on one channel at a time, which makes social interaction very difficult. Given the number of biographical and autobiographical accounts written by AS individuals (who often describe our tendency to be distracted by background sensory information) social interaction that involves accommodating the interests of others could be very uncomfortable.

Attention

NT individuals seem to have a particular capacity that allows them to divide their attention between a number of states. This is regarded as normal development. For example, NTs have the ability to think whilst walking, talking and so on. Having many interests less highly aroused but connected is accepted as normal behaviour. These interests can be placed on hold to accommodate the interests of 'Other'; this is polytropism.

For us (AS individuals), however, the connections between interest and attention flow from a sensory-perception loop that works differently from that of the NT population. The emphasis is upon different rather than deviant. Figure 8.1 illustrates these constructs. The solid filled tree foliage background in AS represents the brain's resultant interests from available single attention as highly focused interests. The 'see through' form in NT represents the brain's resultant connection to attention and diffuse interests. The single curly tree trunk line signifies single attention or focus, while the divided curly line signifies divided attention or focus.

Differences in attention and arousal may underlie some of the primary differences and difficulties seen in the neuro-pathological functioning of

AS individuals (e.g. Bryson *et al.* 2004). Some studies demonstrate that attentional abilities appear to be intact in AS (e.g. Minshew *et al.* 1992). Joseph and Tager-Flusberg (2004) suggested that the performance of AS individuals on ToM tests was connected to issues of attention and perception, and they also found that, with regard to AS, these areas needed more research.

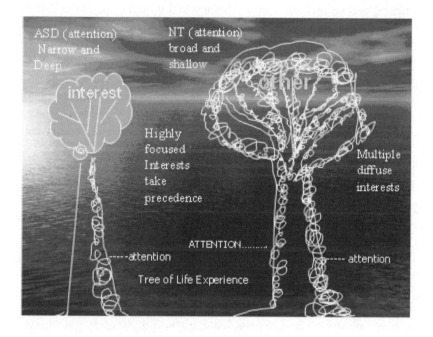

Figure 8.1: Monotropic attention in autistic spectrum (AS) individuals and polytropism attention in neurologically typical (NT) individuals

Gaze following is necessary for the development of joint attention (e.g. Baron-Cohen, Ring *et al.* 2000; Dalton *et al.* 2005; Klin *et al.* 2003). Gaze following has been found to be deficient in autism through observation studies conducted in naturalistic settings (e.g. Klin *et al.* 2003; Leekam *et al.* 2000).

Swettenham *et al.* (2003) have shown that deficits or delays in following eye direction are not due to perceptual or attention deficits, since reflexive responding to eye gaze is intact in autism (Kylliainen and Hietanen 2004). So why would AS individuals avoid sharing in joint attention? Maybe it's sensory overload or our interest system preventing us from doing so with any kind of ease?

Unless I know them well, I hear better whilst not looking at the individual who is talking to me. I also find 'eye contact' quite uncomfortable: all that information coming from another person's facial expression and movement is just too fast to process and to work out what is what!

If the ability to attend is not impaired in AS, maybe the attention, interest and sensory systems in AS are wired up differently from that in NT development. After all, it is a truism that most individuals, AS or NT, will usually look at or attend to something they are interested in. The text books tell us that AS individuals with classic autism lack curiosity, unless something captures their attention. For example, Attwood (2007) states that in autism there is a lack of spontaneous seeking to share the enjoyment, interests or achievements of other people, but at times individuals can be occupied obsessively by their object of interest and seek to share this with others.

Some individuals follow their obsessions consistently and curiously, exploring them from any and every angle and even discussing them exhaustively with others. Interest is the common denominator for us all and, as well as being the key to holding an AS individual's attention, might also enable curiosity at times when nothing else seems to work (Gardner 2008).

There is strong evidence that atypical attention is a feature of autism, but there is disagreement about how this impacts upon AS experience. For example, Happé (1999a, 1999b) suggests AS individuals attend to bits of information and not the whole picture, and Lesser and Murray (1997) suggest attention works as a limited processing resource informed by and informing particular interests.

For us (AS individuals), attention differences can explain a variety of distinctive reactions and behaviours. For example, single interest and single attention might magnify one sense above another, and visual, tactile, hearing and tasting experiences might be overwhelming or underdeveloped. Such behaviours as obsessive thinking, repetitive and/or ritualistic physical activity, distinctive single-sense experiences, such as looking at the world through gaps in our fingers or from the sides of our eyes, and literal reasoning can be explained by attentional differences.

According to Burack et al. (1997), attention can be fully and comprehensibly defined as selectively choosing what you attend to; however 'attention' is used more broadly in this text to refer generally to the resource through which perceptions are processed as well as to its manifestations in focused awareness. In AS, monotropic attention is not seen as a choice but as integral to our learning style. Murray *et al.* (2005) link the role of attention to cognitive processing. They suggest that at any one moment only limited attention is available. This attentional lens allows the individual to view the world in a particular way.

It is known from studies of the brain (e.g. Minshew and Williams 2007) that only a finite supply of metabolites (the products of metabolism) is available to the brain at any given time, meaning we only have so much energy to use on 'attending' at any given time. This is evidenced in the concepts of task demand and task completion. Murray *et al.* (2005) suggest, however, that there is competition between mental processes for the available or scarce attention and that this shapes the cognitive processes individuals live by.

Attentional differences are associated with a number of conditions, and autism is only one of those. For example, obsessive compulsive disorder (OCD) is known to take over an individual's attention totally and dictate compulsions of various kinds, in thought, word and deed. These are well documented (e.g. Fireman *et al.* 2001; Goldstein *et al.* 2001; Schwartz and Begley 2002; Williams 1994). It seems that in both autism and OCD the individual concerned is only able to attend to the issues of concern to them. The fundamental difference, however, between the attentional attributes and the interest system for AS individuals compared to OCD individuals is that the AS individual usually enjoys their interest and does not want it taken away, but for OCD individuals the obsessive attention to an issue is often one they wish they did not have (e.g. Goldstein *et al.* 2001).

The role of attention in focus and selectivity is also highlighted by AS authors of first-hand accounts of living with autism. We often state that we can only attend to one thing at any one time. For example, Stone commented that he felt his life operated more like a train running on a single track. Stone suggests AS individuals are more like trains and NT individuals are more like cars, which can easily change direction, crossing lanes when they want to (H. Stone, personal communication, 7 July 2000).

Attention and brain configuration

Nancy Minshew and her team have demonstrated that the brain is configured differently according to whether or not you are an NT individual or on the autism spectrum (e.g. Minshew *et al.* 2002).

Williams and Minshew (2007) demonstrate how MRI and other ways of creating brain imaging have helped to show the separate brain components involved with AS. They found AS individuals appeared to be using different neural systems to interact socially and to work out intention and connections between facial expressions and emotions, as well as having different systems to appreciate movement, motion and language, 'and, importantly, the difference between automatic processing and deliberate conscious or cognitive processing' (p.496).

Wicker *et al.* (2008) found in their studies that AS individuals showed atypical patterns of connectivity in the prefrontal cortex of the brain. This site is associated with social reciprocity. Some MRI studies where scientists examined brain tissue of AS individuals have revealed visually that AS brains seem configured differently from those of typical individuals (e.g. Just *et al.* 2004).

Other studies have enabled scientists to focus on structures within the brain known as cell minicolumns which play an important role in the way the brain takes in (notes) information and responds to it. The minicolumns of autistic individuals were found to be significantly smaller, but there were many more of them (e.g. Casanova *et al.* 2002). Casanova (2008) said the increased number of cell minicolumns could mean a constant state of over-arousal. Of course, it could also be argued that a state of under-arousal might occur if too much information is bombarding an individual and, in order to cope, they might 'switch off'.

So using functional magnetic resonance imaging (fMRI) scans, numerous differences in the activity of brains of people with normal IQs who have autism have been found (e.g. Casanova *et al.* 2002; Just *et al.* 2004; Minshew *et al.* 2002; Minshew and Williams 2007). The new findings show a decreased level in the coordination among brain areas (e.g. Hadjikhani *et al.* 2007; Minshew and Hobson 2008; Minshew and Williams 2008). The results converge with previous findings of white matter differences in autism compared to typical development (white matter consists of the 'cables' that connect the various parts of the brain to each other).

Therefore, AS could be thought of as a system-wide brain difference that places more limits on the coordination and integration among brain areas than shown in typicals (Casanova *et al.* 2002). These neurological findings help explain an apparent paradox of autism: some people with autism have typical or even superior skills in some areas, while many other types of thinking are not so well connected (O'Connor and Kirk

2008). These findings also support the implications and by-products of monotropism, explored in this text as SAACA.

For if one's cognitive state and subsequent actions are guided by monotropism (the main domain for focused attention) and its subsequent product (for example, being literal, thinking in closed concepts, having difficulties with forward thinking and so on), it implies only being attentive in one direction and in one domain at any one time. Although this might present all kinds of difficulties for an individual it could also be harnessed as a particular learning style. This has implications for many areas in one's life: sensory, emotional, physical, environmental, educational and so on.

Many of us report that the demand of having to pay attention to so many of the usual daily demands of life (conversations, activities, individual and group interactions, decoding instructions, television, radio, people's voices and so on) simultaneously while noting where we ourselves are going, what we are thinking and processing and so on, is a nightmare (e.g. Blackman 2006; Hoy 2007; Lawson 2000; Sainsbury 2000).

Howlin, Baron-Cohen and Hadwin (2007) have noted that some challenging behaviour may be due to difficulties with reading others' facial expressions. Attending to faces, voices and other human communication tools, all at the same time, requires a brain wired up to work with divided attention and a sensory system that is well connected. In AS, however, SAACA is the outcome of a different brain configuration from that seen in the typically developing brain.

Brain configuration should be a consideration in relation to learning style, with particular reference to AS. Brain configuration explains some of the clinical picture seen in AS. It is all too easy to think of 'challenging behaviour' in AS individuals as being their problem and something we need to devise a programme to address. But maybe it is simply a response to the challenge of expectation placed upon us? The challenging behaviour associated with AS is often functional and may be an effort to communicate fear or discomfort. Learning to recognise this might be the first step to helping us (AS individuals) to develop more appropriate communication systems.

Learning style is not impairment in a general capacity; for example Leslie (2000) noted:

If autistic children perform poorly on false-belief tasks because of limited working memory, because of poor executive function, or because of impaired counterfactual reasoning, then why did the photographs/maps tasks not also demand these things? Similarly, for impaired event memory, for poor attention shifting, for poor mental imagery, and for other 'general' impairments, it is hard to see why false-belief problems require the favoured resource while other representation tasks do not. These findings challenge accounts that rely on an impairment in a general capacity. (p.1323)

Looking at AS through the ideas of SAACA provides an alternative explanation for the behaviour we (AS individuals) exhibit, compared to traditional models or explanations of AS.

Monotropism and the sensory system

Being monotropic and having a cognitive style informed by single attention coupled with single interest impacts upon an individual's senses. For example, we might only be able to look at one thing at any one time, or only be comfortable with using one sense at any one time, such as the visual sense (Dalton *et al.* 2005; Grandin 2009). This could mean looking at someone and listening to them (e.g. using two senses) might be difficult, and also helps explain some of the problems we experience with such things as eye contact. I certainly hear better when side-on with someone I don't know very well as opposed to facing them across a table or in a classroom, for example.

In addition, there may not be any available processing resource for modulating and integrating sensory experiences. Sensory dysphoria, whether hypo (underactive) or hyper (overactive), will have a direct impact upon cognition because it can distract from the interest that the other person is trying to share (Lathe 2006). For example, 'Come over and look at this book about animals with me' might not appeal to a child who is playing with water and who is taken over with the feel of water running through their fingers. Instead, to involve a child whose interest is water, one might need to find the kind of book made of water-resistant material so that the sensory dominance (in this instance, water) can be connected to the cognitive shared interest (water-proofed book and sharing of a story).

social coping mechanism

Zaffy can cope better in social settings when he is allowed to draw.

Monotropism has advantages and disadvantages. At the sensory level it can be a disadvantage when it comes to social relationships, because looking but not listening implies lack of interest and can impede the development of a relationship. But monotropism could be an advantage because focus on one sense can be used as a soothing mechanism if the individual is experiencing sensory overload. For example, humming, rocking or stroking a furry cat may help an individual calm down (Scott 2008). Also, monotropism at the cognitive level can be an advantage in the world of concentration, for example students can study an area of interest and not be tempted to party, but it can be seen to be a disadvantage if it prevents the individual from being able to pay attention to the interest of another. However, just as in the above example concerning 'water', when others first join in the interest of the AS individual, such an individual is more likely to be able to make the shift in attention to join in with the other person (Dern and Schuster 2007; Murray *et al.* 2005).

So, even though monotropism might mean not being able to make multiple connections, not being naturally able to identify context or scale and not being able to model alternative possibilities and viewpoints, we can, however, join the interests of others if others first join ours (Gernsbacher *et al.* 2008; Lawson 2008).

Due to being literal (not reading between the lines) and monotropic, and thus experiencing each event as separate and exclusive, we may not link concepts together and inform our experience generally or in an 'open' fashion.

For example, when I was asked to close my eyes and think about the word 'home' and then share what came to mind, I said that I saw my home address on the front of an envelope. When I repeated this exercise with a large audience at a talk on autism and asked the group to feed back to us what came to mind, they said things like family, the lounge, having a family dinner, comfy, safe and so on. The interesting thing is that the group noted thinking states and feeling states compared to my thinking state only. The other thing of interest is that I saw the word H O M E and played with these letters in my thinking. When asked if they had done the same thing, participants said they had not!

This kind of processing style, whilst useful in some situations, can have a negative impact on social relatedness because of these fundamental differences in understanding.

Monotropism and interest

Interest is thought of as any state of arousal that connects an individual to awareness (see Appendix A). For example, one's senses feed information to the brain, the brain then takes note of that information and interest is raised (e.g. if one is in a state of thirst or hunger, one's main interest is to relieve that thirst or hunger).

A long-term interest can also be thought of as a hobby or special project or activity that takes up one's attention and is persistently somewhat aroused. However, in this text, interest is used in a much wider sense than simply the concept of a hobby, because it involves anything that connects the individual to awareness of, understanding of and need or desire to do something about something.

The term *interest* as it refers to a state of arousal, may be prompted by a number of variables (e.g. emotions, such as curiosity or fear; sensory dispositions and/or motor complexities, such as clumsiness, sudden awareness or appreciation of distance). Attention is the scarce resource that supplies local arousal of interest, thus creating enduring individual interests through repeated arousal over time – emotions have a key impact on allocation of attention; where there is feeling there is attention.

Monotropic interest is captivated by attention delivered to one's senses (often to just one single sense) via some attractor. For example, we are often drawn to objects or subjects that have an integral sameness or familiarity (e.g. Thomas the Tank Engine; a historical event; some scientific discovery, such as 'relativity', and so on). Being drawn to attend to any matter is basic to everyone, not just those of us who are AS, but, it is the mono connection within the same interest that is distinctive, rather than the poly inter-relatedness across and between differing interests. For this reason it is very common for us to be drawn, for example, to information technology because of its predictability, reduced stimuli, lack of facial expressions, reduced demand and routine operation (see Appendix E). Other monotropic interests include particular books, plays, television shows, philosophical theories, science debates, maths, history and so on.

In Nicholas Sparks' (2006) novel *Dear John*, he writes a very clear description of single interest and of how eventually the protagonist realised that in order to have a relationship with his father (who had Asperger's syndrome), he had to enter into his father's interest in coin collecting rather than expect his father to share his interests. A clear relationship between father and son followed.

Grandin (2000) and Williams (1994) liken their daily experience to being mono channelled. They report being only able to focus upon one thing at a time and on having one interest that occupies all of their attention. I believe that obsessions, obsessive behaviour, rigid thinking styles and resistance to change (seen in AS) are a product of SAACA. This implies ability to function in the present, which might present difficulties with forward thinking. So, staying with what is familiar and resisting change is more comfortable.

Attention, motivation and interest

It seems common for us to focus on and attend to something for extended periods of time without apparently feeling tired, so long as we are interested. When another who is invited joins my interest, because the two of us are engaged in the same interest (initially mine) we can be happily engaged for long periods of time. At other times though, when we are in the company of people who are chatting about things that are not interesting to us and are therefore difficult for us to attend to, our attention may easily be turned elsewhere or become overwhelmed by the demands placed upon it.

For example, Dinah and I were out walking. In mid-conversation I spotted a bird that captured my attention. The conversation we were having immediately ceased and I only had attention for the bird. I even failed to note where we were walking, what we were conversing about and what we had been doing before. This example appears to be typical for us when we obsess over interests to the point of not being able to notice anything else. In this case it would have been easy for Dinah to feel that her friend was being bad-mannered. Because others might assume that the AS individual is not interested in them and/or that they don't want to talk to them, they might react as if they are feeling rejected, and their reaction can be overwhelming for the AS individual.

I suggest SAACA explains what is happening for me and for other AS individuals because we are using one attentive mode that excludes all others. This would also suggest it is possible to widen the window of attention for us so we can tap into interests outside of our own, by using our interest as a bridge to others, as Kluth (2003) noted in her book when she wrote that interests help connect to other interests.

Kluth gives the example of using an AS student's interest (this particular student was interested in weather systems) as a way of building connection and, therefore, interest in other things. She suggests channelling the weather interest by, for example, showing how the weather is outlined in the newspaper. Over time other sections of the paper can be shown. Eventually, by joining the student's interest first, she was able to cultivate interests in sport and the weather or politics and the weather. It could mean enabling an AS individual to converse with others in ways previously not available to them.

Researchers commonly think of attentional problems in AS as 'disordered attention'; but maybe this is not 'disordered' but 'ordered' attention. According to SAACA, autistic attention is selective, not so much by choice as by it being our default setting.

This is noted by self-reports of AS individuals who indicate that senses and emotive states appear to operate one at a time. Williams (1994) used the analogy for this contrast between herself and ordinary people as that of a busy department store, which in her case can only open one department at a time.

For some AS individuals, it appears that when a number of sensory channels (visual, auditory, tactile, etc.) are challenged simultaneously, they can experience overload and may either close off to further communication or develop what many know as 'challenging behaviour' (Bitsika 2005; Bogdashina 2006).

THE TANTRUM

LIGHTS ... BRIGHT FLASHING
NOISE ... POLYPHONIK SHARP BUZZING
SMELL ... INTENSE INTRUSIVE INVADING
TOUCH ... NEURO INFO CASCADING
WORDS ... PICTURES FILES PUZZLING
CONVERSATION ... EXPECTATIONS - FAST SENSESAAATING
NERVOUS SYSTEM .. COMPUTOR OVERLOADED - JAMMED

SEEEZING

SAACA may also explain the higher performance of AS individuals on visual perception tasks. Burack (1994) suggests that AS individuals responded to the block design task more quickly than typical individuals, as long as they were not distracted. His argument suggests that this is evidence of an inefficient attentional lens. However, it could also be argued as evidence for an efficient attentional lens because these individuals passed the tests and did better than typical individuals. The AS individuals were more focused and used their attention more efficiently, possibly devoting attention to the immediate task more single-mindedly than typical individuals might.

In autism, individuals might not necessarily have an attentional lens that is either too narrow or too wide, so much as one governed by cognitive processes that are dictated by SAACA, leading to: literality; a different appreciation of timing and spatial conjectures; difficulty in correctly predicting outcomes; non-social priorities; non-generalised learning; special interests; ...and passing some tests with higher results than typical controls!

If the deficit model in autism is followed, then professionals, families and autistic individuals alike might only see the AS individual in light of their differences or in terms of disorder and dysfunction. They may fail to see the benefits of being single minded, singly focused and free to harness plentiful attention when interested.

SAACA offers an explanation that helps us understand how and why AS individuals find everyday life rather more complicated than typical individuals do. Although NT individuals may experience similar difficulties to those of us on the AS spectrum, it is the degree and frequency of difficulty that separates us as well as issues of attention.

Triad of impairments or product of SAACA?

I have explained how traditional cognitive theories are formed from a deficit model based on the triad of impairments (impaired social understanding; impaired communication; and impaired imagination or being too rigid in one's thinking) thought to be responsible for the characteristics known as autism spectrum.

I have also suggested that in practical terms, many of us, outside the areas of our specific interest, are not good at dividing attention to accommodate the multiple pieces of information that are coming our way and that may be relevant to multiple different interests. Many typical individuals, on the other hand, are good with dividing their attention and energies, so they can accommodate their own interests and the interests of others. So, rather than AS being the result of specific impairments I have suggested that AS is the result of a particular attention, interest, sensory-motor, perception loop.

However, this will mean we use huge amounts of energy in trying to accommodate a world that insists on multi-tasking, and we are often exhausted by the effort (see, for example, Liane Holliday Willey's book *Pretending to Be Normal* (1999)). This has consequences for us in many different areas of our everyday life. Attwood (2007) tells of one of his clients who is exhausted from socialising and reminds his readers that social exhaustion can contribute to development of clinical depressions.

The difficulties that AS individuals live with each day are why the triad of impairments appeared to explain our problems. But I suggest the reason AS individuals experience difficulties is because we cannot attend simultaneously to all the pressures placed upon us by the expectations of others. Because typical individuals, however, can process information and be actively engaged in a number of events simultaneously, it is often not a problem for them to think and feel at the same time. They chat, walk, process, eat and modify their behaviour all at once. They are even able to put their own interests on hold to accommodate the interests of others.

Unfortunately, because this is viewed as 'normal' we are expected to do and to be the same as typical individuals in a Western society that sees typicality as the only norm. AS individuals, tending not to function well in multi-tasking situations, may give up if their own interests are not harnessed. In our current social climate where AS is not accommodated well, we are not only disadvantaged but defeated before we even begin. With this in mind, I suggest issues of attention and interest are not accommodated by theories such as theory of mind, weak central coherence, executive functioning or enhanced perceptual functioning, as discussed earlier.

Processing style

The sensory system and all of the mental operations just described are involved with information processing (O'Connor and Kirk 2008). As an individual attends to a source that captures their interest, they note and absorb information (Herrera *et al.* 2008). This may be via the eyes, ears, mouth, nose and/or skin. Those who are visually able receive information from seeing. Those who are hearing able take note of sounds heard. Unless individuals have a disability or disease affecting their other senses, they also use their senses of taste, smell and touch. As the brain receives all of the information, the form, or *schema*, of the aroused interest is changed by the new information according to its relevance (Murray 1986). The brain then decides whether or not to retain the information according to its relevance beyond the immediate (i.e. the currently aroused) interest. For example, will it be useful at some later time? Does it enable the individual to feel good about something? Is it something trivial or important? Will this picture aid in daily life encounters?

According to SAACA, the AS processing style will have implications especially when it comes to interacting with others, where it is expected that one will note body language as well as facial expression and tone of voice, in addition to all the external circumstances of the situation. Some of us are not able to block out unwanted information, perhaps because doing so requires a certain low-level investment of subliminal attention. As a result we may be overwhelmed and over-stimulated. If this is the case, the last thing we need is more information that serves only to exacerbate the situation.

Hobson (2008) has argued over time that cognition is based in 'relatedness' and not only in modularity of components located within the brain. However, I disagree with Hobson's general debate (see Hobson 1989) that AS individuals are autistic by nature of their failing to share in the normal world through lack of interest in connecting to the minds of others.

Hobson (2008) suggests AS individuals are not capable of typical relatedness as a means of social referencing and an aspect of cognitive and emotive connection. This view would be inaccurate when explored via the SAACA lens, because it is in fact the opposite that is experienced via monotropism. AS individuals 'connect' and empathise with the object or person they are relating to, almost too much at times, because of single focus. It is only when polytropic interests get in the way of their current focus of interest that they get lost and fail to connect quickly enough.

It is clear from all that has been outlined so far that AS individuals experience life differently from typical individuals. I suggest, however, that the reason for this is that AS individuals are operating via systems, including the sensory system, that might not be well coordinated and integrated. If one's sensory system and, more generally, one's interest system are operating in a more fragmented way, then processing of certain types of information (e.g. social and/or group information) will take longer. For us, the types of information that are processed more slowly will vary according to the interests of the particular individual, and in addition the types of information that are processed more quickly will be related to what the individual is interested in and, therefore, can attend to.

Monotropism and learning styles

When processing information in relation to cognition and attention, the brain forms schemas. A schema is a template (referred to above as the form of an interest) formed from experiences and information and possibly typically influenced by the individual's feelings about the experiences and information (Young and Klosko 1994). As typical individuals broaden their learning and experiences, schemata can be added to and developed over time.

Templates are the basic design or outline that one begins with. For typical individuals, development is presumed to occur progressively, over time and in a relatively predictable order. As children develop they travel through stages of cognitive, physical and moral development. Piaget documented these stages and, although later research suggested they may not be as rigid as Piaget originally stated (Donaldson 1978), they do provide a clear framework from which to understand typical development (see Piaget 1952, 1971).

In AS development, however, there appear to be a number of delays, particularly in the emotional and social domains. This means that although we still travel through the same stages of development, we may be delayed in our starting of a stage and in our completion of a stage. Because of this AS children and adults, although the same age as typical children and adults physically, may be much younger emotionally. If an individual is intellectually disabled as well as autistically delayed, they will always display complex limitations due to their dual disability; however, research has shown that IQ can be improved with learning, practice and repetition of tasks, especially with appropriate communication aids (e.g. Baggs 2008; Emerson, Grayson and Griffiths 2001).

Cognitive psychologists tell us that recalling events from memory will depend upon how those events have been coded in the representation stage of processing. However, according to Attwood (1999) and Happé (1994a), AS individuals do not read for meaning (representation and connection) so much as we read because the words are there. Attwood suggests that when high-functioning AS individuals are tested on a passage they are told to read, if they have been advised that the test will require them to understand what they read (they will be tested for meaning) then they are able to pass the test. If, however, this instruction is omitted, then they may fail the test.

This could be a demonstration of the following factors: first, connecting to meaning aids learning; and second, AS individuals can locate meaning when interest is aroused (i.e. when encouraged prior to a test to look for meaning, AS individuals were able to perform the task).

Complex cognitive skills coupled with interest and attention

Using cognitive skills usually means making use of language, comprehension and memory for text, problem solving, expertise, creativity and decision making (Reed 1996). For the typical population, whose brains are designed to work with divided attention, these processes enable a developing individual to learn from social interaction, role modelling, personal experience, practice, social norms and expectations. For AS individuals, operating with monotropic attention, being literal, thinking in closed concepts and not easily able to generalise our understanding will be the norm.

However, the cognitive skills outlined above (language, comprehension, problem solving and so on) may be underdeveloped, missing or autistically influenced (e.g. monotone voice, lack of intonation, lack of understanding of gaps in conversation, or inappropriate or literal translation).

The issues of literality in language (non-comprehension of metaphor and simile), subsequent problems with comprehension, reading for meaning, viewpoints on problems and problem solving, issues with empathy and social priorities all influence how individuals see and understand the world around them.

Figure 8.2 demonstrates the attributes noted in typical cognition and places them beneath the heading of polytropism or 'normal' development. As the flow chart shows, being able to divide one's attention and 'read' between the lines enables one to align one's interests with those of others, whether in language exchange, in sharing of concepts or simply in being able to appreciate appropriateness. This ability is seen as the norm in typical development, but is not seen as the norm in autistic development.

Polytropism, multiple interests resulting from a brain configuration allowing wider and broader connections leads to:

Non-literality (reads non-literal (social) signs such as face and body language) means not taking things literally. This applies to time, people, words, situations and so on. It allows for the understanding of positive and/or negative criticism (can tell the difference) comprehends the idea of 'joking' and accepts the concept of 'change'

Thinking in open pictures (or concepts) allows for context, scale and intention giving access to relevant information from past, present and/or future

Ability to generalise, for example: actual size, dimensions and wider understanding of generalising all information (social, cognitive, emotional and so on; public and private; yours, mine and/or ours)

Understanding of timing and sequencing (for example: seasons, propriety, conversational chit-chat; first and last and so on)

Forward thinking outside of one's interest (accommodation of interests outside of one's own, even if not personally interested)

accommodation of 'Other'

Figure 8.2: Expected neurotypical development: Multiple connections between senses and interest states. Resulting from the ability to divide attention allowing for multi-tasking and social connectivity

As Murray has said, having a wide spread of interest, and developing a shared pattern of meaning, makes the worldview of most infants progressively more integrated and seamless. For these typical children what does not fit will tend to be invisible; they inhabit a comfortable world (D.K.C. Murray, personal communication, 7 February 2005).

In AS, however, individuals display activity derived from SAACA. Figure 8.3 demonstrates the concepts of SAACA derived from monotropism. The flow chart shows associated issues when one isn't geared to align one's interests with those of others but instead has the ability to focus deeply on a personal interest.

SAACA, derived from monotropism (attention governed by single focus) from which come the following products:

Literality: taking things literally. Could mean having an appreciation of form; being governed by clear cut concepts; having problems with blurry areas; honesty or not knowing when it is socially acceptable to lie.

Thinking in closed pictures (or closed concepts). This could be great for giving attention to details of interest or for being able to stay motivated when tasks might ordinarily pose problems for those typically disposed. But it presents the individual with difficulties connected to a change of circumstances, people, expectations and so on.

Lack of ability to generalise. This could imply specialised abilities with patterns and themes that ordinarily might be missed (for example: the breaking of codes or the ability to plot maps along particular points without being distracted). But it also implies difficulties with the ability to generalise learnings across a variety of domains.

Timing and sequencing could be problematic outside of interest and/or attention because the usual systems in the brain may not be configured to cooperate. In some areas of course this could be useful but in social activity this might be a hindrance unless interest and attention can be shared.

Forward thinking connected with development of focused (single) interest only.

Otherwise this could lead to lack of comprehending 'Other'.

Figure 8.3: Single Attention and Associated Cognition in Autism (SAACA)

I believe being polytropic gives people opportunities of many sorts which are not accessible to people who are monotropic. Developmentally typical children are flexibly able to recognise and exploit opportunities that may pass monotropic children by. Among those missed opportunities are chances to contribute to a common interest, which is at the heart of inclusion (Bailey 1998). While polytropic children will swiftly find out how comfortably to cohabit in shared opportunity space, it may take a monotropic child far longer even to identify distinct cohabitants – let alone figure out how to fit in with them (D.K.C. Murray, personal communication, 21 April 2006).

THE COGNITIVE COMPONENTS OF SAACA

As we have seen, monotropism – single interest and attention – is the foundation of SAACA and lies at its heart. The products of monotropism can be summarised under the following headings:

- literality
- thinking in closed concepts (resistance to change and inability to generalise)
- lack of appreciation of context and scale
- difficulties with timing, sequencing and forward thinking (predicting)
- inappropriate non-social priorities.

These behaviours are described and exemplified below, but the SAACA approach to explaining and dealing with these behaviours will be dealt with in detail in Chapter 9.

Monotropism and literality

Literality is a term to describe being literal and taking things at their logical face value; for example: sentences, concepts, metaphors, similes, words, expressions, situations and people.

Many of us, especially children, tend to understand our world in literal terms. This means that we take the spoken word quite literally and respond accordingly. If individuals related to or working with us do not recognise this and do not understand that we might be taking them literally then they may believe that we are simply out to make life difficult for them.

The following are taken from Lawson (2001) and are examples of words and situations typically taken literally by AS individuals:

- Two teenagers yelling at each other. Father comes into the room and yells, 'We don't have yelling in this house'. The boys keep yelling. They do so because the father's words don't make sense or seem not to apply to them because they are yelling in the house and therefore 'we do have yelling in the house', and also, because the father himself is yelling, the boys might not even appreciate the concept of what yelling is.

- A young girl has her mum's newly baked cake in her hands. Mother says, 'You can't have that'. However, the girl knows that she can because she does have it. She ignores mum and walks away.

- Teacher says to Andrew, 'You do know that your homework is due on Tuesday, don't you?' Andrew says 'Yes', but come Tuesday he does not produce his homework. Teacher only asked if he knew it was due. Teacher did not ask him to give her his homework on Tuesday.

- 'I am bored; can I play a "bored game"?' 'Of course you can, which board game would you like?' 'I want to play cricket.'

- Young man takes too much time to eat breakfast in the morning. Carer complains that because he is so slow, they are often late. However, when they go out for fast food, the young man eats his food quickly and attempts to clear the food from other people's tables too. It seems that the young man believes that 'fast food' should be eaten quickly.

- Store detective says 'You can't take those. You haven't paid for them.' Teenager replies: 'Of course I haven't, I haven't any money.'

Monotropism and thinking in closed concepts

Thinking in closed concepts is a product of monotropic attention and focused interest. It is a way of understanding the world in a static form that does not allow for change. For example, 'we always do cooking on a Friday in the green room'. For AS individuals, if the teacher suggests moving to a different kitchen known as the blue room, the concept of being able to cook there does not exist for some, while it would be very uncomfortable for others, so much so that some would have a tantrum and refuse to go, whilst others might go to the room but become inert and unable to function.

monotone *(mon'otone),n*

1. ability to maintain same tone through entire monologue

Thinking in closed pictures or concepts, therefore, means not connecting ideas or concepts, not being privy to the whole picture but only getting bits of it, which can be rather limiting. Within a social context this makes it hard to read others, anticipate their needs, be spontaneous, work and/or relate without schedules and refocus after being interrupted. Thinking in closed concepts results in difficulties with generalising. For example, a boy learns how to tie his left shoelace and is excited, but then asks his mother, 'Mum, how do I tie my right shoelace?'

Some would argue that the WCC theory explains this. Surely focusing on local details might mean missing the global picture? Yes, this could be so; however, closed concepts can be opened up further when attention is harnessed by interest. For example, an AS individual not really interested in sitting down to watch a television programme, even if their friend is with them, might sit with that friend and watch TV if the programme happens to coincide with their own interests (e.g. if he or she is interested in 'The Simpsons' and that is the show that happens to be on, then they will be happy to join their friend). Other examples would be any situation that harnesses interest and uses it as a medium to drive connection and build understanding. It's as others join our interest that mutual interest can develop. Another example of this might be when an AS individual is interested in maps, or numbers or sport. By joining that interest we have a ready-made vehicle for driving concepts home in a wider capacity. What might start out as an interest in local maps could develop into mapping ones day, week and beyond. Mapping emotions, mapping thinking and mapping social expectation can all grow out of an interest in maps.

In contrast, typical individuals tend to think in open concepts. This means that they can add to their learning relatively easily. They use open pictures to build and integrate their experiences. Piaget (1952) called it 'accommodation'. They can develop concepts or schemas and enable their learning to generalise to a number of settings. For example, if one eats around a table at home, one might expect to eat around a table in restaurants and so on. If you think in closed concepts, however, although you know that you eat at the table in your home, you may not associate a table in a restaurant as a place to eat because that table is in a different context.

Typical individuals think in an open and ongoing manner (e.g. due to having multiple co-active or concurrent accessible interests channelling relevant information as a product of dividing attention). Therefore, they are able to draw on their experiences of the past and utilise these to inform their present and future expectations.

So, generalising for typical individuals usually isn't problematic. For example, when travelling to a particular destination (e.g. school) one might encounter some road works and a diversion sign. Even if one had not experienced this before, a typical individual would understand its implications. By contrast, however, an AS child who notices the car changing direction might think the car is veering away from their school and become very distressed. SAACA would argue this is because the AS individual has problems with thinking in open concepts (e.g. due to single interest and single attention) and thus with forward thinking.

The anxiety might be avoided if we are able to 'conceive' of such a change. This could be organised via photographs of different things that might happen when we travel in the car for example. One could use such photographs of road works, diversions, stopping for petrol or calling at a shop on the way, to show what to expect or where the family are going. Sometimes video games, such as 'The Sims' and 'Sims City' are a useful way to see the outcomes of particular manoeuvres.

For many of us, every time we encounter a situation, if it is not something that happens often or regularly, it is like encountering it for the first time. We tend not to take what has been learnt from one situation and apply it to another. This makes generalising our learnings very difficult. However, many of us can learn to generalise by academically learning the rules for each situation independently (Harchik *et al.* 1990). Again, this is evidence of a particular learning style rather than of an inability to learn.

Monotropism: context and scale

Consider the following story: The fuzzy felt board at my primary school had fuzzy felt animals upon it. These animals, such as goats, cows, sheep and horses, were only about 5–10 cms in size. I noted that the fuzzy felt pig upon the fuzzy felt board was pink, half the size of teacher's hand and didn't move. However, what would I encounter at an animal farm? Would the animals look like those on the fuzzy felt board or would they look and feel different?

On an outing one day we went to a hobby farm, where we were encouraged to get close to and stroke the farm animals. I remember being very reluctant to do so and becoming extremely distressed. It seemed the live pig was not like the fuzzy felt pig upon the fuzzy felt board. I had failed to generalise the ideas expressed upon the fuzzy felt board to the real animals at the farm (taken from Lawson 2001).

I think we often need intention (referring to reading peoples intention from their body language, their words and so on), context (physical, emotional and social) and scale (importance, type of event, big or little, and so on) explained to us in much more detail than typically happens. When using visual supports in education for AS children, it is easier to get a picture in a fuller way. The visuals show what is intended, what the context and the scale of an event or expectation is and so on. As in the example of the fuzzy felt animals above, one needs to make sure that they are accounting for intention context and scale. This could be done using video and photographs which imply a truer reality and show context much clearer.

Monotropism: timing, sequencing and predicting

Some of us can be physically and socially clumsy (Attwood 2007). We may not appreciate the appropriateness of conversational timing and/or physical propriety (Cesaroni and Garber 1991). Some people, like myself, would have difficulties crossing roads due to not working out where the traffic is coming from, or whether it is moving or stationary (Hoy 2007; Lawson 2001, 2008).

During group activities or conversations, for example, in a school classroom, on the playground, in an office at work or at the local shop, we may not be able to judge what it is appropriate to say because we have no interest in the current topic of conversation (Holliday Willey, 1999, 2002). We also have difficulty judging the right time to join a conversation, express an opinion, or just knowing when and how to walk away (Kluth and Chandler-Olcott 2008).

Understanding the context of a conversation means paying attention to more than one's own interest, which according to SAACA will not be easy for AS individuals. We can have lots of issues with time itself and movement through time. This can mean problems with sequencing, timing and/or motor coordination (Baggs 2008). Within everyday life, social concepts such as being prompt, being organised, being apt, being appropriate in conversation and being generally coordinated are difficult for us. Baggs (2008) talks a lot about difficulties with timing and notes that, for her, it is very hard to differentiate between the past, the present and the future because they possess a quality of sameness.

Psychologists note that events stored in long-term memory are usually available when needed to be recalled and brought into working memory. The only time this changes is as one ages when working or short-term memory is less available than long-term memory. In connection with attention and timing, it seems we are not making the same connections between long-term and short-term memory, therefore working memory as an everyday available resource is limited to where our attention and interest is focused. This implies attention may be stagnant or only focused on the present, with little understanding of an application to the future (e.g. Baggs 2008; Kana *et al.* 2006).

For us, having a non-typical brain configuration means using different, or atypical, processes to make sense of the world. It is implied by the research (e.g. Casanova 2005; Koshino *et al.* 2008) that such processes mean either less connectivity between sensory and cognitive processes, or over-connectivity. Therefore it is reasonable to argue that we, who are often good with long-term memory and facts but not so good at short-term memory and its generalised everyday use, will have issues understanding the timing of past, present and future and the connections between them. When, however, interest and single attention for us are harnessed this implied barrier seems to be less troublesome (e.g. Holliday Willey 2002).

The following is an example of harnessing my interest, and therefore my attention, to help me learn about timing. When I was 11 years old I had a puppy. My love for animals has always been a strong interest and my family could get me to do almost anything if it was connected to my pets in some way. So, if Mum had said I had to read my *Janet and John* book for ten minutes, she would align it as follows: 'Wendy, first read your book then you can feed your dog and then walk her for 20 minutes. So, look at the big clock in the lounge room. The clock has two pointers, we call these clock hands. The shorter clock hand is pointing to the hour of the day, the longer clock hand points to the minutes of the day. At the moment the clock is stating it is 4.30 in the afternoon, which means it's after lunch time, but not yet tea time. Read your book until the smaller hand indicates it's 4.40 (40 minutes after 4 o'clock) then you can spend time with Rusty.'

Over time I learnt that the hours and minutes of a day were segments and could be occupied by events and thoughts. Eventually I learnt that these segments of time often lasted for a complete portion of time. Thus

I began to appreciate the timing of certain events. I now know with confidence that some events take more time than others.

I aim to plan my time so I allow enough time for certain things. Because I have trouble forward thinking, however, if things don't go to plan I still panic and have lots of anxiety around 'timing', even though I have now grasped the concept of 'time'.

Having issues with predicting outcomes, for example not learning from experience or being unable to forward think and work out conclusions, is common to so many of us. In social situations this might mean missing social cues, not comprehending the importance of particular or special occasions and possibly not 'getting' the ideas behind concepts such as later, after, yours, mine, theirs, ours, if, when and so on. If AS individuals expect a particular outcome, but an outcome other than the one we might be expecting occurs, we might not cope well with the change.

Although concepts of 'the future' may be very difficult for us, using 'interest' could assist in explaining and in building understanding. For us, other people, events and happenings may move on but, for many, this understanding fails to occur and we feel 'left behind'. Our emotions, feelings and thoughts may all stay fluid, but we don't seem to move on when time changes.

The typical individual, because of being connected to multiple interests via divided attention, appears to know what fits where, when and who with. Even though the minds of AS individuals can hold on to many amazing facts and facets of knowledge, we are not connected to areas outside of our attention and interest, and this can lead to an array of learning difficulties, for example, forgetting what one needs to buy at the shop, but not forgetting the theme of a video, the outfit someone was wearing or the layout of a venue we visited, because some aspect of these other events or places held our attention and interest.

Monotropism and non-social priorities

Non-social priorities will mean a number of things. At times, not having social priorities uppermost in one's mind is appropriate, but knowing when this has to change or knowing the meaning of propriety is vital to social wellbeing. Understanding social priorities and adopting these is crucial and central to all relationships. AS individuals, however, may have a different take on this. For example, choosing preferred clothing (over what is fashionable, practical or the commonsense option) may dominate.

We may not be concerned with appearance, hygiene, being on time or having a tidy home, or we may be quite the opposite and be regimented about these things to the point of distraction (Jackson 2002).

SUMMARY

This chapter has introduced an alternative newly developed cognitive theory called SAACA. SAACA suggests autism is a very different learning style that presents as a result of an attention, interest, sensory-motor perception loop. This alternative theory is in line with the type of development seen in AS and experienced by AS individuals. It is also accommodated by the diagnostic criteria for AS and fits the clinical picture of AS. SAACA fulfils all the requirements for a newly developed theory of autism.

At present there is little empirical supporting evidence for this new approach. However, reports from AS individuals and literature quoted within the text suggest there is merit for further investigation into this potential cognitive style.

The next chapter will highlight some of the relevancy of SAACA as well as demonstrate via case histories how SAACA explains the clinical profile in AS that is not accommodated by the other traditional theories mentioned earlier in this text.

CHAPTER 9

The Relevance
of SAACA

INTRODUCTION

In the previous chapter a newly developed theory concerning the characteristics and clinical picture presented in autism was explored as single attention and associated cognition in autism (SAACA). This chapter will discuss the relevance of SAACA, with reference to individual case studies and as a way of illustrating how SAACA fits the clinical picture in autism.

Also, I hope I have shown that many characteristics can be associated with both typical and AS individuals, but this does not make them mutually exclusive. This will be discussed further in the chapter.

SAACA assumes that individuals with a particular brain configuration will learn in a different way from typical individuals. Typical individuals learn by noting and modelling other people's behaviour, whilst AS individuals often miss and do not note the behaviour of others, unless it is exaggerated or raises their interest. For example, typical individuals, whose brains are configured to notice faces from a very young age and to go on to read facial and body language, learn very quickly the social rules of both family and societal life, whilst we, who often do not notice facial expressions or read body language, have a very difficult time within both family and society. SAACA explains autistic behaviour as monotropism and its products, whilst the ability to divide attention and connect to an integrated sensory system explains typical behaviour (polytropism and its products).

To date, much research about the brain and how it works seems to support the idea that brains can be configured differently. Not only do we see this in the male and female brain (Baron-Cohen 2005) but different brain configurations occur in the typical and in the autistic brain.

EVERYDAY EXPERIENCES FOR AUTISM SPECTRUM INDIVIDUALS

SAACA suggests that almost every characteristic associated with being typical (see Figure 8.1) will be different for AS individuals. One such characteristic is the understanding of the non-literal and metaphorical language that is in daily use by typical individuals; for example, 'I'll just be a minute', which is understood by typical individuals to mean a short amount of time, not literally a minute. This is because typical individuals think in open concepts; for example, they have an appreciation of past, present and future. Typical individuals also generalise learning across differing domains. Understanding social timing and sequencing is a natural part of typical development, as is being appropriate in conversation and forward thinking outside of their own interest.

Thinking ahead and being able to organise oneself and others also seems to come naturally to typical individuals, even though for some being organised might not be their forte. Accommodation of 'Other', for example, social ability (which some say is associated with ToM) and wanting to please other people (i.e. fit in and belong), also seems to come naturally to typical individuals. I argue the above are associated with a typical learning style suited to NT developing individuals whose brains are configured to allow such a learning style to exist for them. I appreciate that everyone is an individual and learns differently, but often NT individuals learn beneath the same 'umbrella' as if they belonged to a particular population.

This means they are able to appreciate and understand what might be happening to another person even if they have not experienced it themselves, (e.g. emotions such as grief, excitement, fear and so on). They can do this because they have a brain that is configured to divide attention and so they notice both external and internal states.

They certainly can be focused and resist interruptions, but this is different from not noting that a potential interruption could occur. Even when they are enjoying a favourite book, sport or hobby they still respond to their name or to words such as 'fire' (Bailey and Snowling 2002), whereas if we are totally focused we might not notice someone speaking to us, even if they are warning us of a dangerous situation.

Because NTs have a brain that is configured to integrate multiple inputs, they also have an integrated sensory system that works with the brain to process information that is seen, heard, tasted, smelt or touched. Therefore, the sensory system and attention system are synchronised with each other. This enables this population to think and feel simultaneously, requiring a brain that is configured to divide attention.

It appears that NTs have little difficulty with multi-tasking and being actively engaged in socialisation at a number of levels (Attwood 2007). These things would be extremely difficult if not impossible for many of us, who might avoid social situations and focus on single interests that are of value to us rather than join the interests of others.

When things change

The following are just a few examples of demonstrated behaviours as a reaction to change for us. Using SAACA to understand these behaviours for each response below, one or more of the products of monotropism would be the reason for the reaction to change.

- Many AS children will become upset if a parent drives them to their destination via a different or unexpected route. They may rock, cover their ears, cry and display strong fear or confusion type responses. Using SAACA allows the recognition of the child's literality and monotropic disposition.

- Moving furniture to a different spot, or changing things (e.g. decor) in the bedroom can cause severe tantrums, rocking, flapping, withdrawal, crying and other distress responses for an AS child. SAACA would suggest that being monotropic implies living in the now and not finding change easy to cope with. Forward thinking relies upon being able to appreciate present time, here and now, as well as having concepts related to the future. This requires dividing one's attention, such as in polytropism.

- Tidying toys or moving something in the child's room can cause the types of distressed responses mentioned above. Typical children might not like this type of change but can usually accommodate it once reasons for it have been given.

- Having visitors arrive unannounced or having an unexpected change of routine can cause the types of responses already outlined above. Once again SAACA would suggest these responses are due to the products of monotropism.

- Changing clothes, because of seasonal changes, can be very distressing. Being told, 'The sun is out today. You need only wear a T-shirt and shorts', is fine in the warm summer months. What, however, does it mean to us when the sun is out during the winter months? SAACA would predict that some of us would wear T-shirts all year round or whenever the sun shone because we might equate sun and T-shirt, rather than equating the changing weather or season with the need for different clothing.

One mother having a conversation with her teenage son about the topic of her being away permanently, as in the event of her death, brought the following response from her son: '…who will take me to McDonalds?'

SAACA would suggest such a comment is not due to lack of ToM or poor central coherence, or even to executive dysfunctioning. Rather, such a response might be due to not being able at that moment to process such information and only able to see the disruption to the routine or expectation.

It could be argued that ToM might account for the above (lack of understanding 'Other') but SAACA also offers a reasonable theory for such a response. When an individual takes life literally, is monotropic and finds the concept of change difficult to understand, such a literal response is almost to be expected.

SAACA suggests that most AS individuals are monotropic and that the monotropic disposition informs AS cognition and subsequent learning styles. This implies only being able to focus on one thing at one time, as long as it's within our interest system. The implication of having a monotropic disposition is that generalising one's experience and understanding is difficult. This could also have an impact upon the understanding of time because time might not be noted as a concept but rather only as a hindrance to being able to stay focused upon the thing that is holding our attention.

The concept of time

The knowledge of how long something lasts (e.g. a moment; a few minutes; an hour, etc.) can initially be learnt by many within the neurotypical population, as one comprehends the length of a day or night, or minutes and seconds, or learns to tell the time by reading a watch or clock. As typical individuals get older, they will have almost an instinctive ability to 'read' their inner clock to tell whether or not an hour has passed, or just a few minutes. This process, however, seems to elude many of us. Being singly channelled, placing all our energy and thinking into doing one thing at one time, can mean missing the cues that time can offer. For some of us this may mean not noticing when we are hungry, tired, need to go to the bathroom or are in pain. For others, this may mean difficulties with moving on emotionally. To imagine what it might be like for AS individuals maybe typical individuals might reflect on the times when they have been totally focused, and consequently have been quite surprised at how much time has gone past without their noticing it!

Imagine yourself lost in a desert without signposts. How can you know the right way to turn? How would you decide what to do? This is what it might feel like for an AS child at school, or the young adult starting work. Typical individuals know how long to wait for gaps in the conversation, or when it's the other person's turn to speak. For us, the idea that 'it's time to stop now' might be bewildering.

The sense of 'timing' typical individuals have is inherently different from ours. So what do you do when you don't have it? I suggest we use other means to stay in control. We rely upon routine, ritual and repetitive behaviours. If there are no rules then we may invent some. There have to be guidelines. How else can we know what to expect? A monotropic learning style explained by SAACA implies that we learn differently from typical individuals. Therefore, teaching us as if we learnt in the same way as typical individuals might only cause more confusion.

SAACA'S EXPLANATION OF WHY AUTISM SPECTRUM AND NEUROTYPICAL PERCEPTIONS ARE DIFFERENT

I believe that our perception can be quite unlike that of the neurotypical population, not just cognitively but in many different domains. SAACA explains this is because the typical population can shift attention easily and the brain can decide which bits of information to register, keep or let go of. Perception is influenced by what is seen, heard, felt and experienced but it is also influenced by emotional feeling and belief.

For example, in the perception of shape and form the brain needs to access many pieces of information from senses (vision and other perceptive lenses). These are then filtered through one's belief system and form an understanding. When we consider our visual sense alone, it is better when we use both our eyes rather than just one. Two eyes gives us a better perspective of depth and distance. I am stating this not to explore it in any detail but just to note, as Georgieva *et al.* (2008) suggest: '…because motion and stereo are such powerful sources of information, especially when presented in combination, it should not be surprising that they are of primary importance for the perception of 3D shape in natural vision' (p.116).

They use the word 'stereo' which implies 'two channels of information being broadcast and received'. The explanation given by SAACA is that AS individuals are using mono sense, not stereo. This leads to deep intense attention and interest singly focused upon whatever is capturing the attention at that time. The broader picture might be missed, not because of central cohesion problems or over-focusing but because our default setting is to have single attention captured by single interest rather than divided attention capturing broader interests.

Zaffy likes the facts.

In one example used by Attwood he states that although AS individuals have a reputation for their factual and 'long memories', it is more likely that 'they have the inability to forget' (T. Attwood, personal communication, 8 April 2005).

It is possible that being able to store facts and factual information does not necessitate one's ability to generalise them. In fact one can have factual information without necessarily understanding it or interacting with it in any way. This could mean, though, that we may use facts inappropriately as a way of trying to connect or communicate with another person. Facts are facts, and although one may learn them or may also be taught through therapies and interventions to introduce them at appropriate times, it might not be useful to be taught this way if an individual doesn't learn in the way that typical individuals usually do.

The social aim of conversation is not to know how to place facts into a conversation, but to appreciate the know-how of 'small talk' and to be able to align one's interests with those of the other person. Therefore, those of us who know lots of facts may have difficulties when conversing in the social or emotional arena when factual input is not the focus. However, there are situations where ability to focus upon facts without being bombarded by social demand is an asset.

SAACA explains the rationale behind many of the issues that dominate our lives and accounts for a diversity of situations which is often lacking in other cognitive theories.

Using SAACA the following case studies demonstrate monotropic attention and how this impacts upon perception.

Case studies

Although the examples used in these case studies appear as anecdotal evidence and this puts them into the non-scientific basket they are nonetheless important because they originate from actual lives of AS individuals. The following are some more examples of not forward thinking, of taking things literally and of not generalising, therefore leaving us to try to adapt to change and work out alternative ways of coping, or of understanding. This also leaves us with certain behaviours and thought patterns that SAACA would assume to predict. Some of the examples first appeared in Lawson (2001).

JANE AND THE TOILET ROLL

Jane, an autistic individual, is very good at remembering facts, and her recall of events of interest to her is outstanding. However, when she is otherwise focused or not attending to some minor event that a typical individual will take for granted, not only does Jane not share in the understanding, she can become quite distressed. At times, when it comes to matters of recall and perception, Jane notes her understanding of events and social interactions but they often seem to be different from those experienced by her typically developing peers.

For example, in talking with her case worker, Jane recalls an incident that occurred one night when she had difficulty sleeping. She remembered thinking that the available toilet paper sheets on the toilet roll were diminishing but there was no need to replace it with a new roll at that time. A few hours later during the night Jane got up and saw that the toilet roll was full. 'How could this be?' Jane wondered if she had been mistaken earlier in thinking that the toilet roll was almost finished. Jane spoke of several incidents that had happened for her throughout her life that had led her to perceive or believe certain things about particular events, people and situations. Many of these events had left Jane feeling confused, lost or unsure because she was unaware of possible alternative explanations or propositions.

In the case of the toilet roll incident another family member had got up during the night and had replaced the toilet roll. This possibility did not occur to Jane because of her difficulty with forward thinking (a direct product of monotropic learning styles) and she was distraught because she could not understand what had happened. The case worker's exploration of the incident with Jane included the idea of other possible events, including the fact that someone else in the family had changed the toilet roll. This helped Jane realise she had assumed her perception of events was the only one but that there could be other reasons why things happen. It took the case worker quite a while, using video footage of role playing changing a toilet roll, to explain that there may be alternative explanations of events that might not be noticed by an individual.

The above illustrates a way of thinking that is not unusual in the lives of AS individuals (Lawson 2001, 2008). The products of a monotropic learning style affect individuals in different ways.

GETTING LOST

Jenny is quickly lost in towns and finds it difficult to negotiate roads and traffic. Giving her a map does not help, it only compounds her confusion. Jenny is good with words and tends to be an auditory learner who works with one concept at any one time. It is interesting that although she can multi-task she can only do so within areas of her interest.

SAACA explains these types of scenarios whilst theory of mind, central cohesion, executive functioning and enhanced perceptual functioning do not, because each fails to consider the role of attention and interest. For example, ToM only suggests AS individuals might have difficulty with concepts concerning reading the intentions or emotional states of others. For Jenny, negotiating road crossings and directions may not reflect issues with ToM although EF might come into this situation. However, crossing roads safely due to noticing traffic conditions appropriately might be more to do with only noting the one goal (crossing the road) and not the other (safely) which has to do with what one is able to attend to more than it does with being able to connect both concepts and, therefore, making the right choice (crossing the road and doing so safely).

EPF might imply that an AS individual would be really good with directions, maps and not getting lost, which for some AS individuals is the case. Usually, though, such individuals may have a special interest in maps, directions, travel and the like. SAACA suggests this ability is more to do with attention and interest than EPF. If EPF were the reason for AS, then it fails to explain Jenny's difficulties.

WRITTEN WORDS, SPOKEN WORDS

Don, another autistic individual, who is very good at reading and using maps and has no problem with roads, traffic or negotiating busy places, is quite different from Jane and Jenny. Although he does well when travelling alone or in familiar cities with regard to finding his way around physically, he becomes quite lost when it comes to comprehending conversations, words and social interaction.

So using words and story to explain the toilet roll incident above to Don would not have helped him understand, whereas mapping or diagramming the incident would have done. It is argued in this text that Jane, Don and Jenny's brains are connecting details of things that occupy their interest system and make it easier to access the type of information they relate to. For example, if words are not an AS individual's interest or are not able to hold their attention, they have difficulty processing them. In such situations role play, photographs and visual story might help where words do not. Some AS individuals need words and pictures (Jordan 1999).

SAACA argues that autistic individuals like Don might be processing words with difficulty because their attention and interest are taken over by mapping. If Don's interest was captured by words, he might not have the issues with conversation.

Some research on attention (e.g. Rutherford *et al.* 2007) suggests that AS individuals divide attention as well as NTs because participants in their study (where AS individuals were matched with typical controls and had to divide their attention between a central word 'READY' and notice smaller peripheral letters on a computer screen) did as well as the controls. SAACA suggests AS individuals only do this well when their interest and/or attention connects them to the activity. It's interesting that a computer screen was used for the experiments conducted. Such a medium does not present with the distracters that ordinary everyday life encounters might.

Such research fails to take into account factors of interest and attention as an explanation of difficulties with aspects of cognition. For example, Kuhl *et al.* (2005) found that young AS children have a difficult time recognising ordinary words, and more of their brains are occupied with this kind of task compared to typically developing youngsters.

> Rather than becoming an expert in recognizing words, their brains slow down, and because these children can't distinguish what should be a familiar word their brains work too hard and they are unable to focus on new words. When they can't understand a word, they miss everything else that follows in a sentence (Kuhl *et al.* 2005, p.175).

In contrast to Kuhl *et al.* (2005), it has been observed that AS individuals who appear not to have access to language but who are triggered by interest, learn and hold words better in their working memory and learn new words too. For example Gardner (2008) demonstrated that her son learnt concepts concerning daily issues and developed typical language once his interest (Thomas the Tank Engine) was used in a script to explain what was happening; if the character of 'Thomas' had to sleep, then so did Gardner's son. In this way, 'Thomas sleep' began to build the concept associated with the word 'sleep'.

Words can be typed and for some of us typed words are easier to understand than spoken language. For example, some of us have confirmed to those around us, that we can and do know 'language' if computers speak for us (Baggs 2008); see also Appendix E. Of course, this implies access to the appropriate mediums that we need to be enabled to do this.

In Gernsbacher *et al.* (2008) a case study revealed a similar scenario. Gernsbacher *et al.* (2008) showed that the individual she studied could think and understand speech but could not express himself by using spoken language. She also pointed out that this had implications for the idea of joining attention via gaze and speech. SAACA would suggest that monotropism and its products play a role here too. None of the above dispositions, however, can be explained by ToM, CC, EF or EPF theory.

THE WASHING

Sharon sat in the kitchen looking out of the window. In one corner of the room the wet washing lay in the blue plastic clothes basket. The sky looked cloudy. 'Will it rain?' thought Sharon. 'It looked like rain yesterday, but the clouds remained unopened,' her thoughts continued. It had been the same situation all week. The now partly damp washing was still in the basket. The dirty linen basket was full. Sharon had been sitting in the kitchen all morning. It was the same yesterday. It was just too difficult to make a decision. She needed to know what to do. But even organising to contact someone to ask their advice seemed beyond her. Sharon continued to sit in the kitchen.

Using SAACA helps us to understand Sharon's behaviour. Sharon's attention would have been so occupied with what the weather might bring that it disabled her from making any decisions at all. Assisting Sharon by means of written alternatives could be helpful. For example, in a note book or written down for Sharon in a place she felt comfortable with and could access easily could be written 'You can put the washing upon a drying rack whatever the weather'.

TAKING TOO LONG IN THE SHOWER

John was in the shower. 'Come on John, you're taking too long in the shower. There won't be any hot water left for anyone else!' said Paul.

John always took his time to get ready in the mornings and quite often the rest of the household suffered too. 'Oh John, come on, we'll all be late now,' said Jane. Paul came to the autism workshop. 'How can I organise John so that he doesn't take too long in the shower?' he asked. Paul and the workshop facilitator talked together at some length. It was agreed John took words literally. Telling him not to 'take too long' in the shower was as meaningless as saying 'how long is a piece of string?' Instead, it was suggested that Paul devise a way of letting John know the timing of each showering preparation and activity.

To do this, a short story was prepared as an instructive outline detailing the procedure. John likes 'The Simpsons', so a comic strip story about Homer Simpson having his shower was used. It was then suggested John does the same as Homer does in the story. For example: 'Once inside the bathroom John takes off his clothes and places them onto the chair. Next, he turns on the taps, makes sure the water is a nice warm temperature and not too hot or too cold. He steps into the shower, picks up the soap and rubs it over his body. John then counts to 60 whilst he places the sponge with the soapy water on it all over him. He washes as far down as possible (a family term that John liked) from his face, neck, shoulders, arms, etc. Then he washes as far up as possible (toes, feet, legs and thighs). Then he washes between the tops of his legs and all around. By the time he reaches 60 he will have washed all of himself, except his hair. Sometimes Homer or John will wash their hair also. So, counting to 60 again, John puts his head under the water spray and gets his hair wet. Then John picks up the shampoo container, squeezes about a spoonful of shampoo onto his hands and rubs this into his hair. Now, as John counts down from 60 to 1, he washes all the shampoo and soap off his body. When John gets to number 1, the soapiness is gone from his body and he turns off the taps. Now John steps out of the shower, picks up the towel and dries himself. When John is dry he can come out of the bathroom with his towel tucked in around his waist.

To help John with his shower timing, Paul was to knock upon the bathroom door. One knock was to advise John it was time to use the soap. Two knocks meant it was time to turn the taps off and dry himself. Three knocks meant it was time to put the towel around himself and exit the bathroom. Two weeks after Paul began to use this technique, John was taking, on average, only ten minutes to have his shower. He was a much happier teenager and the rest of the household were happier too!

In the story of John, SAACA can give an explanation of John's behaviour. That is, John's attention and interest were occupied by the story of 'The Simpsons' so using this story and counting (structure) enabled John to work through the process of showering. It captured his interest (allowing motivation) and attention (allowing him to observe and work through the process). SAACA also allowed an intervention technique which was to give structure or a way of working out what John needed to do to work his way through the process of having a shower.

We need everyday life to be structured and orchestrated (Jordan 1999). Structuring life is helpful because we have huge amounts of anxiety and fear predicting outcomes. For example, an AS child's need to line up objects or engage in other ordered tasks and obsessions might be born from the need to know what will come next and to be sure that this will always happen.

Although we may not 'see' the reasoning, or rationalisation, of events in the same way as the typical population does, as outlined in the examples, SAACA argues this is due to having a different brain configuration and thus a different learning style.

THROWING STONES

A young AS lad aged 12 was talking to a policeman. The youth had been down at a local railway station with some bigger lads throwing rocks at a passing train. Upon questioning, the lad was emphatic that he hadn't thrown rocks, they were stones, and that he hadn't done anything wrong because he had thrown them over the train, not at the train. Difficulties to predict an outcome or fully understand consequences can be a strong component of the AS personality.

Generalising, or sharing in the learning from one situation to another, may not occur easily for us. Learning from mistakes or from being told about something might not build the same connection to understanding if it occurs outside of interest (motivation) and attention (awareness). It could mean we might perform a similar behaviour over and over again, even when it ends in punishment or pain.

Understanding SAACA would allow educational strategies that could work alongside AS individuals, such as the youth above, and deliver different outcomes. Perhaps via video and/or story or even safe role play using the youth's interest, exploring how easily 'stone throwing' might miss its mark or be taken to mean something different from that which was intended could be achieved.

WENDY AND THE BUILDER

The following story aims to show how I took the issue of 'time' very literally and believed the builder to mean what he said quite literally about the timing of his arrival to do some work for me. I realised some time later that I had failed to accommodate the social understanding needed to adapt my thinking concerning the idea that 'time' can be given as an approximation. I was also so taken over by my belief that the builder would arrive at the time he stated that I was unable to focus upon anything else. This experience is offered up as an example of monotropic thinking.

Wendy says to the builder, 'I really am anxious for you to finish off the living room. My parents are coming to visit next week.' The builder replies, 'Yes, I'm able to give you some time to do that. I am off all day on Friday and there will be plenty of time to come over and finish those doors.' However, by 11 am on Friday, the builder hasn't arrived. Wendy is pacing up and down the corridor feeling very anxious and upset. She wonders why the builder, who promised to be at her house all day on Friday, is not there, and she is unable to concentrate on any of her assignments for university because she is waiting for the builder.

At 12 noon, Wendy can wait no longer and she telephones the builder. 'Why aren't you here?' Wendy asks the builder. The builder explains that he has some other jobs to finish, not just the ones for Wendy. He tells Wendy that the doors will only take a couple of hours to finish off and that he will be there after lunch, around 2 pm. Wendy puts the phone receiver down and feels a mixture of emotions. She feels silly and very cross. Cross, because the builder didn't explain things to her properly, and silly, because the builder's subsequent explanation made sense. However, unfortunately, she hadn't been able to see that for herself and she now felt very frustrated. Wendy should have been studying but was unable to concentrate because of her confusion and disappointment with the day.

SAACA suggests this state of being for Wendy is not due to ToM, WCC, EF or EPF, but rather to monotropism and its products (such as being literal and taking things literally).

TRACY GOES TO CAMP

The Year 7s had enjoyed their first camp together and now, as they sat relaxing around the camp fire, Linda, the PE teacher, began to play her guitar. Kim produced an enormous bar of Cadbury's chocolate. As it passed between each camper, participants broke off pieces of the chocolate and passed it on. Eventually the decreasing bar of chocolate reached Tracy.

Tracy, a 12-year-old with Asperger's syndrome, received the chocolate, held it in her hands and looked down at it. There was silence over the rest of the group as they watched Tracy and waited. It seemed like an eternity, but finally Jane broke the silence: 'You can't have the chocolate, Tracy.' Tracy looked up. 'Yes I can!' she exclaimed. Jane reached over to take the chocolate away from Tracy. Tracy jumped up and began to run away. Half a dozen members of the group chased Tracy for almost 20 minutes around the campfire and the tent site.

Eventually, out of breath, Jane called out to Tracy: 'Trace…take a couple of squares from the chocolate bar and please pass it on to Jill.' As the other girls stopped and watched, Tracy stopped running. She bent over the chocolate bar and calmly broke off exactly two squares. She then looked up to locate Jill and moved across to give her the chocolate bar. Murmuring spread through the group as they returned to their tents. 'Why is Tracy so difficult?' one child grumbled. 'She really pushes her luck,' another muttered. 'I'm glad I'm not one of her friends,' echoed a third.

Seen through the eyes of SAACA, the story illustrating issues for Tracy shows how she is taking things literally, is not generalising her understanding and is failing to forward think. For example, how can someone tell Tracy that she can't have the chocolate, when she actually does have it? Also, for Tracy, holding on to the chocolate was a time of processing what she needed to do next. Her processing time was interrupted and she lost her train of thought. Without clear instruction and structure Tracy has no real idea of how to behave. However, if Tracy had been given a clear instruction, for example, 'please take two squares from the chocolate bar to have for yourself, and then pass the chocolate bar to the camper next to you on your right', this scene may never have occurred.

Tracy has some great qualities. She is loyal, trustworthy, truthful and well committed to doing the tasks she chooses. She would make a good friend. However, because of her literality, as well as having difficulty with her own understanding of everyday issues, she is often misunderstood. This only adds to Tracy's feelings of isolation. She would be a prime candidate for depression, mental illness or even juvenile delinquency.

Research conducted by Grossman *et al.* (2000) suggests: 'Individuals with Asperger syndrome may be utilizing compensatory strategies, such as verbal mediation, to process facial expressions of emotion...' (p.369). This means they use different clues to enable them to read others. An interpretation of Grossman *et al.* (2000) is that AS individuals may need to listen rather than look because the words people use might be the key that enables understanding or 'paints an accessible picture'. Alternatively, if people do not use clear language, then many of us will find it hard to work out what they mean.

Through the SAACA lens, it is easy to understand why someone might need more processing time (they only have single attention available to them so cannot look, listen, think and act all at the same time). This type of processing requires divided attention and the products of polytropism or of being a typical individual. In Tracy's case, listening to an explanation rather than looking at what to do with the chocolate would have been clearer for her.

AUTISM SPECTRUM COMPREHENSION

The ability to understand that other people have their own thoughts and beliefs, quite separate from one's own, belongs with typical development. By the time a typical child is three or four years old, many can appreciate second-order beliefs (Sullivan *et al.* 1994). However, this may not be the case for us. SAACA would argue that brain configuration where connectivity between senses, attention and interest (where interest competes for attention and misses areas not attended to) accounts for such scenarios.

For example, Kluth and Chandler-Olcott (2008) and Gernsbacher *et al.* (2008) use the AS individual's particular interest as a vehicle to carry their attention to where they need that individual to go. This might be a study project for school, a structured activity or family time together. If the AS individual's attention is harnessed and they are motivated via interest they can and do achieve things way beyond others' expectations (Sanjay 2008). This is not because they suddenly gain a ToM, or connect to the EFs needed for understanding, so much as it is because their particular learning or cognitive style is utilised (attention and interest enable the connection to a concept to be learnt).

The difficulty of 'putting oneself into another's shoes' (i.e. can only view life from own experience and cannot appreciate how someone else might experience life) can be quite central to being autistic. SAACA would suggest this is an outcome of monotropism and its products. For this reason, many of us are seen to be egocentric and may even appear selfish. The assumption of SAACA is that egocentricity, eccentricity and emotional immaturity in AS individuals might be due to having a different learning style to that of typical individuals (Gernsbacher *et al.* 2008; Minshew *et al.* 2008). This also implies we may not be having access to learning in the way that we need to.

Thus SAACA argues polytropic attention and its products are not available in the same way to us as they are to the typical population. Single attention can account for the difficulty in comprehending 'Other' because attention is only available for one thing at any one time within the attention tunnel (e.g. might notice person is speaking but not notice tone of voice). This is quite different from it being a theory of mind problem, or a problem of executive functioning, central cohesion or enhanced perceptual functioning.

In many ways being selfish concerns an ability to choose 'Self' over 'Other'. For us, however, being only aware of 'Self' is not so much a choice as a predetermined existence. Biologically, this may be one of the outcomes of the way our mind is organised (Minshew and Williams 2007). Having the cognitive disposition to comprehend the idea of 'Other' is not missing altogether, as 15 per cent of AS children do comprehend 'Other', even though it might be in a limited way (Baron-Cohen 1989; Baron-Cohen *et al.* 1985; Baron-Cohen, Joliffe *et al.* 1997). Rather, comprehending other, needs to be developed over time with the right learning tools. SAACA would suggest using our interest because this is where our attention is.

Most typical people appear to have social priorities. That is, they prefer the company of others to being alone (but can choose to be alone when they need to be) and their decisions encompass their own wants, needs and opinions as well as those of others. This is quite different from the priorities apparent in AS. For us, it is not uncommon to think that 'everyone knows what we need because we know' or because we have said that it is so (Gerland 1997; Jackson 2002; Lawson 2000). This implies one is unaware that others are separate to self. Theory of mind may not be responsible for this thinking so much as specific brain design might be.

However, not operating beneath the banner of 'social priorities' poses a range of problems for a socially minded typical world, as well as for the AS individual having to share the polytropic world of others. For instance, mutual human interaction tends to demand emotional and cognitive understanding as a matter of 'right'. It views intolerance and indifference towards others as undesirable and bad. Therefore, when one encounters an egocentric individual in the classroom, schoolyard or work place, one forms a judgement about them. Egocentric becomes self-centred then selfish, demanding, mean, not useful, non-productive and not worth investing in.

But, when individuals view someone as being eccentric and egocentric (without moving to self-centred or selfish) they might tend to think 'artist, savant, genius, musician, mathematician, professor…' This could mean seeing focus, concentration and lack of sociability as a good thing in such people and even being able to forgive their difficulties with being sensitive to the needs or opinions of others.

Using the SAACA lens as a means of seeing AS individuals and the behaviour we might display will assist in realising that different strategies are needed to help us join the typical world. In fact, joining our interest first and using it as a way to build a relationship with us could open doors to learning, and may even widen our attentional lens.

Within the autistic spectrum there are many individuals who have lots of ability, but this can be overshadowed if all that is seen is 'lack of theory of mind'. Being taught the social skills of sharing, listening, being polite, being considerate and affording to others the right to be different would enable so many to live active and meaningful lives (Jordan 1999; NAS 2008). The cognitive awareness of 'Other' and other concepts that those in the polytropic world seem to access so easily could also be available to many individuals along the AS spectrum if SAACA was seen as the 'missing link'.

I believe having a different learning style is more to do with brain configuration and interaction with the environment than with brain dysfunction. The following examples and stories demonstrate some of the practical problems that many of us experience, and an interpretation of the behaviour is given from the theoretical viewpoint of SAACA.

Problems with autism spectrum comprehension (if using a neurotypical lens)

When a school programme has been organised and then fails to happen as timetabled, planned or expected, we might believe that the organiser is incompetent, is mean, is not very intelligent or should simply give their job to someone else who will do it efficiently! The thought that plans can change due to a variety of reasons is not automatically processed.

Using the SAACA lens with this example, a teacher might not only have access to a different understanding of the AS individual's interpretation and behaviour, but might also access tools that enable the student to interpret the situation differently. For example, a timetable that is colour-coded with events outlined as A, B or C could be useful. A could be the usual event, perhaps coded in the colour orange, and the other events, not so usual but allowed, could be coloured differently. A tick could be placed against the event that will occur that day and crosses against the events that will not. The point is that the AS individual could visually see that alternatives are allowed and might happen. All of this would need to be explained in ways that make sense to the student.

An AS child may be fascinated by any number of interesting encounters, but may fail to recognise the effect of such endeavours. For example: David is fascinated with the knowledge that tears come from tear ducts and when crying begins the tear ducts open and water runs down one's face. David will initiate this experience by poking the eyes of young children or animals with his finger or with a stick. When he succeeds in making the tears appear, David is overjoyed! The thought that he is hurting someone else and that this is not appropriate is not automatically processed.

SAACA would suggest that this young man's interest and attention is focused upon the fascination of how things work. There would be many different ways to explore tear ducts and other phenomena that might capture this young man's interest. It could also be made a rule that poking eyes of animals and humans is not allowed or is out of bounds. If explaining these things with words does not build the right concepts then using IT, photographs, role play and other imaginative ideas might be useful.

Amy loves to eat McDonalds' hot chips. When taken to the fast food outlet, Amy does not restrict her eating of chips to her own portion. Amy will endeavour to eat any other person's lunch as well as her own. The concept of ownership, this is mine and that is yours, is not typically processed.

SAACA would argue that Amy does not have a concept of 'yours but not mine' and vice versa. Individuals go to McDonalds and there they eat hot potato chips. If someone says, 'Let's go to McDonalds as a treat', typical individuals know that this means they are only allowed to eat what they have paid for or have been given because they have access to the bigger picture through brain activity that has allowed them to learn this concept. They appear more connected to the various systems that need to function together in order to build the concepts of non-literality, etc. (Attwood 2007; Casanova 2005; Myin and O'Regan 2002).

A newly married couple, one of whom has a diagnosis of AS, are coming to the end of an evening of television. The wife says, 'Darling, I'm going to bed now.' The husband says, 'Goodnight.' The wife replies, 'Aren't you coming too?' To which the husband retorts, 'You're a big girl now, surely you can go to bed by yourself!' The thought that his wife wants him to come to bed because she wants to cuddle up with him and enjoy his being with her is not automatically processed. Other cognitive theories would suggest the AS husband lacks a ToM or has poor executive functioning or central cohesion so he isn't able to see the whole picture. EPF might argue the AS husband is overly focused upon either his television programme or another activity of interest, or that he hasn't processed the information enough due to over-attention to other things.

SAACA would argue that although all of the above might be relevant they each fail to note that the husband might only have single attention available, which keeps him focused upon whatever has captured his interest at that time. SAACA would also argue (unlike other cognitive theories) that if the husband wanted to be with his wife and if he understood that she wanted this too, a time to go to bed and be together could be negotiated (Bogdashina 2005).

What might it mean when an expectation is not fulfilled?

When typical individuals have an understanding of 'Other', it might mean that they can cope with change. They can work out an alternative action or solution to a problem. They will be able to predict what an individual might do, think or choose, if not always accurately. This is a coping strategy that compensates for changes occurring that are outside of one's control. This skill, however, is quite difficult for us who are operating from processes informed by SAACA.

We may need strategies that work best with an interest system informed by single attention, such as the kind of structure a colour-coded timetable might provide. Being encouraged to ask questions (via own language or by pictures or technology) can help direct that individual to an understanding. Using a software program such as PowerPoint or other visual means to explain scenarios for nonverbal individuals should be mandatory in our educational system. Giving access to technology that can enable an AS individual to present their point of view also gives them 'speech' and power that is so often taken away because the individual is not 'enabled' typically.

Preparing for anticipated or expected change will mean that one has time to devote to the necessary issues. However, it is important to remember that although time is a positive factor, too much time or advance warning for some of us may create unnecessary anxiety. It is important to get to know the individual concerned. Sometimes only a day's notice is necessary, sometimes a week or just a few seconds. How much notice of change an individual needs will depend upon their personality, emotional, social and physical needs and their own adjustment factors towards change in their environment.

When an individual is nonverbal, visual supports are very important. Showing photographs of intended change, sequencing events, showing the unfolding stages and so on are vital to gaining an appreciation of what is to come. Even those of us with good language skills may benefit from photos or visual attempts to show expected change. For the older individual, cartoons or comic strip stories can be useful tools to demonstrate anticipated changes. Using virtual reality tools via a computer often engages an individual, capturing attention and interest (e.g. Herrera *et al.* 2008), and all of the above can be implemented into fun activities in this way (Kluth and Chandler-Olcott 2008).

For unexpected change, when there is no time for preparation, thinking ahead can be useful. For example, just as one might carry sweets or a puzzle book in one's bag for a neurotypical child in case of emergencies, one can be equally prepared for unexpected change for us. For example, having a particular electronic game or something that is of interest to the individual concerned can be very useful for compensating or even creating a positive encounter for times when unexpected events occur.

Problem-solving ideas using SAACA

A young mum says to her counsellor, 'My ten-year-old autistic son is so jealous of his baby sister, I can't leave him alone with her. He tries to hurt her at every opportunity and I'm not coping with his behaviour.' With her words in mind it would be easy to conclude that her son is jealous of his baby sister. This might be the case in typical development and, if so, needs to be handled typically.

But, in AS there could be different reasons for his behaviour. Maybe he enjoys the spectacle of the baby's contorted expression as she cries? Maybe he enjoys the response he receives from his parents when he hurts the baby? Maybe he doesn't understand the interaction from the baby's perspective? Has he any concepts to build an understanding that his hurting the baby is uncomfortable for her, is undesirable and is not appropriate? If any of the above are possibilities, then by giving the boy attention (as one might in the case of jealousy) one might actually be increasing the boy's potential to do harm to the baby. Rather than relieving the cause of the boy's behaviour, one might be reinforcing it.

Using SAACA, it might be more useful to teach this boy how to be appropriate by using his interest through the use of a digital camera to take a picture of the child as he was about to poke the baby. This could be used as a tool to show the potential problems poking the baby might cause. When you have your picture it needs to be given a Velcro backing. You can make a board to put the picture on and you can have red markers to use to put a big red cross over the picture. This indicates 'No, hurting the baby.' Your next photo can be of the child with his arm gently around the baby. With your red marker you can place a red tick over the picture. This says 'Yes, loving the baby.' When the boy chooses to be nice to the baby he should be rewarded. The reward should motivate him and give him more pleasure than the show from a tormented baby and her parents. This means knowing and using only things that are of interest to him. A reward that does not interest him is not a reward.

The above, and the case studies and examples discussed earlier in this chapter, demonstrate that learning can occur for us but it needs to be facilitated differently from that for typical individuals. In 2010 Asperger's syndrome and classic autism are judged to be more alike than they are different (Attwood 2007). The difficulties are essentially of the same nature, whichever diagnosis an AS individual receives. Each and every individual, wherever they are on the continuum, will need support and encouragement. This means viewing their behaviour through a non-typical lens, such as SAACA.

TOM'S STORY – AN EXTENDED CASE STUDY

Tom is a 15-year-old who was diagnosed as being AS when he was nine years old. Tom is third generation Australian, and there is a history of learning difficulties in both his paternal and maternal families. After repeated concerns over Tom's behaviour (he seemed anti-social and was finding it hard at school), Tom's parents consulted with a multi-disciplinary team at a major hospital near their home in Australia.

Tom has an IQ within the normal range and attends the local secondary college. Due to the fact that Tom is not intellectually disabled and he is not considered either a danger to himself or to others, he does not fulfil criteria for an aide at school. However, Tom is part of an integration programme that has been developed for him, and his teachers are aware of his disability.

Tom has a sister who is two years younger than him, and Tom's mother reports that the two children get along relatively well. Tom's mother (Sharon) and father (John) both have a career. Sharon is a local primary school teacher and John is a bank manager. John is able to take Tom to school in the morning on his way to work and Sharon brings Tom home. Sharon is more available to Tom because her working hours allow her to spend more time at home. However, John supports both of the children in their recreational activities (e.g. his daughter Sue loves netball and horse riding, while Tom enjoys computer games, chess, basketball and walking).

Tom is usually a very happy and amiable young man but dislikes change. Therefore, in order to avoid the fear and confusion of change Tom has developed certain routines, rituals and coping strategies. For Tom, it appears that maintaining routine and structure are consistent needs that dictate his sense of wellbeing and motivation. Therefore, if his routines and structure are interrupted or interfered with Tom can respond with outbursts of aggression.

Some of Tom's routines and rituals generally do not interfere with daily functioning. For example, Tom always wakes up at seven in the morning and goes to bed at ten in the evening. He eats only toast for breakfast and insists on three sugars in his tea. However, other compulsive desires can cause problems with social interaction. For example, Tom obsessively smells everything, even when it happens to be the perfume on a stranger in the supermarket. SAACA would argue that Tom has some sensory issues (smelling strong attractive odours takes over Tom's attention and disables attention allowing for propriety).

Tom would like to have a friend with whom to share his interest in chess. Unfortunately, Tom does not make friends easily and when he does they usually do not remain friendly for long. This seems to happen because Tom does not appreciate the social cues of normal interaction. Therefore, Tom appears self-centred and egocentric. According to Sharon, Tom's associates view him as being odd and poor company. According to SAACA Tom can relate from his interest (e.g. chess) but would find it difficult to shift attention fast enough (if at all) to follow the social expectations associated with building friendships.

Frith (1991) suggests that AS individuals do not appear to be 'socially tuned', that is they lack the theory of mind that enables them to comprehend how another person is feeling. Frith also states that some AS persons have 'all the trappings of socially adapted behaviour' (p.23), but this is learnt behaviour that only resembles normal functioning and is born from 'abnormal functioning processes'.

Through SAACA it is argued this is not abnormal but different and can be accommodated once understood. Seeing 'pathology' rather than brain configuration might not be helpful. Too often this is the case and we are inappropriately medicated (Bogdashina 2006; Lathe 2006; Lawson 2008).

Another challenge that faces Tom is his literal translation of language. 'Literal use of language is an important feature of autistic communication' (Happé 1991). It would appear that just as Tom perceives his need for structure and routine, literality correlates with Tom's stage of cognitive development. According to Tonge, Dissanayake and Brereton (1994) such communication difficulties and aberrant cognitive skills are central to the autistic condition. However, there is much debate as to why this is so. ToM, EF and WCC theory each offer an explanation, but they all fail to consider attention and interest. The SAACA lens suggests that being literal is a monotropic product. As such it needs to inform all educational tools and processes to which Tom is exposed.

As stated in Chapter 2, AS, as described by Kanner (1943) and as further outlined in the DSM-IV, is diagnosed in children as young as two years of age. However, although Tom has had challenging behaviour and stereotyped interests as far back as his mother can remember (e.g. he only lined up his toy cars, never played typically with them), he did not receive a diagnosis of classic autism. Tom was diagnosed with Asperger's syndrome at the age of nine. This was probably because Tom does not have an intellectual disability and he developed typically in areas of cognition and physical growth. That is, he walked, talked and progressed through childhood developmental milestones like any other child. In fact, at kindergarten Tom seemed particularly bright and capable.

The fact that Tom did not play with his peers but preferred to line up his toy motor cars and place them in order, according to their colour, was seen by his teachers as being simply idiosyncratic to Tom. Also, because he has good verbal skills, this masked other problems that he had with interpretation. His primary school teacher reported that Tom seemed selective in his hearing. He only responded to instruction when he wanted to. Through SAACA, however, it is argued that he could only attend to one thing at any one time so his responses were not out of choice but out of what captured his available attention and subsequent interest system.

Also, according to Tantam, Holmes and Cordess (1993) it is more likely that Tom did not respond because he did not understand what was being asked of him. It could be argued that this might be partly due to poor eye contact and, therefore, poor interpretation of expectations. However, it would be difficult for Tom to look and listen at the same time. Seeing this through the SAACA lens it would be argued Tom could only do one or the other. He needs to learn via structure and visual support using his interest to capture his attention. He does not learn typically, any more than a left-handed person can learn to write easily with their right hand.

According to Bartak (1994), due to good verbal skills individuals with Asperger's autism may not be diagnosed early because they have unimpaired speech. In fact their language skills most likely mask the true picture of their problems.

Tom's condition means that he has both strengths and difficulties. His strengths are:

- *Behavioural*: Tom is consistent and loyal. His single-mindedness is endearing and it is easy to relate to him on matters of mutual interest. When Tom is interested in a topic he stays focused, which can be a useful aid in his learning process.

- *Communicative*: Communicating with Tom is often best when it centers around a topic of his interest. This can be thought of as a strength if we consider that he cannot 'hear' you when you try to talk to him outside of his interest. It's as if interest is the trigger that heightens Tom's senses and he can attend to what is being said. Tom is fascinated by cars. So, for example, saying 'the red car wants to go slow just now, how does Tom feel about this? Is Tom feeling rushed?' If cars are in the conversation Tom's ability to identify what is happening for him will be more accessible.

- *Social/emotional*: Tom is very clear about what he likes and what he does not like. It is very difficult for Tom to lie or be dishonest because he is very literal in his life concepts. When Tom is feeling good about life he is cooperative and wants social contact, but when he is confused, afraid or unwell he can be difficult to please, aggressive and withdrawn. This means that usually it is easy to tell Tom's emotional status.

- *Cognitive/academic*: Tom appears to operate at the concrete operational level. Knowing this enables Tom's workers to explore learning strategies for him that consider his concrete thinking. For example, Tom needs to explore a situation physically to understand how it is made or what it can do. Tom's 'black-and-white' thinking means that many things are easy for him to accept. For example, basic rules of hygiene; TV watching times; the rules of a chess game; eating three meals a day.

Tom's difficulties are:

- *Behavioural*: Because it is easy for Tom to stay focused on matters of interest, it is very difficult to encourage him to do something that he is not interested in. Also, because Tom hates change, any alteration in his routine or interruption of a ritual can mean fear and confusion for him. This could lead to aggressive outbursts or uncooperative behaviour. However, using Tom's interests means he is more likely to be cooperative.

- *Communicative*: Tom loves to talk about his interests but he is not able to understand the interests of others. This means that reciprocal communication is difficult and could lead to Tom having difficulty with relationships.

- *Social/emotional*: Socially Tom seems unaware of the needs and wants of others. This makes social interaction very difficult.

Possibly Tom's lack of eye contact is related to this deficit. Tom can completely miss the cues that another person is giving him. SAACA argues again this is due to monotropism and its product. Helping Tom 'see' the emotions of others through games related to his interest and pictures and so on, would be very useful and could lead to Tom feeling confident and valued.

monologue...
is my dialogue

Why does Tom have his difficulties?

According to Wainwright-Sharp and Bryson (1993), visual orientating deficits in high-functioning AS people may be due to a spatial neglect-like phenomenon. This implies we fail to note or select the piece of visual information needed to make sense of social stimuli (e.g. facial expression). However, Powell and Jordan (1992) suggest that high-functioning AS individuals lack a self-concept and therefore, cannot judge the minds of others. The latter would therefore suggest that some individuals could be taught a self-concept and could also learn to better judge the intentions of others. SAACA explains Tom's strengths and weaknesses differently, suggesting a different brain configuration meaning Tom is using different parts of his brain to problem-solve, and this needs considering in all of Tom's educational and relational interaction.

Can we help Tom cope with change?

Change for us can be very difficult and problematic for all concerned. In their research Cesaroni and Garber (1991) note that change for AS individuals appears to be very traumatic, unless the individuals concerned are adequately prepared for it in advance. Unfortunately, though, life can be quite unpredictable and advance warning or preparation for change may not always be possible. Therefore, equipping Tom with a coping strategy for change is a better option long term.

When and how do we execute an intervention for Tom?

Howlin (1997, 2000, 2003) found that appropriate intervention skills, learnt during adolescence, continued on into adult life. When talking about behaviour modification Wing (1992) suggests that a step-by-step approach is more likely to be successful. This approach, termed 'shaping', is used when the behaviour is not in the student's behavioural repertoire. Foxx (1982) suggests that target behaviour needs to be heavily reinforced. This means it should be combined with a discriminative stimulus, physical guidance, usually using an imitative prompt and then fading that prompt away. However, first a baseline measurement of the target behaviour needs to be established. I suggest that this occur over a two-week period. Any unusual stimuli should be recorded (e.g. ill health, extra pressure or stress not usual in the individual's daily living).

Wing and Attwood (1987) suggest that the active-but-odd autistic individual (like Tom) is more likely than the aloof autistic individual to want to seek out friendships. This, therefore, is a genuine motivator for wanting to learn social skills and strategies that help create an understanding of 'Self' and 'Other'.

According to Powell and Jordan (1992), there is some evidence that we acquire an understanding through the process of working it out (which implies understanding from observation); however, this can be tedious and exhausting if we are expected to multi-task outside our area of interest.

What about generalising Tom's learning?

We do not generalise our learning in the same way as NT individuals do (e.g. Harchik *et al.* 1990). For example, we may learn to sit down at the table to eat at school, but not automatically do the same at home. However, Tom could learn to generalise his learning. For example, he could be taught that it is common practice to sit down to eat, whether he is at home, at school, at a friend's house or in a café or restaurant, via story and pictures using his interest.

Reasoning behind using IT, visuals and structure

It is not helpful to use plastic zoo animals to prepare AS children for a visit to the zoo. For example, how big are the plastic animals? Do they compare with real life-size animals at the zoo? If one understands SAACA, the problems with doing this are easier to appreciate. Rather, issues of what to expect can be addressed by using photos or video clips that give a truer sense of context and so on.

Tom needs to encounter his environment in habitual or routine ways that make sense to him. He may form rules about the way life should be; for example, the traffic should move when the light is green, even if a road accident is causing traffic delay in being able to go through the traffic lights. SAACA suggests understanding Tom's learning style would help others to realise Tom is being literal and needs further explanation in a way he can relate to.

According to Butera and Haywood (1992) cognitive strategies (e.g. direct teaching concerned with theory via verbal communication i.e., being encouraged to actively do or become involved with) are more likely to produce generalisable learning, than simply reading information from the text. This method teaches us higher-functioning AS individuals to think for ourselves and gives us a sense of control. For Tom this may mean that he needs to explore the traffic situation and understand why the traffic is not moving (of course this must be done in a safe way, possibly via re-enactment via a computer game such as 'The Sims'). Just telling Tom that the car cannot move yet would seem like a direct contradiction to traffic light rules unless an explanation is demonstrated (e.g. Herrera *et al.* (2008) found the participants in their study learnt certain concepts more easily once they were enacted via computer games).

Harchik *et al.* (1992) suggest that maintenance and generalisation tend to occur on cue and independently when the learning has taken place in a structured environment. They also suggest that some behaviours will be maintained by naturally existing environmental contingencies. For Tom this will mean that he needs to practise his learning often and make direct connections to outcomes and consequences. As predicted by SAACA, we have difficulties with foreseeing outcomes as part of either our experiences or our intuition.

NEUROTYPICAL PARENTING

The idea of drawing upon past experiences, knowledge and understanding is part and parcel of most developing typical individuals' life experiences. Parents, therefore, can use their experiences to educate and assist their typical children towards their becoming competent individuals, because they can draw upon their own experiences. If, however a child who is monotropic is not privy to the bigger picture, does not draw upon their experience and does not naturally and intuitively generalise their learning, then any parental intervention based upon neurotypical experience might not actually correlate to that child's understanding and might deepen their confusion, rather than alleviate it. This will mean that the usual parental learning support that parents utilise with their offspring is not as available to them as it might be to the parenting of typical children.

In AS, however, highly focused interest takes precedence over presentation of self. The image we present to the word often is not our first priority, unless it's out special interest. Generally we are not governed by 'presentation of self' but, governed by being honest. This will cause conflict in families where fashion, achievement and keeping up with The Jones's is seen as the norm. This is compared to the use of monotropic attention in Figure 8.1, which presents the result of single attention only allowing for a narrow focus. This may cause conflict between the individual who is monotropic and the parent who is polytropic. An AS individual might only be interested in their interest and not able, naturally, to accommodate the interests of 'Other', which a parent might interpret via their polytropic lens as rejection.

For the non-AS parents of an AS individual, polytropism (divided attention able to accommodate diffuse interests) might present as an impediment or barrier to understanding their monotropic child. A child who is so different and does not accommodate interest in the same way as the parent (i.e. highly focused and not having diffuse interests) will not be informed by any neurologically typical need to conform to social expectation. Having a child who is not governed by the same motivational design will present as a difficulty to parent/child interaction.

Parents might be embarrassed by their children, will consider their child's behaviour to be rude and insensitive and will feel unappreciated by their offspring. This feeling will be based upon the parents' own understanding of human behaviour and will fail to accommodate SAACA or the autistic disposition. When understanding does occur and parents and society at large comprehend the importance and influence of SAACA for the AS individual, it can radically change the parents' perception of their child and can potentially release them from neurologically typical expectation.

Polytropism is stressful in itself. For example, the need to accommodate the interests of others, whilst taking care of 'Self', and being aware of the wider world of divided attention, will cause stress for parents of AS individuals. In contrast AS individuals are inclined towards presentation of single interest that does not accommodate 'Other' and, therefore, have little or no spare attention for concepts not within their interest system.

For AS individuals, this leads to difficulties appreciating the concepts that rule the world of NT individuals. This non-understanding between parent and child increases parental distress. We often live in sensory overloading and cognitively overwhelming daily experiences that cause us discomfort and confusion. Therefore, the more parents struggle to assist their AS individual in typical ways the more demand the individual may perceive and the higher the distress levels become for all concerned.

SUMMARY

SAACA builds upon the concept that autism depends upon an atypical attentional style known as monotropism. Monotropism is the term used to describe single attention where the attentional tunnel can be compared to an intense narrow beam of light. Polytropism, or the ability to use divided attention (associated with typical development), can be depicted as a wide beam of light, less intense but enabling the viewer to see more of the picture than the narrow beam.

If AS individuals are only able to utilise monotropic attention then the information available to them for processing everyday concepts will be limited. This suggests that we, rather than 'lacking a theory of mind', have reduced access to connecting to 'Self' and 'Other' due to our differing learning style. However, when we are viewed through the SAACA lens, our behaviour is understandable and the appropriate environmental and educational resources can be implemented. This would enable the facility of attention for the AS individual to encompass their interest and potential development of understanding of 'Self' and 'Other' could ensue.

CHAPTER 10

Looking to the Future

INTRODUCTION

This chapter briefly summarises the ideas expressed throughout this book. It mentions current cognitive theory in AS, echoing aspects of the debate in this area, and outlining the limitations of SAACA. It also restates some of the research concerning brain configuration and AS experiences, along with further ideas for the future. The concluding few paragraphs of this chapter will draw attention to the areas that SAACA seems unable to answer and will offer some suggestions as to why this is so.

There are still many questions as to why certain behaviours occur in AS. For example, are they to do with the usual discrepancies seen in families (e.g. relational and occupational issues; personality clashes; education; culture of expectation; genetics)? There is a need for further research into these areas. Much of this is happening, and some researchers suggest answers to such questions are not far away.

A DIFFERENT LEARNING STYLE

Professionals working with parents of AS individuals require work practices that are evidence-based. SAACA is a newly developed cognitive theory that not only explains AS but also enables a new understanding of AS individuals. SAACA explains autism as a different learning style, and this is currently supported by the recent understandings of brain configuration differences and by anecdotal evidence provided by the AS population.

Researchers Gernsbacher and Frymiare (2005) and Björne (2007) have raised multiple questions about the idea that the brain can only be modular and that genetics act alone to inform the learning styles of individuals. Instead, they suggest individuals, neurotypical or otherwise, are living and learning through a variety of interactions with their environments. Björne suggests learning should be thought of like this:

> Cognitive processes never reside exclusively in one circumscribed part of the brain, but rather depend on the synchronized functioning of interconnected areas, and we should be looking for modules neither in the infant nor the adult brain…development depends on a complex interaction of multiple factors in the interaction between the organism and its environment. (p.24)

Björne (2007) also points out that:

> In developmental theory, some key concepts are those of equifinality, multifinality and nonlinearity. Equifinality means that organisms with different initial states can reach the same endpoint, or that similar initial conditions can take different routes or pathways to a common endpoint (Gottlieb 1991, 1998; Lickliter 2000; Wagman and Miller 2003). That is, different structural and causal patterns can underlie common overt patterns of behaviours, cognition, and emotion. (p.26)

As a way of combating the issue of change, many of us form stringent routines and rules. For example, we aim to organise our lives to follow the same structure every day. Therefore, our everyday lives need to consider a healthy balance of structure and strategy. Williams (1994) uses the analogy of a department store where, for the individual with AS, only one department is open at a time. Murray (1996) uses this example to explain that neurotypical individuals can have several interests (i.e. departments) open all at once and still function; and that it is this spreading of attention that allows the typical individual to cope with a complex world and be ready for change.

Unfortunately, within most of our education systems, AS is often misunderstood (thought of as challenging behaviour; laziness; stubbornness and so on). This may present difficulties at schools that only see students through the eyes of typical development and don't look beyond it. Currently most school systems are designed for those individuals who can be multi-channelled and enabled to multi-task even outside areas of their own interest systems.

Most neurotypical youngsters enjoy learning a variety of things as well as socialising with their peers. However, when we are faced with the school curriculum, having to learn to read, write and socially interact with peers, we may quickly become overloaded and unable to cope. This inability to cope might show itself via our behaviour, which may become agitated, aggressive, frustrated, scared and manipulative. However, when one understands why an AS individual is demonstrating inappropriate behaviour and involves that student in exploring this themselves, the student and school can only benefit (Bitsika 2005).

Therefore, by seeing and translating behaviour through the SAACA lens, differing educational, familial and social practices can help make learning accessible to AS individuals. Also, as echoed previously, technology, visual structure, the development of social skills and mutual understanding can aid in supporting such learning. Using strengths and skills related to an AS individual's interest can become the engine that drives mutual understanding.

Completing tasks

There are a number of steps that all individuals need to take in order to complete a task, for example, writing an essay. Most neurotypical individuals hardly notice these steps and, unless the task is very complex, would rarely need to break tasks down in a particular order to complete them. However, as one AS individual (Sullivan 2002) has reported, for her to be able to organise and complete a task, interest is not enough. Sullivan states individuals must also have the motor skills and various sensory connections necessary to complete any given task. For example, individuals need to:

- notice they can make a choice

- notice what options are possible in their situation

- determine how they feel about the various options

- bring 'online' any skills that will be needed to carry out those steps (e.g. if their choice requires standing up, they'll need to bring 'online' whatever motor skills are involved in standing up;

if their choice involves writing an essay, they'll have to bring 'online' all the pieces of knowledge and manners of thought involved in essay-writing)

- begin (i.e. actually start moving, in response to thought, if applicable).

Sullivan (2002) describes what can happen if any of these steps are missed:

> Since we may be configured differently to a neuro-typical person and since if any of the…steps fail to eventuate in a given situation, the person will be inertial in that situation, it is perhaps not surprising that AS individuals tend to become overcome by inertia. Also, since removing various skills from that list will only result in a disconnection between intention and action, this will have rather different internal dynamics. It is perhaps not surprising that the details of how the person is inert, and of what changes make sense to address that, vary widely from person to person. (online blog)

Interest is not enough, nor is it a matter of attention, suggests Sullivan (2002), who finds herself in periods of inertia that seem to have little connection to executive functioning. AS and other conditions can co-occur (Curran 2008), which means disorders such as depression and other mental disabilities can concurrently impact upon an individual. The issues, therefore, might not be related to AS but will add complications to addressing the overall needs of the AS individual.

Normality

Normality means different things to different people. Being black is normal for black swans. However, being white is normal for white swans. All individuals are different, but each comes from the same species.

The medical model for AS views autism as a dysfunction; SAACA puts forward an alternative view that AS is a different learning style associated with neuro-diversity and brain configuration with its interaction between senses and environmental experience. Yes, genetics has a role to play in this scenario and this is a good thing.

Vismara and Lyons (2007) demonstrated that AS individuals (young children in their work) increased joint attention when motivation was furthered by using the child's interest. This deepens the conviction that attention, interest and the points for information contact (senses) are interconnected and assist an AS individual with their learning. All of these ideas support SAACA and add questions about current cognitive theories that discuss dysfunction, disorder and mental conditions that need remediation rather than appropriate educational access.

The cognitive learning style in AS called SAACA is not only at the heart of being autistic but is also at the heart of how AS individuals learn. This being so it makes sense to use the individual's learning style and associated interest system in all educational settings and as inducements to support in employment and relational settings too.

Potentially, understanding the AS population from the viewpoint of SAACA would result in a different outcome for all AS people. Thirty years ago many families would have been advised by doctors to put their beloved AS children into an institution and forget them.

Today, with a different understanding of autism as explained by SAACA, our families could be encouraged to use our interest to motivate our attention and enable connections to be built. It will only be as professionals do this that young AS individuals will have a positive and fulfilling future.

I hope this book will help make AS all the more reasonable, make the understanding of what and why someone does something obvious to others, and ultimately change the way AS individuals are treated and give them back the power that has been taken away from them in the past. In 2010 there are computers and other IT equipment to assist individuals with learning.

This type of technology suits a SAACA learning style because it allows for single focus without the interruption of facial expression or body language, overwhelming stimuli such as perfumes and so on. IT appeals to so many of us because it is stimuli reduced (currently comes without perfume), structured, uncluttered, usually predictable and autism friendly.

So, what is normal? (taken from Lawson 2008)

The definition of normal has many sides and aspects to it that range from behaviour (e.g. moral and sexual behaviours) to institutions, such as marriage and social convention. Normal refers to 'a lack of significant

deviation from the average' and the phrase 'not normal' is often applied in a negative sense (asserting that someone or some situation is improper or sick).

The word comes from the Latin *normalis* (f) and implies that the most common behaviour in a society is considered normal. Of course, there are many sub-groups in any given society where 'the group' sets out the rules for what is usual, typical or normal for that group. If one is a collector of coins, stamps, fine china, vintage cars or superhero magazines, one could argue that this is normal for the individual collector or the special interest group to which they belong, whilst it might not be normal for another individual who does not have that interest or occupation. So, in every respect the idea of normal must always be implicitly relative to a point of view or interest.

The other way of looking at normal is to think of what is most commonly occurring in any mainstream situation. This means that the ordinary or usual practice for the majority could be considered 'normal'. There are difficulties with this definition as history has shown there have been times when whole societies were involved in destructive and abominable practices that were considered normal, by many, at the time. However, with the current figures of incidence with AS individuals increasing it only makes sense to explore how best to support and work with this population rather than isolate and further deepen the problems that exist already (such as those mentioned earlier).

The debate concerning autism, disability, neuro-diversity and typicality poses some ongoing challenges. Disability presents itself in a variety of ways and for many living with disability, 'who' they are is normal for them. With regard to AS, which is certainly very disabling in a world that does not accept, value or accommodate difference, being handicapped is an everyday reality for many.

I argue that the right to exist as oneself, with or without disability, should be part of the norm. I do not argue for the right to exist in order to upset, displace, disrespect or disenfranchise another. Having a respectful understanding of one another should include accessibility to appropriate resources, support, safe places and sincere appreciation of difference in learning styles. Anything less is not acceptable.

It's in everyone's interest

SAACA suggests that understanding individuals' cognitive styles takes AS out of the deficit model of disability and into the realm of human difference and variation. Although for many AS will still be disabling, individuals can ultimately take back control over a wider societal understanding of 'normal', enabling them to create a more inclusive schema or way of thinking. Society as a whole can be thought of as consisting of a vast system of overlapping communities of interest each made up of individuals with their own sets of interests. Every interest is what it is as a result of a learning history during which relevant facts have informed it. Thus schemata can be thought of as the forms of interests. With this understanding in mind it is easier to comprehend how humans interact with one another and why we are so controlled by what we think others are thinking of or wanting from us.

With the idea of 'people first' it has become common to think of individuals with autism rather than of autistic individuals. Many individuals feel that their autism is not some added on appendage but is who they are (Muggleton 2008). Within the idea of SAACA it is argued autism is not a deficit but a different way of learning. Through the SAACA lens, when it is understood that AS individuals learn differently, typical thinking and all that follows regarding the challenges AS individuals face on a daily basis must change.

EXPERIMENTS TO REFUTE
OR SUPPORT SAACA

Experiments using interest and attention in a sensory-friendly environment for AS individuals would assist in exploring if SAACA is a 'stand alone' theory that explains AS. In this book statements and explanations have been made via case studies and by reinterpreting the AS literature, but scientific statistical analysis has not been conducted to put this theory to the test. However, experiments considering the SAACA lens and that of neurotypical development need to be undertaken.

To falsify SAACA experiments with other clinical populations to examine the level of monotropism, attention and interest should be conducted to determine whether other populations exhibit SAACA characteristics, or if this is only seen in autism. Further experiments might also look at the extent of SAACA in high-functioning individuals who appear to shift attention, or multi-task. It is argued from the SAACA lens that AS individuals only shift attention within their scope of interest. This researcher very much hopes that others will take up this challenge and explore ways to make this happen.

There are many naturalistic settings that might provide suitable opportunities for scientific tests for SAACA; these include classrooms; clubs; sports activities and the like. These could consist of small groups of children, adolescents or adults, some NT individuals and other AS individuals. The project would need to look for areas of divided attention and shared interest outside of one's own particular interest. Experiments could include the ideas set out below:

- A researcher could note responses to individual name calling during times of intense attention. A chart could be drawn up and teachers (for example) could be asked to record responses from both NT and AS individuals. Records could be made of when, how often, in what situations and so on the individual responds to their name.

- Research could note the responses to, for example, the call of 'Fire' whilst AS and NT individuals are otherwise occupied. This again could be recorded on a chart noting responses. Such experiments could be conducted at college or university or sheltered placements.

- Projects could record responses to an individual offer of shared attention (e.g. pointing) by age 18 months through to two years, in both the AS and NT populations. Work could focus upon when individuals are motivated by interest and in situations of apparent non-interest, for that age group. This could explore ideas based around sharing attention for the social connection with another or only when one's own interest is triggered.

- Research could test for age-appropriate literal language (polytropic understanding versus monotropic understanding) of metaphor appreciation. If AS individuals find it difficult to decode metaphor and only show interest in doing so when it's 'in their interest' compared to wanting to please the examiner even if not interested, this might be significant.

- Research could explore social responsiveness to same, own or shared interest in small group situations. The differences could be measured and statistical relevance sought.

- Tests for ability to shift attention and interest in common activities when not interested could be conducted in both groups of individuals (e.g. examiners could look for and record quality and quantity of sharing eye gaze, reading body language, noting voice intonation and associated intention).

The research ideas expressed above are a few of the many ideas that could be taken up by future research.

When it comes to looking ahead and considering areas of further research into concepts surrounding learning styles, neuro-diversity and autism, I hope that the area of interconnection between interests, senses and attention will be given some priority. Further research into the brain's connections to the various systems of the human body and their relationship to attention and interest might show that human diversity is the common 'normal' for humans and that Western social priorities (Björne 2007; Bowler 2007; Lawson 2008) are more of a Western societal development rather than a universal human condition.

LIMITATIONS OF SAACA

Questions SAACA fails to answer concern the areas where SAACA is practised and the AS individual appears to be making their needs understood and those working with them appear to be meeting those needs, and yet despite this some individuals continue with obsessive or extremely challenging behaviours. Might this be due to other influences than the autistic condition? For example, physical illness, such as digestive tract disturbances, arthritis, infections and pain; or mental illness, such as depression, oppositional defiance disorder, obsessive compulsive disorder, various phobias and even psychotic dispositions. Might it be due to intellectual disability and/or learning difficulties? How might epilepsy or any other medical condition impact upon an individual's 'attentive' resource? What about established learnt behaviour, paranoia or personality? How might these contribute to an individual's belief systems? All of these conditions that plague so many families need exploring.

Much more research is needed in all of the areas concerned with AS and attention. I ask for other researchers to disprove SAACA and to show how it cannot be the cognitive theory that explains AS. If this cannot be done, or until it is, maybe this newly developed theory should be considered as appropriate and AS individuals seen through the SAACA lens.

List of Publications

BOOKS AND CHAPTERS IN BOOKS

Lawson, W. (2008) 'Understanding and Enjoying Successful Social Relationships.' In G. Edmonds and L. Beardon (eds) *Asperger Syndrome and Social Relationships: Adults Speak Out about Asperger Syndrome* (pp.97–112). London: Jessica Kingsley Publishers.

Lawson, W. (2008) *Concepts of Normality: The Autistic and Typical Spectrum.* London: Jessica Kingsley Publishers.

Lawson, W. (2006) *Friendships: The Aspie Way.* London: Jessica Kingsley Publishers.

Lawson, W. (2006) *ASPoetry: Illustrations from an Aspie Life.* London: Jessica Kingsley Publishers.

Lawson, W. (2005) 'Coming Out Various.' In D. Murray (ed) *Coming Out Asperger: Diagnosis, Disclosure and Self-confidence* (pp.200–213). London: Jessica Kingsley Publishers.

Lawson, W. (2004) *Sex, Sexuality and the Autism Spectrum.* London: Jessica Kingsley Publishers.

Lawson, W. (2003) *Build Your Own Life: A Self-help Guide for Individuals with Asperger's Syndrome.* London: Jessica Kingsley Publishers.

Lawson, W. (2003) 'Remembering School.' In M. Prior (ed) *Learning and Behavioural Problems in Asperger's Syndrome* (pp.177–205). New York: Guilford Press.

Lawson, W. (2001) *Understanding and Working with the Spectrum of Autism: An Insider's View.* London: Jessica Kingsley Publishers.

Lawson, W. (2000) *Life Behind Glass: A Personal Account of Autism Spectrum Disorder.* London: Jessica Kingsley Publishers.

Murray, D. and Lawson, W. (2007) 'Inclusion Through Technology for Autistic Children.' In R. Cigman (ed) *Included or Excluded: The Challenge of the Mainstream for Some SEN Children* (pp.151–157). London: Taylor & Francis.

JOURNAL ARTICLES

Lawson, W. (2008, Spring) 'ASPoetry.' *Popular Narrative Media 1*, 1, 87–102.

Lawson, W. (Spring 2002/Summer 2003) 'Growing potential.' *Journal of Mental Health*, Queensland, 30–35.

Lawson, W. (2002) 'Autism and attention.' *Good Autism Practice 3*, 2, 38–42.

Lawson, W. (2001/2002, December/January) 'Growing up with autism.' *Social Spectrum 2*, 4–5.

Murray, D., Lesser, M. and Lawson, W. (2005) 'Attention, monotropism, and the diagnostic criteria for autism.' *Autism: The International Journal of Research and Practice 9*, 2, 139–156.

References

American Psychiatric Association (1980) *Diagnostic and Statistical Manual of Mental Disorders* (3rd edn) Washington, DC: Author.

American Psychiatric Association (1987) *Diagnostic and Statistical Manual of Mental Disorders* (3rd Rev. edn). Washington, DC: Author.

American Psychiatric Association (1994) *Diagnostic and Statistical Manual of Mental Disorders* (4th edn). Washington, DC: Author.

American Psychiatric Association (2000) *Diagnostic and Statistical Manual of Mental Disorders* (4th Rev. edn). Washington, DC: Author.

Attwood, T. (1998) *Asperger's Syndrome: A Guide for Parents and Professionals.* London: Jessica Kingsley Publications.

Attwood, T. (1999) 'The pattern of abilities and development of girls with Asperger's syndrome.' Information sheet, Autism Queensland, Australia.

Attwood, T. (2000) 'Strategies for improving the social integration of children with Asperger syndrome.' *Autism 4*, 1, 85–100.

Attwood, T. (2007) *The Complete Guide to Asperger's Syndrome.* London: Jessica Kingsley Publishers.

Bacon, A., Fein, D., Morris, R., Waterhouse, L. and Allen, D. (1998) 'The responses of autistic children to the distress of others.' *Journal of Autism and Developmental Disorders 28*, 129–142.

Baddeley, A. and Wilson, B. (1988) 'Frontal amnesia and the dysexecutive syndrome.' *Brain and Cognition 7*, 212–230.

Baddeley, A.D. and Wilson, B.A. (eds) (1995) *Handbook of Memory Disorders.* New York, NY: Wiley.

Baggs, A. (2008) 'Ballastexistenz.' Retrieved 2 February 2009 from http://amanda. autistics.org

Bailey, A., Le Couteur, A., Gottesman, I., Bolton, P., Simonoff, E., Yuzda, E. *et al.* (1995) 'Autism as a strongly genetic disorder: Evidence from a British twin study.' *Psychological Medicine 25*, 63–77.

Bailey, J. (1998) 'Australia: Inclusion Through Categorisation.' In T. Booth and M. Ainscow (eds) *From Them to Us: An International Study of Inclusion in Education* (pp.171–183). New York, NY: Routledge.

Bailey, P.J. and Snowling, M.J. (2002) 'Auditory processing and the development of language and literacy.' *British Medical Bulletin 63*, 135–146.

Baird, J.A. (2008) 'Thinking outside the smarties box: A broader perspective on theory of mind commentary on Wellman and Miller.' *Human Development 51*, 2, 143–147.

Baron-Cohen, S. (1987) 'Autism and symbolic play.' *British Journal of Developmental Psychology 5*, 139–148.

Baron-Cohen, S. (1989) 'The autistic child's theory of mind: A case of specific developmental delay.' *Journal of Child Psychology and Psychiatry 30*, 2, 285–297.

Baron-Cohen, S. (1997) *Mindblindness: An Essay on Autism and Theory of Mind.* Cambridge, MA: MIT Press.

Baron-Cohen, S. (2000) 'Theory of Mind and Autism: A Fifteen Year Review.' In S. Baron-Cohen, H. Tager-Flusberg and D.J. Cohen (eds) *Understanding Other Minds: Perspectives from Autism* (pp.466–480). Oxford: Oxford University Press.

Baron-Cohen, S. (2001) 'Theory of mind in normal development and autism.' *Prisme, 34*, 174–183.

Baron-Cohen, S. (2002) 'The extreme male brain theory of autism.' *Trends in Cognitive Sciences 6*, 248–254.

Baron-Cohen, S. (2005) 'The Empathizing System: A Revision of the 1994 Model of the Mindreading System.' In B. Ellis and D. Bjorklund (eds) *Origins of the Social Mind* (pp.1–44). New York, NY: Guilford Press.

Baron-Cohen, S., Ashwin, E., Tavassoli, C. and Chakrabarti, B. (2009) 'Talent in autism: Hyper-systemizing, hyper-attention to detail and sensory hypersensitivity.' *Philosophical Transactions of the Royal Society of London, Series B, Biological Sciences 364*, 1377–1383.

Baron-Cohen, S., Bolton, P., Wheelwright, S., Scahill, V., Short, L., Mead, G. *et al.* (1998) 'Does autism occur more often in families of physicists, engineers, and mathematicians?' *Autism 2*, 3, 296–301.

Baron-Cohen, S., Cox, A., Baird, G., Swettenham, J., Nightingale, N., Morgan, K. *et al.* (1996) 'Psychological markers in the detection of autism in infancy in a large population.' *British Journal of Psychiatry 168*, 58–163.

Baron-Cohen, S., Golan, O., Chakrabarti, B. and Belmonte, M.K. (2008) 'Autism Spectrum Conditions.' In C. Sharp, P. Fonagy and I. Goodyer (eds) *Social Cognition and Developmental Psychopathology* (pp.29–56). Oxford: Oxford University Press.

Baron-Cohen, S., Joliffe, T., Mortimore, C. and Robertson, M. (1997) 'Another advanced test for theory of mind: Evidence from very high functioning adults with autism or Asperger's syndrome.' *Journal of Child Psychology and Psychiatry, 38*, 813–822.

Baron-Cohen, S., Leslie, A.M. and Frith, U. (1985) 'Does the autistic child have a theory of mind?' *Cognition 21*, 37–46.

Baron-Cohen, S., Leslie, A.M. and Frith, U. (1986) 'Mechanical, behavioural and intentional understanding of picture stories in autistic children.' *British Journal of Developmental Psychology 4*, 113–125.

Baron-Cohen, S., Richler, J., Bisarya, D., Gurunathan, N. and Wheelwright, S. (2003) 'The systemising quotient (SQ): An investigation of adults with Asperger syndrome or high functioning autism and normal sex differences.' *Philosophical Transactions of the Royal Society of London, Series B, Biological Sciences 358*, 361–374.

Baron-Cohen S., Ring, H., Bullmore, E., Wheelwright, S., Ashwin, C. and Williams, S. (2000) 'The amygdala theory of autism.' *Neuroscience Biobehaviour 24*, 355–364.

Baron-Cohen, S., Ring, H., Moriaty, J., Schmitz, B., Costa, D. and Ell, P. (1994) 'Recognition of mental state terms: Clinical findings in children with autism and a functional neuro-imaging study of normal adults.' *British Journal of Psychiatry 165*, 640–649.

Baron-Cohen, S., Wheelwright, S., Cox, A., Gillian, B., Charman, T., Swettenham, C. *et al.* (2000) 'Early identification of autism by the Checklist for Autism in Toddlers (CHAT).' *Journal of the Royal Society of Medicine 93*, 521–525.

Baron-Cohen, S., Wheelwright, S., Stott, C., Bolton, P. and Goodyer, I. (1997) 'Is there a link between engineering and autism?' *Autism: An International Journal of Research and Practice 1*, 153–163.

Bartak, L. (1994) 'Briefing notes on autism and Asperger's syndrome.' National Association for Autism. Melbourne University, Australia.

Behrmann, M., Thomas, C.P. and Humphreys, K. (2006) 'Seeing it differently: Visual processing in autism.' *Trends in Cognitive Science 10*, 258–264.

Belmonte, M., Cook, E., Anderson, G., Rubenstein, J., Greenough, W., Beckel-Mitchener, A. *et al.* (2004) 'Autism as a disorder of neural information processing: Directions for research and targets for therapy.' *Molecular Psychiatry 9*, 646–663.

Bertone, A., Mottron, L., Jelenic, P. and Faubert, J. (2005) 'Enhanced and diminished visuo-spatial information processing in autism depends on stimulus complexity.' *Brain 128*, 10, 2430–2441.

Bitsika, V. (2003) 'But I'm not really bad: Using an idiographic versus a nomothetic approach to understand the reasons for difficult behaviour in children.' *Australian Journal of Guidance and Counselling 13*, 1, 54–68.

Bitsika, V. (2005) 'Beyond nomothetic classification of behavioural difficulties: Using valued outcomes analysis to deal with behavioural problems that occur in the classroom.' *British Journal of Guidance and Counselling 33*, 2, 213–225.

Bitsika, V., Sharpley, C. and Orapeleng, S. (2008) 'An exploratory analysis of the use of cognitive, adaptive and behavioural indices for cluster analysis of ASD subgroups.' *Journal of Intellectual Disability Research 52*, 11, 973–985.

Björne, P. (2007) *A Possible World: Autism from Theory to Practice.* Lund University, Sweden.

Blackman, L. (2006) *Lucy's Story: Autism and Other Adventures.* London: Jessica Kingsley Publishers.

Blair, R.J. (1995) 'A cognitive developmental approach to morality: Investigating the psychopath.' *Cognition 57*, 1, 1–29.

Blair, R.J. (1996) 'Morality in the autistic child.' *Journal of Autism and Developmental Disorders 26*, 571–579.

Blair, R.J. (1999) 'Psychophysiological responsiveness to the distress of others in children with autism.' *Personality and Individual Difference 26*, 477–485.

Blair, R.J. (2005) 'Responding to the emotions of others: Dissociating forms of empathy through the study of typical and psychiatric populations.' *Conscious Cognition 14*, 698–718.

Blair, C., Zelazo, P.D. and Greenberg, M. (2005) 'The assessment of executive function in early childhood: Prospects and progress.' *Developmental Neuropsychology 28*, 561–571.

Blakemore, S.J. and Choudhury, S. (2006) 'Development of the adolescent brain: Implications for executive function and social cognition.' *Journal of Child Psychology and Psychiatry 47*, 3/4, 296–312.

Bloom, P. and German, T.P. (2000) 'Two reasons to abandon the false belief task as a test of theory of mind.' *Cognition 77*, 1, 25–31.

Bogdashina, O. (2005) *Communication Issues in Autism and Asperger Syndrome: Do We Speak the Same Language?* London: Jessica Kingsley Publishers.

Bogdashina, O. (2006) *Theory of Mind and the Triad of Perspectives on Autism and Asperger Syndrome: A View from the Bridge.* London: Jessica Kingsley Publishers.

Bonnel, A., Mottron, L., Peretz, I., Trudel, M., Gallun, E. and Bonnel, A.M. (2003) 'Enhanced pitch sensitivity in individuals with autism: A signal detection analysis.' *Journal of Cognitive Neuroscience 15*, 2, 226–235.

Bowler, D.M. (2001) 'Autism: Specific Cognitive Deficit or Emergent End-point of Multiple Interacting Systems?' In J.A. Burack, T. Charman, T.N. Yirmiya and P.R. Zelazo (eds) *The Development of Autism: Perspectives from Theory and Research* (pp.219–235). Mahwah, NJ: Lawrence Erlbaum.

Bowler, D.M. (2007) *Autism Spectrum Disorders: Psychological Theory and Research.* Chichester: Wiley.

Bowler, D.M., Briskman, J., Gurvidi, N. and Fornells-Ambrojo, M. (2005) 'Understanding the mind or predicting signal-dependent action? Performance of children with and without autism on analogues of the false-belief task.' *Journal of Cognition and Development 6*, 2, 259–283.

Bowler, D.M., Gaigg, S.B. and Gardiner, J.M. (2008) 'Effects of related and unrelated context on recall and recognition by adults with high-functioning autism spectrum disorder.' *Neuropsychologia 46*, 4, 993–999.

Bowler, D.M., Gardiner, J.M. and Gaigg, S.B. (2007) 'Factors affecting conscious awareness in the recollective experience of adults with Asperger's syndrome.' *Consciousness and Cognition.*

Brereton, A.V., Tonge, B.J. and Einfeld, S.E. (2006) 'Psychopathology in children and adolescents with autism compared to young people with intellectual disability.' *Journal of Autism and Developmental Disorders 36*, 7, 863–870.

Brosnan, M.J., Scott, F.J., Fox, S. and Pye, J. (2004) 'Gestalt processing in autism: Failure to process perceptual relationships and the implications for contextual understanding.' *Journal of Child Psychology and Psychiatry 45*, 3, 459–469.

Brown, T. (2006) 'Executive functions and attention deficit hyperactivity disorder: Implications of two conflicting views.' *International Journal of Disability, Development and Education 53*, 1, 35–46.

Bryson, S.E., Landry, R., Czapinski, P., McConnell, B., Rombough, V. and Wainwright, A. (2004) 'Autistic spectrum disorders: Causal mechanisms and recent findings on attention and emotion.' *International Journal of Special Education 19*, 1, 14–22.

Bull, R., Phillips, L.H. and Conway, C. (2008) 'The role of control functions in mentalizing: Dual task studies of theory of mind and executive function.' *Cognition 107*, 663–672.

Burack, J.A. (1994) 'Selective attention deficits in persons with autism: Preliminary evidence of an inefficient attentional lens.' *Journal of Abnormal Psychology 103*, 3, 535–543.

Burack, J.A., Enns, J.T., Stauder, J.E.A., Mottron, L. and Randolph, B. (1997) In D.J. Cohen and F.R. Volkmar (eds) *Handbook of Autism and Pervasive Developmental Disorder* (pp.226–247). New York, NY: Wiley.

Burgess, P.W. and Simons, J.S. (2005) 'Theories of Frontal Lobe Executive Function: Clinical Applications.' In P.W. Halligan and D.T. Wade (eds) *Effectiveness of Rehabilitation for Cognitive Deficits* (pp.211–231). Oxford: Oxford University Press.

Butera, G. and Haywood, H.C. (1992) 'A cognitive approach to the education of young children with autism.' *Focus on Autistic Behaviour 6*, 6, 1–14.

Caron, M.J., Mottron, L., Berthiaume, C. and Dawson, M. (2006) 'Cognitive mechanisms, specificity and neural underpinnings of visuospatial peaks in autism.' *Brain 129*, 7, 1789–1802.

Carpenter, C., Pennington, B. and Rogers, S. (2002) 'Interrelations among social-cognitive skills in young children with autism.' *Journal of Autism and Developmental Disorders 32*, 2, 91–106.

Carter, A.S., Black, D.O., Tewani, S., Connolly, C.E., Kadlec, M.B. and Tager-Flusberg, H. (2007) 'Sex differences in toddlers with autism spectrum disorders.' *Journal of Autism and Developmental Disorders 37*, 1, 86–97.

Casanova, M.F. (2005) 'Autistic brains out of synch?' *Science Neurology 308*, 1856–1858.

Casanova, M.F. (2008) 'The Significance of Minicolumnar Size Variability in Autism: A Perspective from Comparative Anatomy.' In A.W. Zimmerman (ed) *Autism: Current Theories and Evidence* (pp.349–360). Totowa, NJ: Humana Press.

Casanova, M.F., Buxhoeveden, D.P., Switala, A.E. and Roy, E. (2002) 'Minicolumnar pathology in autism.' *Neurology 58*, 3, 428–432.

Casanova, M.F., Switala, A.E., Trippe, J. and Fitzgerald, M. (2007) 'Comparative minicolumnar morphometry of three distinguished scientists.' *Autism 11*, 6, 557–569.

Cascio, C., McGlone, F., Folger, S., Tannan, V., Baranek, G. *et al.* (2008) 'Tactile perception in adults with autism: A multidimensional psychophysical study.' *Journal of Autism and Developmental Disorders 38*, 1, 27–137.

Castelli, F., Frith, C., Happé, F. and Frith, U. (2002) 'Autism and brain mechanisms for the attribution of mental states to animated shapes.' *Brain 125*, 1839–1849.

Cesaroni, L. and Garber, M. (1991) 'Exploring the experience of autism through firsthand accounts.' *Journal of Autism and Developmental Disorders 21*, 3, 303–313.

Chakrabarti, S. and Fombonne, E. (2005) 'Pervasive and developmental disorders in preschool children: Confirmation of high prevalence.' *Journal of Psychiatry 162*, 6, 1133–1141.

Chamak, B., Bonniau, B., Jaunay, E. and Cohen, D. (2008) 'What happens when we ask autistic persons what is wrong with them?' *Journal of Psychotherapy and Psychosomatics 77*, 5, 271–279.

Charman, T. and Swettenham, J. (2001) 'The Association Between the Repetitive Behaviours and Social-communicative Impairments in Children with Autism: Implications for Developmental Theory.' In J.A. Burack, T. Charman, N. Yirmiya and P.R. Zelazo (eds) *Development and Autism: Perspectives from Theory and Research* (pp.325–346). Mahwah, NJ: Lawrence Erlbaum.

Charman, T., Swettenham, J., Baron-Cohen, S., Cox, A., Baird, G. and Drew, A. (1997) 'Infants with autism: An investigation of empathy, pretend play, joint attention, and imitation.' *Developmental Psychology 33*, 5, 781–789.

Chawarka, K., Klin, A. and Volkmar, F. (2003) 'Automatic attention cueing through eye movement in 2-year-old children with autism.' *Child Development 74*, 1108–1123.

Chiavarino, C., Apperly, I.A. and Humphreys, G.W. (2008) 'The effect of action goal hierarchy on the coding of object orientation in imitation tasks: Evidence from patients with parietal lobe damage.' *Cognitive Neuropsychology 25*, 7, 1011–1026.

Cigman, R. (ed) (2007) *Included or Excluded? The Challenge of the Mainstream for Some SEN Children.* London: Routledge.

Clark, L. (2008) 'Introduction.' In W. Lawson (ed) *Concepts of Normality: The Autistic and Typical Spectrum* (pp.9–11). London: Jessica Kingsley Publishers.

Clift, S., Stagnitti, K. and DeMello, L. (1998) 'A validational study of the test of pretend play (ToPP) using correlational and classificational analyses.' *Child Language and Teaching Therapy 14*, 199–209.

Clift, S., Stagnitti, K. and DeMello, L. (2000) 'A developmentally appropriate test of kinder/school readiness.' *Australian Journal of Early Childhood 25*, 22–26.

Craig, J. and Baron-Cohen S. (1999) 'Creativity and imagination in autism and Asperger syndrome.' *Journal of Autism and Developmental Disorders 29*, 4, 319–326.

Curran, J. (2008) 'Diversity is the spice of life: Working to improve the emotional and mental health assessment of people with developmental disabilities and mental health problems.' ASSID Conference, 24–26 November 2008 (p.60) Melbourne, Australia.

Dahlgren, S.O., Sandberg, A.D. and Hjelmquist, E. (2003) 'The non-specificity of theory of mind deficits: Evidence from children with communicative disabilities.' *European Journal of Cognitive Psychology 15*, 1, 129–155.

Dahlgren, S.O. and Trillingsgaard, A. (1996) 'Theory of mind in non-retarded children with autism and Asperger's syndrome: A research note.' *Journal of Child Psychology and Psychiatry 37*, 759–763.

Dakin, S. and Frith, U. (2005) 'Vagaries of visual perception in autism.' *Neuron 48*, 497–507.

Dalton, K.M., Nacewicz, B.M., Johnstone, T., Schaefer, H.S., Gernsbacher, A., Goldsmith, H.H. *et al.* (2005) 'Gaze-fixation and the neural circuitry of face processing in autism.' *Nature Neuroscience 8*, 519–526.

Dawson, G., Toth, K., Abbott, R., Osterling, J., Munson, J., Estes, A. *et al.* (2004) 'Early social attention impairments in autism: Social orienting, joint attention, and attention to distress.' *Developmental Psychology 40*, 2, 271–283.

Dawson, M., Mottron, L. and Gernsbacher, M. (2008) 'Learning in Autism.' In J. H. Byrne (Series ed) and H. Roediger (Vol. ed) *Learning and Memory: A Comprehensive Reference: Cognitive Psychology* (pp.759–772). New York, NY: Elsevier.

Dawson, M., Mottron L., Jelenic, P. and Soulières, I. (2005, June) 'Superior performance of autistics on RPM and PPVT relative to Wechsler scales provides evidence for the nature of autistic intelligence.' Poster session presented at the International Meeting for Autism Research, Boston, MA.

Dawson, M., Soulières I., Gernsbacher, M. and Mottron, L. (2007) 'The level and nature of autistic intelligence.' *Psychological Science 18*, 8, 657–662.

Decety, J. and Lamm, C. (2007) 'The role of the right temporoparietal junction in social interaction: How low-level computational processes contribute to meta-cognition.' *The Neuroscientist 13*, 580–593.

Dern, S. (2008) 'Autistic intelligence.' Retrieved 14 October 2008, from http://www.autismusundcomputer.de/Dern_GG_2007.pdf

Dern, S. and Schuster, N. (2007) 'Unterschätzte Außenseiter.' *Gehirn und Geist 7–8*, 50–54. Retrieved 12 November, 2008, from http://www.gehirnundgeist.de/artikel/874917

Dewey, J. (1913) *Interest and Effort in Education*. Boston: Houghton Mifflin.

Dewey, J. (1938) *Experience and Education*. New York, NY: Macmillan.

Dewey, J. (1956) *The Child and the Curriculum and the School and Society*. Chicago, IL: Phoenix.

Diehl, S., Silliman, E., Chisholm, T., Bouchard, C. and Friedman, S. (2003) 'A new look at performance on theory of mind tasks by adolescents with autism spectrum disorder.' *Language, Speech, and Hearing Services in Schools*, 236–252.

Doherty, M. (2001) 'Selecting the wrong processor: A critique of Leslie's theory of mind mechanism–selection processor theory.' *Developmental Science 2*, 1, 81–85.

Donaldson, M. (1978) *Children's Minds*. New York, NY: Norton.

Donovan, S. and Bransford, J.D. (2005) *How Students Learn: History, Mathematics, and Science in the Classroom*. National Academies Press

Duncan, J. (1986) 'Disorganization of behavior after frontal lobe damage.' *Cognition and Neuropsychology 3*, 271–290.

Dworzynski, K., Ronald, A., Hayiou-Thomas, M.E., Rijskijk, F., Happé, F., Bolton, P. *et al.* (2007) 'Developmental path between language and autistic-like impairments: A twin study.' *International Journal of Language and Communication Disorders 42*, 3, 273–92.

Dworzynski, K., Ronald, A., Hayiou-Thomas, M.E., McEwan, F., Happé, F., Bolton, P. *et al.* (2008) 'Developmental path between language and autistic-like impairments: A twin study.' *Infant and Child Development 17*, 2, 95–202.

Dziobek, I., Fleck, S., Rogers, K., Wolf, O.T. and Convit, A. (2006) 'The "amygdala theory of autism" revisited: Linking structure to behavior.' *Neuropsychologia 44*, 10, 1891–1899.

Eisenmajer, R. and Prior, M. (1991) 'Cognitive linguistic correlates of "theory of mind" ability in autistic children.' *British Journal of Developmental Psychology 9*, 351–364.

Emerson, A., Grayson, A. and Griffiths, A. (2001) 'Can't or won't? Evidence relating to authorship in facilitated communication.' *International Journal of Language and Communication Disorders 3*, 6, 98–103.

Fireman, B., Koran, L.M., Leventhal, J.L. and Jacobson, A. (2001) 'The prevalence of clinically recognized obsessive-compulsive disorder in a large health maintenance organization.' *American Journal of Psychiatry 158*, 11, 1904–1910.

Flavell, J.H. (1988) 'The Development of Children's Knowledge about the Mind: From Cognitive Connections to Mental Representations.' In J. Astington, P. Harris and D.R. Olson (eds) *Developing Theories of Mind* (pp.244–270). Cambridge: Cambridge University Press.

Fletcher-Watson, S., Leekam, S.R., Turner, M.A. and Moxon, L. (2006) 'Do people with autistic spectrum disorder show normal selection for attention? Evidence from change blindness.' *British Journal of Psychology 97*, 4, 537–554.

Fletcher-Watson, S., Leekam, S.R., Findlay, J.M. and Stanton, E.C. (2008) 'Young adults with autism spectrum disorder show normal attention to eye-gaze information – evidence from a new change blindness paradigm.' *Journal of Autism and Developmental Disorders 38*, 9, 1785–1790.

Fodor, J. (1983) *The Modularity of Mind.* Cambridge, MA: MIT Press.

Foxx, R.M. (1982) *Decreasing Behaviours in Severely Retarded and Autistic Persons.* Champaign, IL: Research Press.

Francisco, D. (1991) 'Love is not a feeling, it's an act of your will.' Retrieved 13 November 2008 from www.rockymountainministies.org

Frith, U. (1989) *Autism: Explaining the Enigma.* Oxford: Blackwell.

Frith, U. (1991) *Autism and Asperger Syndrome.* Cambridge: Cambridge University Press.

Frith, U. (2004) 'Emanuel Miller Lecture: Confusions and controversies about Asperger syndrome.' *Journal of Child Psychology and Psychiatry 45*, 672–686.

Frith, U. and Frith, C.D. (2003) 'Development and neurophysiology of mentalising.' *Philosophical Transactions of the Royal Society of London, Series B, Biological Sciences 358*, 459– 473.

Frith, U., Morton, J. and Leslie, A. (1991) 'The cognitive basis of a biological disorder: Autism.' *Trends in Neuroscience 14*, 433–438.

Gallese, V. and Goldman, A. (1998) 'Mirror neurons and the simulation theory of mind reading.' *Trends in Cognitive Sciences 2*, 493–501.

Gardner, N. (2008) *A Friend Like Henry.* Sydney: Hachette.

Garner, I. and Hamilton, D. (1999) 'Susceptibility to illusion in ASD.' Paper given at the Autism Conference, Adelaide, South Australia.

Garner, I. and Hamilton, D. (2001) 'Evidence for Central Coherence: Children with Autism Do Experience Visual Illusions.' In J. Richer and S. Coates (eds) *Autism: The Search for Coherence* (pp.75–85). London: Jessica Kingsley Publishers.

Gazzola, V., Aziz-Zadeh, L. and Keysers, C. (2006) 'Empathy and the somatotopic auditory mirror system.' *Humans Current Biology 16*, 1824–1829.

Georgieva, S.S., Todd, J.T., Peeters, R. and Orban, G.A. (2008) 'The extraction of 3D shape from texture and shading in the human brain.' *Cerebral Cortex 18*, 10, 2416–2438.

Gerland, G. (1997) *A Real Person: Life on the Outside.* London: Souvenir Press.

Gernsbacher, M.A. and Frymiare, J.L. (2005) 'Does the autistic brain lack core modules?' *Journal of Developmental and Learning Disorders 9*, 3–16.

Gernsbacher, M.A., Stevenson, J.L., Khandakar, S. and Goldsmith, H.H. (2008) 'Why does joint attention look atypical in autism?' *Child Development Perspectives 2*, 38–45.

Gerrans, P. (2002) 'The theory of mind module in evolutionary psychology.' *Biology and Philosophy 17*, 305–321.

Gerrans, P. (2008) 'Rethinking modularity.' *Journal of Language and Communication 22*, 3, 259–268.

Gerrans, P. and Stone, V.E. (2008) 'Generous or parsimonious cognitive architecture? Cognitive neuroscience and theory of mind.' *British Journal for the Philosophy of Science 59*, 2, 121–141.

Geurts, H.M., Verté, S., Oosterlaan, J., Roeyers, H. and Sergeant, J.A. (2004) 'How specific are executive functioning deficits in attention deficit hyperactivity disorder and autism?' *Journal of Child Psychology and Psychiatry 45*, 836–854.

Gillberg, C. (2003) 'Deficits in attention, motor control, and perception: A brief review.' *Archives of Disease in Childhood 88*, 10, 904–910.

Gillberg, C. and Coleman, M. (2000) *The Biology of the Autistic Syndromes* (3rd edn). Cambridge: Cambridge University Press.

Goldstein, G., Johnson, C. and Minshew, N. (2001) 'Attentional processes in autism.' *Journal of Autism and Developmental Disorders 31*, 4, 433–446.

Goldstein, S. and Schwebach, A.J. (2004) 'The comorbidity of pervasive developmental disorder and attention deficit hyperactivity disorder: Results of a retrospective chart review.' *Journal of Autism and Developmental Disorders 34*, 3, 329–339.

Gomot, M., Belmonte, M.K., Bullmore, E.T., Bernard, F.A. and Baron-Cohen, S. (2008) 'Brain hyper-activity to auditory novel targets in children with high-functioning autism.' *Brain 131*, 9, 2479–2488.

Goodale, M.A. and Milner, A.D. (1992) 'Separate visual pathways for perception and action.' *Trends in Neuroscience 15*, 20–25.

Grandin, T. (1996) *Thinking in Pictures and Other Reports from My Life with Autism.* New York, NY: Vintage Books.

Grandin, T. (2000) 'My mind is a web browser: How people with autism think.' *Cerebrum 2*, 1, 14–22.

Grandin, T. (2009) 'Visual abilities and sensory differences in a person with autism.' *Biological Psychiatry 65*, 1, 15–16.

Grandin, T. and Deesing, M. (2003) 'Distress in animals: Is it fear, pain or physical stress?' Paper given at the American Board of Veterinary Practitioners Symposium, 17 May 2002, Manhattan Beach, California. Retrieved 5 April 2010 from www.grandin.com/welfare/fear.pain.stress.html

Grandin, T. and Scariano, M. (1986) *Emergence: Labelled Autistic.* Novato, CA: Arena Press.

Grant, A.D. and Berg, E.A. (1948) 'A simple objective test for measuring flexibility in thinking.' *Journal of General Psychology 39*, 15–22.

Grant, C.M., Boucher, J., Riggs, K.J. and Grayson, A. (2005) 'Moral understanding in children with autism.' *Autism 9*, 3, 317–331.

Green, S., Pring, L. and Swettenham, J. (2004) 'An investigation of first-order false belief understanding of children with congenital profound visual impairment.' *British Journal of Developmental Psychology 22*, 1, 1–17.

Greenaway, R. and Plaisted, K. (2005) 'Top-down attentional modulation in autistic spectrum disorders is stimulus-specific.' *Psychological Science 16*, 987–994.

Griffin, R., Friedman, O., Ween, J., Winner, E., Happé, F. and Brownell, H. (2006) 'Theory of mind and the right cerebral hemisphere: Refining the scope of impairment.' *Laterality: Asymmetries of Body, Brain and Cognition 8911*, 3, 195–225.

Griffith, E.M., Pennington, B.F., Wehner, E.A. and Rogers, S.J. (1999) 'Executive functions in children with autism.' *Journal of Child Development 70*, 4, 817–832.

Grossman, J.B., Klin, A., Carter, A.S. and Volkmar, F.R. (2000) 'Verbal bias in recognition of facial emotions in children with Asperger syndrome.' *Journal of Child Psychology and Psychiatry, and Allied Disciplines 41*, 3, 369–379.

Hadjikhani, N., Joseph, R.M., Snyder, J. and Tager-Flusberg, H. (2007) 'Abnormal activation of the social brain during face perception in autism.' *Human Brain Mapping 28*, 441–449.

Hale, C.M. and Tager-Flusberg, H. (2005) 'Social communication in children with autism: The relationship between theory of mind and discourse development.' *Autism 9*, 57–178.

Happé, F. (1991) 'The Autobiographical Writings of Three Asperger Syndrome Adults: Problems of Interpretation and Implications for Theory.' In U. Frith (ed) *Autism and Asperger Syndrome* (pp.207–242). Cambridge: Cambridge University Press.

Happé, F. (1994a) 'An advanced test of theory of mind: Understanding of story characters: Thoughts and feelings by able autistic, mentally handicapped and normal children and adults.' *Journal of Autism and Developmental Disorders 24*, 129–154.

Happé, F. (1994b) *Autism: An Introduction to Psychological Theory*. London: UCL Press.

Happé, F. (1995) 'The role of age and verbal ability in the theory of mind task performance of subjects with autism.' *Child Development 66*, 3, 843–855.

Happé, F. (1996) 'Studying weak central coherence at low levels: Children with autism do not succumb to visual illusions. A research note.' *Journal of Child Psychology and Psychiatry 37*, 873–877.

Happé, F. (1999a) 'Autism: Cognitive deficit or cognitive style?' *Trends in Cognitive Sciences 3*, 6, 216–222.

Happé, F. (1999b) 'Understanding assets and deficits in autism: Why success is more interesting than failure.' *The Psychologist 12*, 540–555.

Happé, F., Briskman, J. and Frith, U. (2001) 'Exploring the cognitive phenotype of autism: Weak "central coherence" in parents and siblings of children with autism: I. Experimental tests.' *Journal of Child Psychology and Psychiatry 42*, 299–307.

Happé, F. and Frith, U. (2006) 'The weak coherence account: Detail-focused cognitive style in autism spectrum disorders.' *Journal of Autism and Developmental Disorders 35*, 1, 5–25.

Happé, F. and Ronald, A. (2008) 'Fractionable autism triad: A review of evidence from behavioural, genetic, cognitive and neural research.' *Neuropsychology Review 18*, 287–304.

Happé, F., Ronald, A. and Plomin, R. (2006) 'Time to give up on a single explanation for autism.' *Natural Neuroscience 9*, 10, 1218–1220.

Harchik, A.E., Harchik, A.J., Luce, S.C. and Jordan, R. (1992) 'The special educational needs of children with Asperger syndrome.' Educational Research into Autism Group. Paper given at the Wakehurst Study Weekend on Asperger Syndrome, University of Hertfordshire.

Harchik, A.E., Harchik, A.J., Luce, S.C. and Sherman, J.A. (1990) 'Teaching autistic and severely handicapped children to recruit praise: Acquisition and generalization.' *Research in Developmental Disabilities 11*, 77–95.

Heaton, P., Hudry, K., Ludlow, A. and Hill, E. (2008) 'Superior discrimination of speech pitch and its relationship to verbal ability in autism spectrum disorders.' *Cognitive Neuropsychology 25*, 6, 771–782.

Hermelin, B. (2001) *Bright Splinters of the Mind.* London: Jessica Kingsley Publishers.

Hermelin, B. and O'Connor, N. (1970) *Psychological Experiments with Autistic Children.* Oxford: Pergamon Press.

Herrera, G., Alcantua, F., Jordan, R., Blanquer, A., Labajo, G. and De Pablo, C. (2008) 'Development of symbolic play through the use of virtual reality tools in children with autistic spectrum disorders: Two case studies.' *Autism 12*, 27, 143–157.

Hesmondhalgh, M. (2006) *Autism, Access and Inclusion on the Front Line.* London: Jessica Kingsley Publishers.

Hill, E.L. (2004) 'Executive dysfunction in autism.' *Trends in Cognitive Science 8*, 1, 26–32.

Hobson, R.P. (1989) 'Beyond Cognition: A Theory of Autism.' In G. Dawson (ed) *Autism: Nature, Diagnosis, and Treatment* (pp.22–48). New York, NY: Guilford Press.

Hobson, R.P. (2008) 'Interpersonally situated cognition.' *International Journal of Philosophical Studies 16*, 3, 377–397.

Holland, A. (Producer) (2008) 'Neurological gait keepers.' *Catalyst* [Television broadcast]. Melbourne, Australia. ABC Network. Retrieved 5 April 2010 from www.abc.net.au/catalyst/stories/2389736.htm

Holliday Willey, L. (1999) *Pretending to Be Normal: Living with Asperger's Syndrome.* London: Jessica Kingsley Publishers.

Holliday Willey, L. (2002) *Asperger's Syndrome in the Family: Redefining Normal.* London: Jessica Kingsley Publishers.

Howlin, P. (1997) *Autism: Preparation for Adulthood.* London: Routledge.

Howlin, P. (2000) 'Outcomes in adult life for more able individuals with autism or Asperger's syndrome.' *Autism 4*, 1, 63–68.

Howlin, P. (2003) 'Outcome in high functioning adults with autism with and without early language delays: Implications for the differentiation between autism and Asperger syndrome.' *Journal of Autism and Developmental Disorders 33*, 3–13.

Howlin, P., Baron-Cohen, S. and Hadwin, J. (2007) *All about Emotions.* London: Wiley.

Howlin, P., Mawhood, L. and Rutter, M. (2000) 'Autism and developmental receptive language disorder – a follow-up comparison in early adult life II: Social, behavioural and psychiatric outcomes.' *Journal of Psychiatry and Allied Disciplines 41*, 561–578.

Hoy, R. (2007) *Autism and Me.* London: Jessica Kingsley Publishers.

Hughes, C. (1998) 'Executive function in pre-schoolers: Links with theory of mind and verbal ability.' *British Journal of Developmental Psychology 16*, 233–253.

Hughes, C. and Ensor, R. (2007) 'Executive function and theory of mind: Predictive relations from ages 2 to 4 years.' *Developmental Psychology 43*, 1447–1459.

Hughes, C. and Leekam, S. (2004) 'What are the links between theory of mind and social relations? Review, reflections and new directions for studies of typical and atypical development.' *Social Development 13*, 590–619.

Hughes, C. and Russell, J. (1993) 'Autistic children's difficulty with mental disengagement from an object: Its implications for theories of autism.' *Developmental Psychology 29*, 498–510.

Jackson, L. (2002) *Freaks, Geeks and Asperger's Syndrome: A User Guide for Adolescence.* London: Jessica Kingsley Publishers.

Joliffe, T. and Baron-Cohen, S. (1999) 'The strange stories test: A replication with high-functioning adults with autism or Asperger syndrome.' *Journal of Autism and Developmental Disorders 29*, 395–406.

Jordan, R.R. (1999) *Autistic Spectrum Handbook: An Introductory Handbook for Practitioners.* London: David Fulton.

Jordan, R.R. (2008) 'Autism spectrum condition.' Awares International online conference. Retrieved 11 October 2008 from www.awares.org/conferences

Joseph, R.M. and Tager-Flusberg, H. (2004) 'The relationship of theory of mind and executive functions to symptom type and severity in children with autism.' *Development and Psychopathology 16*, 137–155.

Just, M., Cherkassky, V., Keller, T. and Minshew, N. (2004) 'Cortical activation and synchronization during sentence comprehension in high-functioning autism: Evidence of underconnectivity.' *Brain 127*, 8, 1811–1821.

Kaland, N., Mortensen, E.L. and Smith, L. (2007) 'Disembedding performance in children and adolescents with Asperger syndrome or high-functioning autism.' *Autism 11*, 1, 81–92.

Kampe, K., Frith, C.D. and Frith, U. (2003) '"Hey John": Signals conveying communicative intention towards the self activate brain regions associated with mentalising regardless of modality.' *Journal of Neuroscience 23*, 5258–5263.

Kana, R., Keller, T., Cherkassky, V., Minshew, N. and Just, M. (2006) 'Sentence comprehension in autism: Thinking in pictures with decreased functional connectivity.' *Brain 129*, 9, 2484–2493.

Kanner, L. (1943) 'Autistic disturbances of affective contact.' *Nervous Child 2*, 217–250.

Kanner, L. (1971) 'Follow-up study of eleven autistic children originally reported in 1943.' *Journal of Autism and Childhood Schizophrenia 1*, 2, 119–145.

Kassim, M.A., Hanafi, S.R. and Hancock, D.R. (2007) 'Test Anxiety and Its Consequences on Academic Performance among University Students.' In R. Nata (ed) *Progress in Education: Volume 15* (pp.17–37). Huntington, NY: Nova Science.

Keay-Bright, W. (2007) 'Tangible technologies as interactive play spaces for children with learning difficulties: The reactive colours project.' *International Journal of Technology, Knowledge and Society 4*, 1, 111–120.

Kennett, J. (2002) 'Autism, empathy and moral agency.' *The Philosophical Quarterly 52*, 340–357.

Kern, J.K., Garver, C.R., Carmody, T., Andrews, A.A., Mehta, J.A. and Trivedi, M.H. (2008) 'Examining sensory modulation in individuals with autism as compared to community controls.' *Research in Autism Spectrum Disorders 2*, 85–94.

Kern, J.K., Trivedi, M.H., Garver, C.R., Grannemann, B.D., Andrews, A.A., Salva, J.S. *et al.* (2006) 'The pattern of sensory processing abnormalities in autism.' *Autism 10*, 480–494.

Klin, A., Jones, W., Schultz, R. and Volkmar, F. (2003) 'The enactive mind or from actions of cognition: Lessons from autism.' *Philosophical Transactions of the Royal Society of London, Series B, Biological Sciences 358*, 345–360.

Kluth, P. (2003) *You're Going to Love This Kid: Teaching Students with Autism in the Inclusive Classroom.* Baltimore, MD: Paul H. Brookes.

Kluth, P. and Chandler-Olcott, K. (2008) *A Land We Can Share: Teaching Literacy to Students with Autism.* Baltimore, MD: Paul H. Brookes.

Koshino, H., Kana, R.K., Keller, T.A., Cherkassky, V.L., Minshew, N.J. and Just, M.A. (2008) 'fMRI investigation of working memory for faces in autism: Visual coding and underconnectivity with frontal areas.' *Cerebral Cortex 1*, 289–300.

Kourkoulou, A., Findlay, J.M. and Leekam, S.R. (2008) 'Implicit memory of visual context is intact in autism spectrum disorders (ASDs).' *Perception 37*, 6, 959–968.

Kuhl, P.K., Coffey-Corina, S., Padden, D. and Dawson, G. (2005) 'Links between social and linguistic processing of speech in preschool children with autism: Behavioral and electrophysiological measures.' *Developmental Science 8*, 1, 9–20.

Kylliainen, A. and Hietanen, J.K. (2004) 'Attention orienting by another's gaze direction in children with autism.' *Journal of Child Psychology and Psychiatry 45*, 435–444.

La Malfa, G., Lassi, S., Bertelli, M., Salvini, R. and Placidi, G.F. (2004) 'Autism and intellectual disability: A study of prevalence on a sample of the Italian population.' *Journal of Intellectual Disability 48*, 3, 262–267.

Lathe, R. (2006) *Autism, Brain and Environment.* London: Jessica Kingsley Publishers.

Lawson, W. (1998) 'My life as an exchange student with Asperger syndrome on an exchange programme from Monash University, Australia to the University of Bradford, England.' *Autism 2*, 3, 290–295.

Lawson, W. (2000) *Life Behind Glass.* London: Jessica Kingsley Publishers.

Lawson, W. (2001) *Understanding and Working with the Spectrum of Autism: An Insider's View.* London: Jessica Kingsley Publishers.

Lawson, W. (2006) *Friendships: The Aspie Way.* London: Jessica Kingsley Publishers.

Lawson, W. (2008) *Concepts of Normality: The Autistic and Typical Spectrum.* London: Jessica Kingsley Publishers.

Leekham, S.R., Lopez, B. and Moore, C. (2000) 'Attention and joint attention in preschool children with autism.' *Developmental Psychology 36*, 2, 261–273.

Leslie, A.M. (1987) 'Pretence and representation: The origins of theory of mind.' *Psychological Review 94*, 412–426.

Leslie, A.M. (1994) 'ToMM, ToBy, and Agency: Core Architecture and Domain Specificity.' In L.A. Hirschfeld and S.A. Gelman (eds) *Mapping the Mind: Domain Specificity in Cognition and Culture* (pp.119–148). New York, NY: Cambridge University Press.

Leslie, A.M. (2000) '"Theory of Mind" as a Mechanism of Selective Attention.' In M. Gazzaniga (ed) *The New Cognitive Neurosciences* (2nd edn) (pp.1235–1247). Cambridge, MA: MIT Press.

Leslie, A.M. and Roth, D. (1993) 'What Autism Teaches Us about Representation.' In S. Baron-Cohen, H. Tager-Flusberg and D.J. Cohen (eds) *Understanding Other Minds: Perspectives from Autism* (pp.83–111). Oxford: Oxford University Press.

Lesser, M.J. and Murray, D.K.C. (1997) 'Mind as a dynamical system: Implications for autism.' Psychobiology of autism: Current research and practice. Durham Research Conference, April 1998, University of Sunderland.

Mann, T.A. and Walker, P. (2003) 'Autism and a deficit in broadening the spread of visual attention.' Journal of Child Psychology and Psychiatry and Allied Disciplines 44, 274–284.

Marshall, K. (2008) 'Reaching the reluctant learner: At your service.' Educational Leadership 65, 6, 1–9.

Martin, D. (2007, 9 July) 'One in 58 British children will be on the autism spectrum.' Daily Mail. Retrieved 9 October 2008 from www.dailymail.co.uk/health/article-466966

McAlister, A. and Peterson, C. (2007) 'A longitudinal study of child siblings and theory of mind development.' Cognitive Development 22, 2, 258–270.

Mesibov, G., Shea, V. and Schopler, E. (2000) The TEACCH Approach to Autism Spectrum Disorders. New York, NY: Springer.

Milne, E., Swettenham, J., Hansen, P., Campbell, R., Jeffries, H. and Plaisted, K. (2002) 'High motion coherence thresholds in children with autism.' Journal of Child Psychology and Psychiatry and Allied Disciplines 43, 255–263.

Milne, E., White, S., Campbell, R., Swettenham, J., Hansen, P. and Ramus, F. (2006) 'Motion and form coherence detection in autistic spectrum disorder: Relationship to motor control and 2:4 digit ratio.' Journal of Autism and Developmental Disorders 36, 225–237.

Minshew, N.J., Goldstein, G., Muenz, L.R. and Payton, J.B. (1992) 'Neuropsychological functioning in nonmentally retarded autistic individuals.' Journal of Clinical Experimental Neuropsychology 14, 5, 749–761.

Minshew, N.J. and Hobson, J.A. (2008) 'Sensory sensitivities and performance on sensory perceptual tasks in high-functioning individuals with autism.' Journal of Autism and Developmental Disorders 38, 8, 1485–1498.

Minshew, N.J., Meyer, J. and Goldstein, G. (2002) 'Abstract reasoning in autism: A dissociation between concept formation and concept identification.' Neuropsychology 16, 3, 327–334.

Minshew, N.J. and Williams, D.L. (2007) 'The new neurobiology of autism: Cortex, connectivity, and neuronal organization.' Archives of Neurology 64, 945–950.

Minshew, N.J. and Williams, D.L. (2008) 'Brain Behavior Connections in Autism.' In K.D. Buron and P. Wolfberg (eds) Learners on the Autism Spectrum: Preparing Highly Qualified Educators (pp.44–87). Shawnee, KS: Autism Asperger Publishing.

Mitchell, P. and Lacohee, H. (1991) 'Children's early understanding of false belief.' Cognition 39, 107–127.

Miyake, A., Friedman, N.P., Emerson, M.J., Witzki, A.H., Howerter, A. and Wager, T.D. (2000) 'The unity and diversity of executive functions and their contributions to complex "frontal lobe" tasks: A latent variable analysis.' Cognitive Psychology 41, 49–100.

Moore, D.S. (2001) The Dependent Gene: The Fallacy of 'Nature vs. Nurture'. New York, NY: Owl Books.

Mottron, L. and Burack, J.A. (2001) 'Enhanced Perceptual Functioning in the Development of Persons with Autism.' In J.A. Burack, T. Charman, N. Yirmiya and P.R. Zelazo (eds) *The Development of Autism: Perspectives from Theory and Research* (pp.131–148). Hillsdale, NJ: Lawrence Erlbaum.

Mottron, L., Burack, J.A., Iarocci Belleville, G.S. and Enns, J. (2003) 'Locally oriented perception with intact global processing among adolescents with high functioning autism: Evidence from multiple paradigms.' *Journal of Child Psychology and Psychiatry 44*, 906–913.

Mottron, L., Burack, J.A., Stauder, J.E. and Robaey, P. (1999) 'Perceptual processing among high-functioning persons with autism.' *Journal of Child Psychology and Psychiatry 40*, 203–211.

Mottron, L., Dawson, M., Soulières, I., Hubert, B. and Burack, J.A. (2006) 'Enhanced perceptual functioning in autism: An update, and eight principles of autistic perception.' *Journal of Autism and Developmental Disorders 36*, 1–43.

Mottron, L., Mineau, S., Martel, G., Bernier, St. C., Berthiaume, C., Dawson, M. *et al.* (2007) 'Lateral glances toward moving stimuli among young children with autism: Early regulation of locally oriented perception?' *Development and Psychopathology 19*, 23–36.

Mottron, L., Pertz, I. and Ménard, E. (2000) 'Local and global processing of music in high-functioning persons with autism: Beyond central coherence?' *Journal of Child Psychology and Psychiatry, and Allied Disciplines 41*, 8, 1057–1065.

Muggleton, J. (2008) 'Make school make sense. An intervention by the National Autistic Society.' Retrieved 9 September 2008 from www.mugsy.org/josh/hocspeech.htm

Murray, D.K.C. (1986) 'Language and interests.' Unpublished doctoral dissertation, University of London.

Murray, D.K.C. (1992) 'Attention Tunnelling and Autism.' In P. Shattock and G. Linfoot (eds) *Living with Autism: The Individual, the Family and the Professional* (pp.89–97). Sunderland: Autism Research Unit, University of Sunderland.

Murray, D.K.C. (1995) 'An autistic friendship.' In *Psychological Perspectives in Autism. Durham Research Conference, April 1995* (pp.183–193). Durham: University of Sunderland.

Murray, D.K.C. (1996) 'Shared attention and speech in autism.' Therapeutic Intervention in Autism. Durham Research Conference, 1–3 April 1996 (pp.361–369). Durham: University of Sunderland.

Murray, D.K.C. (2006) 'One that got away.' In D.K.C. Murray (ed) *Coming Out Asperger: Diagnosis, Disclosure and Self-confidence* (pp.108–124). London: Jessica Kingsley Publishers.

Murray, D.K.C. and Lesser, M. (2006) 'Confidence, Self-confidence and Social Confidence.' In D.K.C. Murray (ed) *Coming Out Asperger: Diagnosis, Disclosure and Self-confidence* (pp.53–66). London: Jessica Kingsley Publishers.

Murray, D.K.C., Lesser, M. and Lawson, W. (2005) 'Attention, monotropism and the diagnostic criteria for autism.' *Autism 9*, 2, 139–156.

Myin, E. and O'Regan, J. (2002) 'Perceptual consciousness, access to modality and skill theories. A way to naturalize phenomenology?' *Journal of Consciousness Studies 9*, 1, 27–45.

National Autistic Society (Producer) (2008) *Being Me: A Self-development Resource Pack for People on the Autism Spectrum.* [Motion picture] London: National Autistic Society.

Newson, E. (2000) 'The social development of the young autistic child.' *Good Autism Practice 1*, 1, 92.

O'Connor, K. and Kirk, I. (2008) 'Atypical social cognition and social behaviours in autism spectrum disorder: A different way of processing rather than an impairment.' *Journal of Autism and Developmental Disorders 38*, 1989–1997.

Ozonoff, S. (1995) 'Executive Functions in Autism.' In E. Schopler and G. Mesibov (eds) *Learning and Cognition in Autism* (pp.199–220). New York, NY: Plenum Press.

Ozonoff, S., Strayer, D.L., McMahon, W.M. and Filloux, F. (1994) 'Executive function abilities in autism and Tourette syndrome: An information-processing approach.' *Journal of Child Psychology and Psychiatry 35*, 1015–1032.

Perner, J. (1996) 'Simulation as Explicitation of Predication-implicit Knowledge about the Mind: Arguments for a Simulation–Theory Mix.' In P. Carruthers and P.K. Smith (eds) *Theories of Theory of Mind* (pp.90–104). Cambridge: Cambridge University Press.

Peterson, C.C., Peterson, J.C. and Webb, J. (2000) 'Factors influencing the development of a theory of mind in blind children.' *British Journal of Developmental Psychology 18*, 3, 431–447.

Piaget, J. (1952) *The Child's Conception of Number.* London: Routledge and Kegan Paul.

Piaget, J. (1971) *Biology and Knowledge.* Chicago, IL: University of Chicago Press.

Plaisted, K.C., Dobler, V., Bell, S. and Davis, G. (2006) 'The microgenesis of global perception in autism.' *Journal of Autism and Developmental Disorders 36*, 1, 107–116.

Plaisted, K.C., O'Riordan, M.A. and Baron-Cohen, S. (1998) 'Enhanced visual search for a conjunctive target in autism: A research note.' *Journal of Child Psychology and Psychiatry 39*, 777–783.

Plaisted, K.C., O'Riordan, M.A., Driver, J. and Baron-Cohen, S. (2001) 'Superior visual search in autism.' *Journal of Experimental Psychology: Human Perception and Performance 27*, 719–730.

Plaisted, K.C., Swettenham, J. and Rees, L. (1999) 'Children with autism show local precedence in a divided attention task and global precedence in a selective attention task.' *Journal of Child Psychology and Psychiatry 40*, 733–742.

Powell, S.D. and Jordan R.R. (1992) 'Remediating the thinking of pupils with autism: Principles into practice.' *Journal of Autism and Developmental Disorders 22*, 3, 413–418.

Premack, D. and Woodruff, G. (1978) 'Does the chimpanzee have a theory of mind?' *Behavioral and Brain Sciences 1*, 4, 515–526.

Prince-Hughes, D. (ed) (2002) *Aquamarine Blue 5: Personal Stories of College Students with Autism.* Athens, OH: Swallow Press.

Pring, L., Hermelin, B. and Heavey, L. (1995) 'Savants, segments, art and autism.' *Journal of Child Psychology and Psychiatry 36*, 1065–1076.

Purkis, J. (2006) *Finding a Different Kind of Normal.* London: Jessica Kingsley Publishers.

Reed, S.K. (1996) *Cognition* (4th edn). New York, NY: Brooks/Cole Publishing.

Riby, D.M. and Hancock, P.J.B. (2008) 'Viewing it differently: Social scene perception in Williams syndrome and autism.' *Neuropsychologia 46*, 2855–2860.

Riby, D.M. and Hancock, P.J.B. (2009a) 'Do faces capture the attention of individuals with Williams syndrome or autism? Evidence from tracking eye movements.' *Journal of Autism and Developmental Disorders 39*, 3, 421–431.

Riby, D.M. and Hancock, P.J.B. (2009b) 'Looking at movies and cartoons: Eye-tracking evidence from Williams syndrome and autism.' *Journal of Intellectual Disability Research 53*, 2, 169–181.

Rinehart, N.J., Bellgrove, M.A., Tonge, B.J., Brereton, A.V., Howells-Rankins, D. and Bradshaw, J.L. (2006) 'An examination of movement kinematics in young people with high-functioning autism and Asperger's disorder: Further evidence for a motor planning deficit.' *Journal of Autism and Developmental Disorders 36*, 757–767.

Rinehart, N.J., Tonge, B.J., Iansek, B.I., McGinley, J., Brereton, A.V., Enticott, P. *et al.* (2008) 'Gait function in newly diagnosed children with autism: Cerebellar and basal ganglia related motor disorder.' *Developmental Medicine and Child Neurology 48*, 10, 819–824.

Robins, B., Dickerson, P., Stribling, P. and Dautenhahn, K. (2004) 'Robot-mediated joint attention in children with autism: A case study in robot–human interaction.' *Interaction Studies 5*, 2, 161–198.

Robinson, E.J. and Mitchell, P. (1995) 'Masking of children's early understanding of the representational mind: Backwards explanation versus prediction.' *Child Development 6*, 1022–1039.

Robison, J.E. (2008) *Look Me in the Eye.* Sydney: Random House.

Ropar, D. and Mitchell, P. (1999) 'Are individuals with autism and Asperger's syndrome susceptible to visual illusions?' *Journal of Child Psychology and Psychiatry, and Allied Disciplines 140*, 8,1283–1293.

Ropar, D. and Mitchell, P. (2001) 'Do individuals with autism and Asperger's syndrome utilise prior knowledge when pairing stimuli?' *Developmental Science 4*, 4, 433–441.

Roth, I. (2007) 'Imagination and Awareness of Self in Autistic Spectrum Poets.' In M. Osteen (ed) *Autism and Representation* (pp.145–165). New York, NY: Routledge.

Royall, D.R., Lauterbach, E.C., Cummings, J.L., Reeve, A., Rummans, T.A., Kaufer, D.I. *et al.* (2002) 'Executive control function: A review of its promise and challenges for clinical research a report from the committee on research of the American Neuropsychiatric Association.' *Journal of Neuropsychiatry Clinical Neuroscience 14*, 4, 377–405.

Russell, J. (1997) 'How Executive Disorders Can Bring about an Inadequate "Theory of Mind".' In J. Russell (ed) *Autism as an Executive Disorder* (pp.256–304). Oxford: Oxford University Press.

Rutherford, M.D., Young, G.S. Hepburn, S. and Rogers, S.J. (2007) 'A longitudinal study of pretend play in autism.' *Journal of Autism and Developmental Disorders 37*, 6, 1024–1039.

Sainsbury, C. (2000) *Martian in the Playground.* London: The Book Factory.

Sally, D. and Hill, E. (2006) 'The development of interpersonal strategy: Autism, theory-of-mind, cooperation and fairness.' *Journal of Economic Psychology 27*, 73–97.

Sanders, J., Johnson, K.A., Garavan, H., Gill, M. and Gallagher, L. (2007) 'A review of neuropsychological and neuroimaging research in autistic spectrum disorders: Attention, inhibition and cognitive flexibility.' *Research in Autism Spectrum Disorders 2*, 1, 1–16.

Sanjay, G. and *CNN* Medical Unit Producers (2008) 'Technology gives girl with autism a voice.' Retrieved 5 November 2008 from www.carlysvoice.com

Schwartz, J.M. and Begley, S. (2002) *The Mind and the Brain: Neuroplasticity and the Power of Mental Force.* Sydney: HarperCollins.

Scott, L. (2008) 'The growing trend of pets as therapy.' Retrieved 31 January 2008 from www.eioba.com/a27950/the_growing_use_of_pets_as_therapy

Scott, F. and Baron-Cohen, S. (1996) 'Imagining real and unreal objects: An investigation of imagination in autism.' *Journal of Cognitive Neuroscience 8,* 400–411.

Scott, F., Baron-Cohen, S. and Leslie, A.M. (1994) '"If pigs could fly": An examination of imagination and counterfactual reasoning in autism.' Unpublished manuscript, University of Cambridge.

Sergeant, J.A., Geurts, H.M. and Oosterlaan, J. (2002) 'How specific is a deficit of executive functioning for attention-deficit/hyperactivity disorder?' *Behavioural Brain Research 130,* 3–28.

Shah, A. and Frith, U. (1993) 'Why do autistic individuals show superior performance on the block design task?' *Journal of Child Psychology and Psychiatry 34,* 1351–1364.

Shallice, T. and Burgess, P. (1991) 'Higher-order Cognitive Impairments and Frontal Lobe Lesions in Man.' In H.S. Levin, H.M. Eisenberg and A.L. Benton (eds) *Frontal Lobe Function and Dysfunction* (pp.125–138). New York, NY: Oxford University Press.

Shallice, T., Marzocchi, G.M., Coser, S., Del Savio, M., Meurter, R.F. and Rumiati, R.I. (2002) 'Executive function profile of children with attention deficit hyperactivity disorder (ADHD).' *Developmental Neuropsychology 21,* 75–86.

Shattock, P., Kennedy, A., Rowell, F. and Berney, T.P. (1990) 'Role of neuropeptides in autism and their relationships with classical neurotransmitters.' *Brain Dysfunction 3,* 5, 328–345.

Shore, S. (2002) 'Dating, marriage and autism.' *Advocate 4,* 3, 24–27.

Shore, S. (ed) (2004) *Ask and Tell: Self-advocacy and Disclosure for People on the Autism Spectrum.* Shawnee Mission, KS: Autism Asperger Publishing.

Silberman, S. (2008) 'Genius, genes and autism.' Retrieved 7 January 2009 from www.stevesilberman.com

Stagnitti, K. (1998) *Learn to Play: A Program for the Development of a Child's Imaginative Play Skills.* Melbourne: Coordinates Publications.

Stagnitti, K. (2004) 'Understanding play: The implications for play assessment.' *Australian Occupational Journal 51,* 1, 3–12.

Stanley, M. (2007) 'What really are the divorce rates?' Retrieved 9 July 2008 from www.prepinc.com/main/docs/What%20Really%20is%20the%20Divorce%20Rate%208-3-2007.pdf

Sullivan, A. (2002) 'Inertia: From theory to praxis.' Retrieved February 11, 2006, from www.autistics.org/library/inertia.html

Sullivan, K., Zaitchik, D. and Tager-Flusberg, H. (1994) 'Preschoolers can attribute second-order beliefs.' *Developmental Psychology 30,* 3, 395–402.

Swettenham, J., Condie, S., Campbell, R., Milne, E. and Coleman, M. (2003) 'Does the perception of moving eyes trigger reflexive visual orienting in autism?' *Philosophical Transactions of the Royal Society of London, Series B, Biological Sciences 28,* 358, 325–334.

Tager-Flusberg, H. (2001) 'A Re-examination of the Theory of Mind Hypothesis of Autism.' In J.A. Burack, T. Charman, T.N. Yirmiya and P.R. Zelazo (eds) *The Development of Autism: Perspectives from Theory and Research* (pp.173–193). Mahwah, NJ: Lawrence Erlbaum.

Talay-Ongon, A. and Wood, K. (2000) 'Unusual sensory sensitivities in autism: A possible crossroads.' *International Journal of Disability, Development, and Education 47*, 201–212.

Tantam, D., Holmes, D. and Cordess, C. (1993) 'Nonverbal expression in autism of Asperger type.' *Journal of Autism and Developmental Disorders 23*, 1, 111–133.

Tonge, B.J., Dissanayake, C. and Brereton, A.V. (1994) 'Autism: Fifty years on from Kanner.' *Journal of Pediatric Child Health 30*, 2, 102–107.

Torrance, E.P. (1964) 'Education and the creative potential.' *Educational and Psychological Measurement 24*, 707–709.

Torrance, E.P. (1974) *The Torrance Tests of Creative Thinking: Norms – Technical Manual:* Bensenville, IL: Scholastic Testing Services.

Van Lang, N.D.J. (2003) *Autism Spectrum Disorders: A Study of Symptom Domains and Weak Central Coherence.* University of Groningen, Netherlands.

Vidyasagar, T.R. and Pammer, K. (1999) 'Impaired visual search in dyslexia relates to the role of the magnocellular pathway in attention.' *Neuroreport 10*, 1283–1287.

Vignemont, F. and Frith, U. (2007) 'Autism, Morality and Empathy.' In W. Sinnott-Armstrong (ed) *Moral Psychology: Volume 3. The Neuroscience of Morality: Emotion, Disease, and Development* (pp.273–280). Cambridge, MA: MIT Press.

Vismara, L.A. and Lyons, G.L. (2007) 'Joint attention behaviours in young children with autism: Theoretical and clinical implications for understanding motivation.' *Journal of Positive Behavior Interventions 9*, 4, 214–228.

Vogeley, K., Bussfeld, P., Newen, A., Herrmann, S., Happé, F., Falkai, P., *et al.* (2001) 'Mind reading: Neural mechanisms of theory of mind and self-perspective.' *NeuroImage 14*, 1, 170–181.

Vogeley, K., May, M., Ritzl, A., Falkai, P., Zilles, K. and Fink, G.R. (2004) 'Neural correlates of first-person perspective as one constituent of human self-consciousness.' *Journal of Cognition and Neuroscience 16*, 817–827.

Vohs, K.D. and Baumeister, R.F. (2004) 'Understanding Self-regulation.' In R.F. Baumeister and K.D. Vohs (eds) *Handbook of Self-regulation: Research, Theory and Applications* (pp.1–9). New York, NY: Guilford Press.

Wainwright-Sharp, J.A. and Bryson, S.E. (1993) 'Visual orienting deficits in high-functioning people with autism.' *Journal of Autism and Developmental Disorders 23*, 1, 1–13.

Webb, S.J., Dawson, G., Bernier, R. and Panagiotides, H. (2006) 'ERP evidence of atypical face processing in young children with autism.' *Journal of Autism and Developmental Disorders 36*, 881–890.

Wechsler, D. (1997) *Wechsler Adult Intelligence Scale* (3rd edn). New York: Psychological Corp.

Welsh, M.C., Pennington, B.F. and Groisser, D.B. (1991) 'A normative-developmental study of executive function: A window on prefrontal function in children.' *Developmental Neuropsychology 7*, 2, 131–149.

Wicker, B., Fonlupt, P., Hubert, B., Tardif, C., Gepner, B. and Deruelle, C. (2008) 'Abnormal cerebral effective connectivity during explicit emotional processing in adults with autism spectrum disorder.' *Social Cognitive and Affective Neuroscience 3*, 2, 135–143.

Willcutt, E.G., Doyle, A.E., Nigg, J.T., Faraone, S.V. and Pennington, B.F. (2005) 'Validity of the executive function theory of attention-deficit/hyperactivity disorder: A meta-analytic review.' *Biological Psychiatry 57*, 11, 1336–1346.

Williams, D. (1992) *Nobody Nowhere*. London: Jessica Kingsley Publishers.

Williams, D. (1994) *Somebody Somewhere*. London: Jessica Kingsley Publishers.

Williams, D.L., Goldstein, G. and Minshew, N. (2006) 'Neuropsychologic functioning in children with autism: Further evidence for disordered complex information-processing.' *Child Neuropsychology 12*, 4/5, 279–298.

Williams, D.L. and Minshew, N.J. (2007) 'Understanding autism and related disorders: What has imaging taught us?' *Neuroimaging Clinics NA 17*, 4, 495–509.

Wiltshire, S. (1989) *Cities*. London: J.M. Dent.

Wimmer, H. and Perner, J. (1983) 'Beliefs about beliefs: Representation and constraining function of wrong beliefs in young children's understanding of deception.' *Cognition 13*, 103–128.

Wing, L. (1992) 'Manifestations of Social Problems in High-functioning Autistic People.' In E. Schopler and G.B. Mesbov (eds) *High Functioning Individuals with Autism* (pp.129–141). London: Plenum.

Wing, L. (1998a, Winter) 'Classification and diagnosis-looking at the complexities involved.' *Communication*, pp.15–18.

Wing, L. (1998b) 'The History of Asperger Syndrome.' In E. Schopler, G.B. Mesibov and L.J. Kunce (eds) *Asperger Syndrome or High Functioning Autism* (pp.1–28). New York, NY: Plenum.

Wing, L. (2000) 'Past and Future Research on Asperger Syndrome.' In A. Klin, F. Volkmar and S. Sparrow (eds) *Asperger Syndrome* (pp.418–432). New York, NY: Guilford Press.

Wing, L. and Attwood, A. (1987) 'Syndromes of Autism and Atypical Development.' In J. Cohen, A. Donnellan and R. Paul (eds) *Handbook of Autism and Pervasive Developmental Disorders* (pp.3–19). New York, NY: Winston-Wiley.

Wing, L. and Shah, A. (2000) 'Catatonia in autistic spectrum disorders.' *British Journal of Psychiatry 176*, 357–362.

Wozniak, R.H. (1999) *Introduction to Memory by Hermann Ebbinghaus (Classics in Psychology, 1855–1914: Historical Essays)*. Bristol: Thoemmes Press.

Yerys, B.E., Hepburn, S.L., Pennington, B.F. and Rogers, S.J. (2007) 'Executive function in preschoolers with autism: Evidence consistent with a secondary deficit.' *Journal of Autism and Developmental Disorders 37*, 6, 1068–1079.

Young, J.E. and Klosko, J.S. (1994) *Reinventing Your Life: The Breakthrough Program to End Negative Behavior…and Feel Great Again*. Ringwood, Victoria, Australia: Plume, Penguin Group.

Zelazo, P.D. and Muller, U. (2002) 'Executive Function in Typical and Atypical Development.' In U. Goswami (ed) *Handbook of Childhood Cognitive Development* (pp.445–469). Oxford: Blackwell.

A model of mind presented as a dynamical system of interests competing for attention

This concept is illustrated in the equation that follows.

The Model of the Interest System
Retrieved 7 January 2008
From: http://www.autismandcomputing.org.uk/

By Mike Lesser and Dinah Murray 1997

The model is based on the concept of an interest. The word is used with its everyday meaning. It has however the implication of concern rather than advantage, and it covers all deployment of attention, from desire to wonder.

The system comprises two spatially discretised differential equations ($X(i,j)$ and $Y,(i,j)$ arranged as the elements of a Volterra-Lotka equation. Similar to a chemical diffusion reaction model. The state space is closed (toroid). Its metric is cognitive map space with the addition of perception and imagination. Emotion is reduced to a single aversive/attractive value which, in combination with the state of the matrix provides the value of $X(i,j)$. The differential equations are fluctuated to simulate an unknown environment. The brain is modeled as a noisy far from equilibrium network. The dynamic modeled conforms with present psycho-neurological findings.

The quotidian mind is apparently occupied with interests and these interests compete for attention which is Conserved and finite, ie N = supply of metabolites.

Interests are aroused and depressed both by autocatalysis, sensory input and by the state of the rest of the system.

$$\frac{dx_{ij}}{dt} = \left((bf(x_{ij} + wx_{ij}^2) + b\frac{(1-f)}{4}\left((x_{i-ij} + wx_{i+ij}^2) + (x_{ij-l} + wx_{ij-l}^2) + (x_{ij+l} + wx_{ij}^2) \right) \right) \left(1 - \frac{\sum\limits_{i'j'} x_{i,j+l}\, e^{-pd(ij',j)}}{N\sum\limits_{i'j'} e^{-pd(ij',j)}} \right) - mx_{i,j}$$

$$\frac{dy_{i,j}}{dt} = \left(sf(x_{i,j}\, y_{i,j} + wy_{ij}^2) + s\frac{(1-f)}{4}\left((x_{i-ij}\, y_{i-ij} + wy_{i-ij}^2) + (x_{i+ij}\, y_{i+ij} = wy_{i+ij}^2) + (x_{ij-l}\, y_{ij-l} + wy_{ij-l}^2) + (x_{ij-}l + wy_{ij-l}^2 - l) + (x_{ij+l}\, y_{ij+l} + wy_{ij+l}^2) \right) \right)$$

N = attention

$x_{i,j}$ = interest

$y_{i,j}$ = activity

b = the rate at which attention becomes interest

s = the rate at which interest becomes activity

m = the rate at which arousal becomes decays

w = the rate of positive feedback

f = the basal rate of association excitation of interests

p = the decay factor in resource overlap with distance

d (i, j; i', j') = the distance between $x_{i,j}$ and $x_{i',j'}$

The arousal of an interest is its emotional content ie the value of X(i,j).

Emotions are modelled by the extreme reduction of all emotion to a single variable which models an attraction/revulsion spectrum.

In everyday life expression of an interest tends to lower its arousal. Ie the VL part of the equations. N =metabolic resources-> X(i,j) Arousal -> Y(i,j) Action.

The authors of this model propose that mind is a noisy far from equilibrium dynamical system of competing interests and that imagination is an emergent property of the system.

The image of the imaginer is an emergent property of the imagination.

The output of the system need bear no simple relationship to the input.

The equations were implemented as a computer program in C language. The program was run on a Cray computer at the, then, SERC Atlas Computer Centre Didcot Oxon. and on a MasPar multi CPU array at the NASA Goddard Jet Propulsion Laboratories Washington DC. Visualisations of the data produced by these computer simulations demonstrated that the system did indeed have emergent properties. Which is to say that the model would not only produce interests that were present in its initial state. Furthermore the model also produces interests that had no immediate connection with any other interests. (See purple cloud graphic) This can be viewed as analogous to the creative function in a human mind.

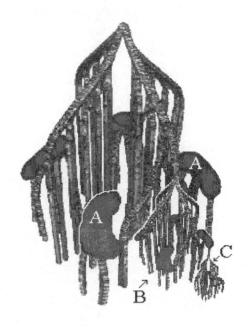

Computer graphic of development of interest system showing sudden events A. With added language system B and ego C.

There is an area of solution space in which the structural attractors generated by the model are few, slow to change and very aroused. This corresponds with the monotropic (attention tunnelled) state found in people described as autistic. (This is what the last paper was about) This area of state space is contiguous with the rest of the space suggesting that autism is part of a normal distribution of personality types.

This is not a model of autism it is a theory about human beings in which autism has a natural role as contributing to essential diversity. The interest model of mind is a new way (graphic, mathematical) of conceiving of people as transient collections of desires/directed energies affecting and being affected by perception, imagination, cognition and action. We think it makes psychological data (people) easier to analyse.

Paraphrase of criteria for autism spectrum disorder

The Diagnostic and Statistical Manual of Mental Disorders IV. (DSM-IV) describes the following diagnostic criteria: classic autism

A.

1. Qualitative impairment in social interaction as manifested by at least two of the following:

   • Marked impairment in the use of multiple nonverbal behaviours such as eye-to-eye gaze, facial expression, body postures and gestures to regulate social interaction;

   • Failure to develop peer relationships appropriate to developmental level;

   • Lack of spontaneous seeking to share enjoyment, interests or achievements with other people (e.g. by a lack of showing, bringing or pointing at objects);

   • Lack of social or emotional reciprocity.

2. Qualitative impairments in communication as manifested by at least one of the Following:

   • Delay in, or total lack of, the development of spoken language (not accompanied by an attempt to compensate through alternative modes of communication such as gesture or mime);

   • In individuals with adequate speech, marked impairment in the ability to initiate or sustain a conversation with others;

- Stereotyped and repetitive use of language or idiosyncratic language;

- Lack of varied, spontaneous make-believe play or social imitative play appropriate to developmental level.

3. Restricted repetitive and stereotyped patterns of behaviour, interests and activities, as manifested by at least one of the following:

- Encompassing preoccupation with one or more stereotyped and restricted patterns of interest that is abnormal either in intensity or focus;

- Apparently inflexible adherence to specific, non-functional routines or rituals;

- Stereotyped and repetitive motor mannerisms (e.g. hand or finger flapping or twisting, or complex whole-body movements);

- Persistent preoccupations with parts of objects.

B. *Delays or abnormal functioning in at least one of the following areas, with onset prior to age 3 years:*

(1) social interaction;

(2) language as used in social communication;

(3) symbolic or imaginative play.

C. *The disturbance is not better accounted for by Rett's disorder or childhood disintegrative disorder.*

Asperger's Autism

- **No delay in language/cognition**; diagnosis requires communicative phrase speech by 3 years; **normal curiosity, adaptive behaviour and self-help skills during first 3 years**;

- **Two to four of four symptoms of abnormal social interaction** (e.g. lack of reciprocity and lack of spontaneous seeking to share enjoyment);

- **Circumscribed interest or stereotyped behaviour**, interest and activities;

- Not attributable to autism, schizophrenia or obsessive compulsive disorder;

- Thus, **a total of three symptoms required**, at least two of which reflect difficulties in reciprocal social interaction.

PDD-NOS or Atypical Autism

- No clear operationalised criteria;

- Suggestion: five or more DSM-IV criteria for autistic disorder, at least one of which relates to areas of difficulties within the social arena;

- Not meeting criteria for autistic disorder or Asperger's disorder.

Non-cognitive theories of autism

Non-cognitive theories of autism taken, with permission, from the work by Lewis Mehl-Madrona MD; PhD Coordinator for Integrative Psychiatry and System Medicine, Program in Integrative Medicine, University of Arizona / College of Medicine. http://www.healing-arts.org/children

Name of Theory	Summary of Theory	References	Comments
Opioid Excess	Excess opioid-like substances (eg. Casomorphine), affect the brain producing autism symptoms. Such substances in their right place in the human body do not cause harm. However, in children with autism they have been found in larger amounts in urine and serum than in controls.	Bauman M., Kemper TL. (1985) Histoanatomic Observations of the Brain in Early Infantile Autism. Neurology 35: 866–874. Panksepp J. (1979) A Neurochemical Theory of Autism Trends in Neuroscience 2: 174–177 Reichelt KL., Hole K., Hamberger A., Saelid G., Edminson P.D., Braestrup C.B., Lingjaerde O. Ledaal P., Orbeck H. (1981) Biologically Active Peptide Containing Fractions in Schizophrenia and Childhood Autism. Adv. Biochem. Psychopharmacol. 28: 627–6 43.	To date only anecdotal evidence exists to suggest dietary intervention maybe helpful for some children with autism. However, such evidence should be taken seriously and it is hoped researchers will conduct scientific experiments to adequately test for this in the near future.
Gluten and Casein	Proteins not properly broken down. cause cells in gut tissues to die prematurely. Casein and gluten may move into the bloodstream. (exorphins) affect the brain causing opioid like effects	Shattock P., Kennedy A., Rowell F., Berney TP. (1990) Role of europeptides in Autism and their Relationships with Classical Neurotransmitters. Brain Dysfunction 3 (5) 328–345.	A strict gluten and casein-free diet does appear to reduce the level of opioid peptides and improve autism for some people. The earlier the implementation of the diet, the better.

Name of Theory	Summary of Theory	References	Comments
Gamma Interferon	Elevated level of interleukin-12 and gamma interferon were found in individuals with autism. It is suggested opioids will increase gamma interferon levels.	Shattock P, Lowdon G. (1991) Proteins, Peptides and Autism. Part 2: Implications for the Education and Care of People with Autism. Brain Dysfunction 4 (6) 323–334. Shaw W., Kassen E.,Chaves E. (1995) Increased Urinary Excretion of Analogues of Krebs Cycle Metabolites and Arabinose in Two Brothers with Autistic Features. Clinical Chemistry 41 (8) 1094–1104.	Once again this theory is linked to the idea that opioids can increase levels of gamma interferon. More research is needed on this topic.
Free Sulphate	Low levels of free sulphate found in the plasma of individuals with autism. Sulphate ions are not absorbed from the gut, therefore proteins not broken down leading to opioid effect or autism symptoms.	Waring RH, &Klovrza LV (2000) Sulphur Metabolism. Journal of Nutrition and Environmental Medicine, 10(1):25–32	Parents have been exploring the use of Epsom Salts placed in the bath water. Anecdotal evidence shows some benefit but also some irritability.
Oxytocin and Vasopressin	An argument that Pitocin (oxytocin) might cause some cases of autism. Pitocin is used to induce labor. Theory is Mothers with sulfation have a higher probability for delayed or desultory labor. Opioid peptides inhibit oxytocin release.	Shaw W., Chaves E., Luxem M. (1994) Abnormal Urine Organic Acids:Fungal Metabolism in urine samples of AS Children. Results: antifungal drugs. Internal Report of University of Ansas.	This theory goes hand in hand with the 'free sulphate' theory suggesting that due to sulphation problems oxytocin and vasopressin will be interfered with and will not allow for normal function.

Name of Theory	Summary of Theory	References	Comments
Autism and amino Acids	Many autistic people have low levels of specific amino acids said to be due to absent or non-functioning enzymes.	Barton, M. & volkmar, F. (1998) How commonly are known medical conditions associated with autism? Journal of autism and Developmental Disorders 28 (4) 273–279	Individuals with autism are not the only individuals to have low-level amino acids. One cannot assume that therefore, the two are connected. There is growing evidence from biochemistry and biophysics that brains of individuals with autism are structurally different.
Methylation	The metabolic process of methylation may be defective in autism. Methylation is important for the control of histamine, protection of DNA. Serotonin production and other brain functions.	Perry, E.K., Lee, M.L., Martin-Ruiz, C.M., Court, J.A., volsen, S,G., Merrit, J., folly, E., Iversen, P.E., Bauman, m.L., Perry, R,H. & Wenk, G.L. (2001). Cholinergic activity in autism: abnormalities in the cerebral cortex and basal forebrain. American Journal of Psychiatry (157 (7): 1058–66	Such biophysical theories of autism fit very well with the cognitive theory of autism expressed in this text.
Stress and Immunity	The effects of stress on immunity are not disputed. Autism as a result of auto-immune disease has been related to excessive Th2 cytokines resulting, in part, from vaccination.	Sharpley, C. Bitsika, V. & Efremidis, B. (1997) 'The influence of gender, parental health, and perceived expertise of assistance upon the well-being of parents of children with autism' Journal of Intellectual & Developmental Disability, Vo. 22, No.1, pp. 19–28.	The correlation between stress and the immune system is well documented. To date there are no studies that specifically link ASD as an outcome of stress. However, there are many studies that show stress to be elevated in ASD and to be a contributing factor to the increase of 'autistic symptoms'.

Name of Theory	Summary of Theory	References	Comments
Autoimmune Theories	Many autistic people demonstrate a mild immunosuppression which could be accounted for by the actions of opioids on T-cells. Opioids decrease T-cell proliferation via the mu-receptors. Faulty immune regulation may play a part in the cause of autism. Immunilogical testing of children with autism has shown a commonality of features also found in individuals with autoimmune diseases such as systemic lupus erythematosus, thyroid disease, ankylosing spondylitis, rheumatoid arthritis, insulin-dependent diabetes, and multiple sclerosis.	Rabin, B.S. (1999) Stress, immune function and health: The connection. New York: Wiley-Liss & Sons. Inc. Capdevia A, Decha-Omphai W, Song KH, Borchardt RT, Wagner C., (1997) Arch Biochem Biophys, 345:1 47–55 Warren RP, et.al. (1986), Immune abnormalities in patients with autism. Journal of Autism and Developmental Disorders 16:189–197.	Anecdotal and experimental evidence suggests that autoimmune disease is higher within the population of autism than in the typical population. However, which comes first? Does autism predispose an individual to the higher possibility of autoimmune disease? There just isn't any hard evidence that faulty autoimmune regulation causes autism, only that it might accompany autism.
Viral Infection Theory	The viral theory of autism relies upon a relative immunosuppression, thought to be in intestinal tract produce symptoms of autism. Secretory immunoglobulin A (SIgA) is an important defense in the intestines against viral infections and is often postulated to be deficient in autism.	A Whiteley, Jacqui Rodgers and Paul Shattock (1998) 'A Review of the records at the Autism Research Unit: Birth, gastrointestinal and viral factors supporting a metabolic hypothesis of autism spectrum disorders'. Presented to Durham Conference, University of Sunderland,	Viral infection is known to be responsible for a number of 'changes' to the human condition. Chicken pox and other mystery viruses are said to be precursors to some incidence of childhood autism where the child seemed perfectly healthy before the infection.

Name of Theory	Summary of Theory	References	Comments
Viral Infection theory	Viral encephalitis is known to give rise to autistic-like disorders, particularly when it occurs early in life. An association between past viral infection (which can be vaccine-derived) and brain auto-antibodies in autism, as well as other neurological diseases, has been found. Elevated titers of anti-measles antibodies, for example, in autistic children could signify a chronic activation of the immune system against this neurotropic virus.	Shattock, P. (2003) Autism: The triggers', Paper presented at 'Autism conference, Missouri, USA. Singh, V.K. (1998) Serological association of measles virus and human herpes virus-6 with brain autoantibodies in autism: Clinical Immunology and Immunopathology, 89 (1): 105–8. Deufemia, P., Celli, M. Finocchiaro, R. et. Al (1996) 'Abnormal intestinal permeability in children with autism. Acta Paediatrica 85. 1076–79.	There is anecdotal and some experimental evidence that the measles virus is a trigger for autism in some children. Shattock (2003) believes that a new sub-group of autistic children are autism triggered due to a reaction of the measles virus and other autoimmune characteristics.
Vaccination Theory	Some AS children exhibit positive titers of measles and MMR antibodies, the majority of cases associated with the presence of MBP (myelin basic protein, or brain) Dr. Wakefield, discovered a possible connection between autism and viral infection associated with the MMR vaccination. The damage from autism provoked an allergic type reaction initiated by the body's reaction to the vaccine. auto-immune response could affect DPP-IV, reducing its levels, connecting vaccines to the opioid theory	Wakefield, A.J. (2003) 'Measles, mumps, and rubella vaccination and autism' English Journal of Medicine (10): 951–4.	Are some children susceptible to the viral promotion of autism? Further research is necessary to address this question of viral approaches to autism. Paul Shaddock (The University of Sunderland) found 10% of urine samples from AS children do NOT have the high IGA. He suspects that the MMR vaccination plays a role in particular AS children. Although many studies to date have failed to demonstrate any connection between the MMR and autism.

Name of Theory	Summary of Theory	References	Comments
Action of secretin Theories	Secretin is a polypeptide hormone involved in the regulation of gastric function. Secretin stimulates pituitary adenylate cyclase (via PACAP) which increases intracellular cAMP in certain brain regions. One thought is that secretin reverses the lowering of cAMP brought about by opioids. There are two divergent opinions on secretin—one that high dose secretin is necessary to obtain CNS binding of secretin to receptors in the brain as opposed to the concept that secretin is a neuropeptide and only small concentrations are required (as per oral secretin administration.	Karoly Horvath, MD, PhD, Gerry Stefatos, DPhil, Kenneth N. Sokolski, MD, Renee Wachtel, MD, Laura Nabors, PhD, and J. Tyson Tildon, PhD. (1998) Autistic Behavior and Secretin. Journal of the Association for Academic Minority Physicians. Vol. 9, No.1. pp.9–15.	Improved social and language skills after secretin administration in three patients with autistic spectrum disorders. Repeat studies have not substantiated claims that: The patients that seem to respond the best are the children characterized by gut problems, dysbiosis, yeast overgrowth, and food allergies'. Some evidence of seizure activity. Secretin not seen to be a long-term viable option for most children with ASD.
Intestinal Permeability	Research on Aboriginal children: gut prone to 'leaky gut syndrome' which causes gastro disease. Maybe the same disposition occurs in AS children. To evaluate this, a non-invasive intestinal permeability test measures the rate: two non digestible sugars, lactose and mannitol, excreted in urine after ingestion. Pediatric specialists in Rome discovered 43% of AS children had increased permeability.	Kukuruzovic RH, Haase A, Dunn K, Bright A, Brewster DR. (1999) 'Intestinal Permeability and Diarrhoeal Disease in Aboriginal Australians'. Arch Dis Child 81:304–308. Horvath K, Papdimitriou CJ, Rabsztyn A, Drachenberg C, Tildon JT. (1999) Gastrointestinal abnormalities in children with autistic disorder. Journal of Pediatrics 135:559–63.	Although 'leaky gut syndrome' may not cause autism it can certainly be present in children with autism. This assessment can be a critical tool for developing holistic intervention strategies to treat autism.

Name of Theory	Summary of Theory	References	Comments
Prenatal Aspartame Exposure	Aspartame appears to play a role in a number of neurological conditions: The methanol toxicity is thought to mimic the symptoms of multiple sclerosis. Systemic lupus erythematosis may be triggered by Aspartame. lupus improves when diet soda consumption is stopped.	Markle. N. (1999) lectured at the World Environmental Council on Aspartame. Blaylock, R. (2000) Excitotoxins: The Taste That Kills. Health Press	Dr. H.J. Roberts in the bookDefense Against Alzheimer's Disease: A Rational Blueprint for Prevention shows how aspartame is a factor involved with the increased incidence of dementia. Although there is no direct link to autism it is a culprit being indicated in many related disorders. Therefore, it should be avoided.
Aspartame Exposure	Symptoms of fibromyalgia, spasms, shooting pains, numbness in the legs, cramps, vertigo, dizziness, headaches, tinnitus, joint pain, depression, anxiety, slurred speech, blurred vision, or memory loss have been attributed to Aspartame. Aspartame changes the dopamine level in the brain, affecting Parkinson's Disease. Therefore, it could also be implicated in autism.	Mar. N. Megson (2003) Pediatric & Adolescent Ability Centre. Highland II Office park, 7229 Forest Avenue Suite 211, Richmond, Virginia Wakefield, A, Murch, S, Anthony, A., et al. Ileal Lymphoid-Nodular Hyperplasia, Nonspecific Colitis And Pervasive Developmental Disorders In Children. Lancet 1998; 351:639	Aspartame has been banned in some countries and, where it still exists should be avoided or used with caution (artificial sweeteners).
Vitamin A Deficiency and Autism	Low vitamin A levels in the central and peripheral nervous system could be the etiology of biological and behavioral abnormalities, such as those seen in autism. Autistic children may have a Vitamin A deficiency because of gastrointestinal inflammation.	Megson, M.N. (2000) Is Autism G-Alpha Protein Defect Reversible with Natural Vitamin A? Defeat Autism Now Conference. The Town and Country Resort and Convention Center	Children with autism may well be deficient in Vitamin A but children without autism may be also. There isn't any scientific evidence to date that demonstrates vitamin A deficiency is a trigger for autism.

Name of Theory	Summary of Theory	References	Comments
Orphanin Protein: Orphanin FQ/ nociceptin (OFQ/N)	Autism may be a disorder linked to the disruption of the G-Alpha protein, affecting retinoid receptors in the brain. A study of 60 autistic children suggests that Autism may be caused by inserting a G-Alpha protein defect, the pertussis toxin found in D.P.T. vaccine, in to genetically at risk children. This toxin separates the G-Alpha protein from the retinoid receptors. Those most at risk report a family history of at least one parent with a pre-existing G-Alpha protein defect, including night blindness, pseudohypo-parthyroid--ism or adenoma of the thyroid or pituitary gland.	Megson, M.N. (2000) Is Autism G-Alpha Protein Defect Reversible with Natural Vitamin A? Defeat Autism Now Conference. The Town and Country Resort and Convention Center	Studies with mice have shown that anxiety is increased when the Orphanin Protein is missing in certain parts of the brain. This coupled with genetic inclination towards anxiety may be operative in some mice with this deficiency. There is some speculation that this might also be the case in autism. Natural Vitamin A may reconnect the retinoid receptors critical for vision, sensory perception, language processing and attention. More research needed.
Smoke and Air Pollution: Relationship to Learning and Behavioural problems	A neurobehavioral toxic effect was found in children who showed evidence of inhibition of pyrimidine-5'-nucleotidase by low hair phosphorus levels and low zinc levels in whom there was enhanced lead absorption. It is well documented that lead poisoning causes increased agitation; aggression and other inability to concentrate. These are behaviours seen in autism.References	Stewart-Pinkham, S.M. (1989)The Effect of Ambient Cadmium Air Pollution on the Hair Mineral Content of Children. Science Total Environment 78:289–96.	Although air pollution may exacerbate learning and behavioural difficulties in children this does not equate to a cause of autism. Many children with autism breath relatively clean air and have had little exposure to chronic air pollution. However, their difficulties are just as prominent.

APPENDIX D

Paintings by an autism
spectrum adult

These paintings have been chosen from part of an exhibition of works originally on display in London in 2003, courtesy of the National Autistic Society.

These show imagination at work in AS.

These four images are from a series of paintings by Peter Myers, 2003. Comment has been made concerning their likeness to some Aboriginal art.

They can be viewed at: www.autismandcomputing.org.uk

They are also sold as postcards in aid of the free magazine by and for people with Asperger syndrome, *Asperger United*, available through the National Autistic Society in London, UK.

APPENDIX E

Summary of communication 'obstacles'

This summary shows how AS individuals and typical individuals might respond to communication tools and which ones might be useful to AS individuals. This summary was devised for a lecture on the use of alternative communication given by Dr Dinah Murray at an Autreach retreat in the UK during the summer of 2008.

Potential issues	Speech	Writing	Symbols	Signs	Computers
Phonology	−1	+1	+1	+1	+1
Intonation	−1	+1	+1	+1	+1
Pragmatics	−1	0	0	0	0
Semantics	+1	+1	+1	+1	+1
Syntax	+1	+1	0	0	+1
Body language	−1	+1	+1	−1	+1
Emotion-in	−1	0	+1	+1	+1
Emotion-out	−1	0	+1	+1	+1
Time pressure to respond	−1	+1	+1	0	+1
Auditory overload	−1	+1	+1	+1	+1
Visual overload	−1	0	0	0	0
Synchronised turn taking	−1	+1	+1	0	+1
Willing discoursers-AS	0	0	0	0	0
Willing discoursers-NT	+1	+1	−1	−1	+1

Potential issues	Speech	Writing	Symbols	Signs	Computers
Rapid topic switching	−1	0	0	0	0
Total	−8	+9	+8	+4	+11

−1 = typically a problem
+1 = typically not a problem
 0 = possibly a problem

Subject Index

'accommodation' (Piaget) 127–8
action of secretin theories 210
amino acids 207
Aspartame exposure 210
Asperger's Autism
  classic autism 31–2, 154
  criteria 202–3
  gait studies 33
  high-functioning autism 31
  interest and attention 31
  joint attention 33
Asperger's Disorder 32, 146–8, 157
attention
  behaviours, distinctive 106
  brain configuration 107–10
  cell minicolumns, and over-arousal 108
  curiosity, and interest 106
  differences, new theory based on 12
  dividing 104, 117
  and EF 67, 70–1, 73, 75
  and emotion 113
  energy for 107
  and EPF 96, 97
  joint 33, 37, 69, 104, 169
  learning style 25, 109–10
  meaning of 106–7
  'ordered' 115
  and other conditions 107
  and SAACA 116
  and WCC 81–2, 85–6
  see also monotropism
attention and interest
  brain configuration 17, 42–3
  case studies 141, 143–5
  cognitive skills 120–3
  cognitive theories 26–7, 42–3
  deficit model, of autism 116
  difference, and normality 28
  and EF 69, 72, 73, 74
  and EPF 93, 94, 97

language, difficulty with 20
  measurement of 24, 25–6
  monotropism 21, 112–4
  obsessive/ritualistic needs 20
  and OCD 107
  psychological theories 24
  and SAACA 23–4, 100–1, 113–4
  'Self' and 'Other' 42, 69
  sensory discomfort 15, 20, 28
  sensory-perception loop 24–5, 104
  traditional theories, of AS 23–4
attention deficit with hyperactivity disorder (ADHD), and EF 70–1
Atypical Autism 203
Autism is (poem) 19
autism spectrum condition (ASC) 23, 27
autoimmune theories 208

behaviour
  'bizarre', and visual differences 36
  challenging 109, 174
  obsessive 20, 106, 113–4
  repetitive/stereotyped 202
block design test (BDT) 94
  HFA-P *versus* HFA-NPindividuals 95
  AS superiority 79, 92, 116
body language 129
brain configuration
  attention 17, 107–10
  attention and interest 17, 42–3
  brain imaging 26, 108
  cognitive style 29
  and EF 71, 73
  and EPF 94, 95
  learning style 17–8, 134, 150

monotropism 17
  and ToM 48, 62
  AS and typical 134

case studies, monotropic attention
  getting lost 141
  Jane and the toilet roll 140
  taking too long in the shower 143–5
  throwing stones 145–6
  Tracy goes to camp 146–8
  the washing 143
  Wendy and the builder 146
  written words, spoken words 141–3
change
  coping strategies 152–3, 160
  reactions to 135–6
  resistance to 72, 102–3, 113–4, 125, 155
  structure and strategy, balance of 166
  visual supports 150–1
childhood disintegrative disorder 202
closed concepts, thinking in
  change, fear of 125
  interest, harnessing 127
  local details, focusing on 127
  open concept thinking 127–8
cognition
  and EF 40
  and EPF 40
  meaning of 39–40
  and senses 40
  and ToM 40
  and WCC 40
cognitive skills
  language, literalism in 120
  monotropic development 120, 123

cognitive skills *cont.*
  neurotypical development
    120–1
  and SAACA 122
cognitive theories
  attention and interest 26–7,
    42–3
  challenges to 27, 38
  cognition 39–40
  complexity, of AS 24
  critique of dominant 12
  methodology, falsification
    as 26–7
  theory, consideration of 40–2
  see also enhanced perceptual
    functioning (EPF);
    executive functioning
    (EF); non-cognitive
    theories; theory of
    mind (ToM); weak
    central coherence
    (WCC)
communication
  'obstacles', summary of
    215–6
  qualitative impairment of
    201–2
  see also language; social
    interaction
comprehension, in AS
  'egocentricity' 149–50
  expectations, not fulfilled
    152–3
  harming, rules about 151
  learning style 150
  neurotypical lens 150–2
  'Other', understanding
    148–9
  ownership concepts 151–2
  problem-solving ideas 153–4
  social priorities 149–50
  visual supports 150–1, 153
compulsive desires 155–6
computers
  computerised tests 83–4, 86
  IT, value of 11–2, 161–2,
    169
  technology, access to 153
  typed words, benefits of 143
context and scale, and
  monotropism 123, 128–9
continuum in AS, evidence
  for 32
conversation 201
creativity *see* imagination;
  paintings, by AS adult;
  poetry

deficit model, of autism
  cognitive theories 27
  deficits, characterising autism
    as list of 11
  and EPF 92
  and SAACA 116–7
  and ToM 97
depression 117, 168
developmental stages, Piaget
  119, 127–8
diagnostic criteria, for autism
  spectrum disorder 30
  Asperger's Autism 32, 202–3
  behaviour, repetitive/
    stereotyped 202
  childhood disintegrative
    disorder 202
  communication, qualitative
    impairment of 201–2
  delays/abnormal functioning
    202
  PDD-NOS (Atypical Autism)
    203
  Rett's disorder 32, 202
  social interaction, qualitative
    impairment of 201
diff-ability, autism as spectrum
  of 17, 31
DSM-IV (Diagnostic and
  Statistical Manual of
  Mental Disorders IV) *see*
  diagnostic criteria, for
  autism spectrum disorder
dyslexia 75
dyspraxia 28

Ebbinghaus illusion task 92
echolalia 31
EF *see* executive functioning (EF)
enhanced perceptual
  functioning (EPF)
  attention, 'subliminal' 97
  attention and interest 93,
    94, 97
  brain configuration 94, 95
  cognition 40
  deficit model, of autism
    92, 97
  definition of 91
  domain-specific tasks 92–3
  focussed attention 96
  higher- and lower-order
    processes 94–5
  learning style 98
  limitations of 98
  local processing, superior 92,
    93, 96

  perception differences 94
  sensory dysphoria 93
  and ToM 97
  touch sensitivity 93
  visual/auditory
    modalities 92
  and WCC 95, 97
EPF *see* enhanced perceptual
  functioning (EPF)
equifinality 166
executive functioning (EF)
  in animals 66
  attention and interest 67, 69,
    72, 73, 74, 75
  belief and reasoning 71
  brain configuration 71, 73
  brain injury symptomo-
    logy 66
  change, resistance to 72
  child development 68
  cognition 40
  cognitive functions,
    regulation of 66, 67
  definition of 65
  impulsive behaviours 66
  as inadequate account 72, 73
  inhibitory control 67
  joint attention 69
  mental states, impaired 73
  neural networks 67–8, 70
  non-executive processes 67
  'noticing' 75
  and other populations
    69–71, 74–5
  planning ahead 67
  private/public separation 66
  as secondary deficit 73–4
  sensory dysphoria 72
  and ToM 71–5
  and WCC 78–9
  working memory 67
eye contact, difficulty with 106,
  110, 157, 159

Facebook 12
facial expressions, difficulty
  reading 109
false belief tests 45–6, 55–6, 57
free sulphate 206
friendship difficulties 156

gait studies 33
gamma interferon 206
gender, and AS
  cognitive profiles, of AS 34
  incidence, of AS 34

multi-tasking 22–3
skills variations 34
generalising, difficulty with
128–9, 136, 145, 161–2
genetic disorder, AS as 27
gluten and casein 205

harming, rules about 151
hobbies, and interest 113

imagination
Interest System, Model
of 197
paintings, by AS adult 213–4
play, symbolic/imaginative
202
and WCC 81
imitation 58
incidence, increased of
autism 31
individual variability, in AS 11,
29–38, 30–1, 32
information processing style
79–80, 84–5, 117–8
intellectual disability, as
characteristic of AS 31
interest
case study 141–2
and curiosity 106
harnessing 127, 130–1
interests of others, joining
114
and language 16–7, 142–3
meaning of 20–1, 42,
112–3, 197
obsessive behaviours 106
others as distraction from
114
preoccupation with 202
schemas (templates) 119,
171
as state of arousal 112, 113,
197, 199
typical *versus* AS 104
see also attention and interest
Interest System, Model of
computer graphic of 199
differential equations 26,
197–200
emotions 197, 199
interest, arousal of 197, 199
monotropic state 200
perception 197
intestinal permeability 210
IQ differences 86, 108, 119
IT, benefits of *see* computers

joint attention 33, 37, 69, 104,
169

Kanizsa triangle 83–4, 88

language
attention and interest 20
delays/abnormal functioning
202
idiosyncratic 31
and interest 16–7, 142–3
literalism 103, 120, 123–5,
146–8, 156
metaphorical language 134
reading 142
spoken language 143
stereotyped/idiosyncratic
202
word recognition difficulties
141–2
see also computers
learning style
action learning 25
autism as 23
brain configuration 17–8,
134, 150
case study 140
developmental delays 119
environmental interactions
165–6
inclusion 35
interest 169, 171–2
IT, value of 11–2, 161–2,
169
normality 168–9
reading, for meaning
119–20
SAACA as 169
schemas (templates) 119
school systems 35, 166–7
task completion 167–8
AS and typical 133
literalism
case study 146–8
language 103, 120, 123–5,
146–8, 156
monotropism 123–5
processing style 112
time, concept of 136–7, 146

memory
and EF 67
factual information 139
long- and short-term 130
methylation 207

monotropism
attention and interest 20–3,
21, 104–5, 105f,
112–4, 164
autistic disposition 23
change, difficulty
encountering 102–3
closed concepts, thinking in
123, 125–8
cognitive skills, complex
120–3
context and scale 123,
128–9
generalising, difficulty with
128–9, 136, 145,
161–2
learning style 119–20
multi-tasking 21, 22–3
non-social priorities 131–2
'Other', understanding of
148–9
processing style 117–9
and sensory system 110–2
single-mindedness 101
social interaction 104
timing and sequencing 123,
129–31
triad of impairments 116–7
tunnel vision 101
see also attention and interest;
literalism
moral judgements 58–9
Müller-Lyer illusion 82, 88
multi-tasking 21, 22–3, 135

neurological disposition, AS
as 24
non-cognitive theories, of
autism 203
action of secretin theories
210
Aspartame exposure 210
autism and amino acids 207
autoimmune theories 208
free sulphate 206
gamma interferon 206
gluten and casein 205
intestinal permeability 210
methylation 207
opioid excess 205
orphanin protein: orphanin
FQ/nociceptin
(OFQ/N) 203
oxytocin and vasopressin
206
prenatal Aspartame exposure
210

non-cognitive theories, of
    autism *cont.*
  smoke and air pollution 211
  stress and immunity 207
  vaccination theory 209
  viral encephalitis 209
  viral infection theory 208
  Vitamin A deficiency, and
    autism 211
normality
  definition of 169–71
  and difference 28
  and disability 171
  learning style 168–9

obsessive behaviours 20, 106,
    113–4
obsessive compulsive disorder
    (OCD) 107
opioid excess 205
organising self 31, 134
orphanin protein: orphanin FQ/
    nociceptin (OFQ/N) 203
'Other' *see* 'Self' and 'Other',
    understanding
ownership concepts 151–2
oxytocin and vasopressin 206

paintings, by AS adult 213–4
parenting, neurotypical 162–3
PDD-NOS (Pervasive
    Developmental Disorder -
    Not Otherwise Specified)
    203
PDD (Pervasive Developmental
    Disorder) 24
perception
  case study 139–48
  emotion and belief,
    involvement of 137–8
  memory, and factual
    information 139
  mono *versus* stereo sense 138
  visual perception tasks 116
  see also enhanced perceptual
    functioning
Pervasive Developmental
    Disorder - Not Otherwise
    Specified (PDD-NOS)
    203
Pervasive Developmental
    Disorder (PDD) 24
planning, difficulty with 67,
    134, 140
  see also timing and
    sequencing

play
  pretend 56–7
  symbolic/imaginative 202
poems
  Autism is 19
  Inclusion 35
  My big picture 78
  Transition 29–30
poetry 18, 19, 60–1
pollution 211
polytropism
  parenting, neurotypical 163
  see also monotropism
prenatal Aspartame exposure
    210

research, need for further 165
Rett's Disorder 32, 202
routine, need for 81, 135–6,
    137
  see also change

SAACA (Single Attention and
    Associated Cognition in
    Autism)
  attention and interest 23–4,
    100–1
  attributes, enhanced 100
  autism, diagnostic categories
    23–4
  case study 155–62
  cognitive components of
    123–32
  cognitive skills 122
  definitions 101
  empathetic responses 100
  everyday experiences, for AS
    individuals 134–7
  limitations of 174
  parenting, neurotypical
    162–3
  perceptions 137–48
  problem-solving ideas 153–4
  research ideas 172–3
  sensory-motor loop 100–1
  visual abilities, superior 100
  see also monotropism
schemas (templates) 119, 171
school systems 35, 166–7
'Self' and 'Other',
    understanding
  attention and interest 42, 69
  comprehension, in AS 148–9
  monotropism 148–9
  SAACA 164
  ToM 44, 48–9, 53–4, 59,
    64–4

sensory-perception loop 24–5,
    37–8, 104, 117
sensory system, and AS
  concentration 112
  and DSM criteria 36
  hyper- and hyposensitivity
    36
  joining interests of others
    112
  processing style, literal 112
  sensory dysphoria 37, 110
  sensory overload 38, 111
  sensory preferences 36
  'skin crawling' sensations 36
  social relationships 111
  sound, as pain 36
  tactile defensiveness 36–7
sexuality, and gender 22–3
short-term memory 130
sickness, autism as 27
Single Attention and Associated
    Cognition in Autism *see*
    SAACA
social interaction
  emotional reciprocity 201
  'monotropic' forms of 12
  nonverbal behaviours 201
  peer relationships 201
  and prefrontal cortex 108
  as problematic 20
  sharing 201
  social impairment 31
social model, of disability 41–2
social priorities 149–50
stress and immunity 207
structures, need for 145

technology *see* computers
tests, computerised 83–4, 86
'The Sally-Ann task' 55–6
theory of mind (mechanism)
    module (ToMM) 44,
    46–7
theory of mind (ToM)
  areas of mind 45
  behaviours as innate 57–8
  bigger picture, failure to
    connect with 56
  brain configuration 48, 62
  cognition 40
  definition of 44–5
  development of 50–2
  and EF 71–5
  and EPF 97
  false belief tests 45–6, 55–6,
    57
  genetic factors 48

imagination 45, 50–1, 59–61, 62
as insufficient explanation, for AS 57–8, 61
interest system 59
lack of, in autism 45
'mentalising' 45
'mind reading' 45, 49, 54–5
modular *versus* non-modular theorists 62
moral judgements 58–9
and other populations 48–50
pretend play 50, 56–7
rigid development view of 51–2
'Self' and 'Other' concept 44, 48–9, 53–4, 59, 64–4
social interaction 45, 46
'theory theory' *versus* simulation theory 62–3
ToM tests, passing of by AS individuals 50
triad of impairments 59
time, concept of 136–7, 146
timing and sequencing 123
interest, harnessing 130–1
predicting outcomes, difficulty with 131
social awkwardness 129
ToM *see* theory of mind (ToM)
Tom's story: case study
behavioural difficulties 155, 158, 160
change, strategies for 155, 160
communicative difficulties 158
compulsive desires 155–6
AS diagnosis 155, 156–7
eye contact, poor 157, 159
family background 155
friendship difficulties 156
interventions, appropriate 160–1
IT, visuals and structure, using 161–2
language, literal use of 156
learning style 157
routines and rituals 155
self-concept, teaching 160
single attention 157
social/emotional 158–9
spatial neglect-like problem 160
strengths 157–8

Torrance Test 60
traditional theories, of AS 16, 23–4
Transition (poem) 29–30
triad of impairments
attention, dividing 117
cognitive theories 27
deficit model, of autism 116–7
developmental disorder, AS as 40
as diagnostic criteria 24
multi-tasking, and expectations of others 117
sensory-perception loop 117
social exhaustion 117
and WCC 77

vaccination theory 209
viral encephalitis 209
viral infection theory 208
visual supports
nonverbal individuals, visual supports for 153
timetable changes 150–1
Vitamin A deficiency, and autism 211

weak central coherence (WCC)
alternative explanation to 86, 87–8
and attention 81–2, 85–6
big picture, failure to see 78–9, 80–1, 84–5
block design test (BDT) 79, 92
brain insult, evolutionary outcome of 81
cognitive development 40, 82, 86–7
'cognitive development stream' theories 82
definition of 77
and EF 78–9
and EPF 95, 97
gestalt, difficulties with 77, 82
global processing 86, 88–90
imagination and creativity 81
information processing 79–80, 84–5
Kanizsa triangle study 83–4, 88
'mind-blindness' 81
multi-tasking 87

neurotypical and AS populations, application in 83–90
triad of impairments 77
visual illusions 88, 89
Wechsler Intelligence Scales 79
Wisconsin Card Sorting task 70

Author Index

Apperly, I.A. 66
Attwood, T. 34, 35, 101, 106, 117, 129, 135, 139, 152, 154
Aziz-zadeh, L. 95

Bacon, A. 58
Baddeley, A.D. 56
Baggs, A. 72, 119, 129, 130, 143
Bailey, A. 27
Bailey, P.J. 135
Baird, J.A. 58
Baron-Cohen, S. 26, 29, 30, 34, 40, 45, 46, 49, 50, 51–2, 51f, 55, 58, 60, 61, 62, 89, 100, 101, 105, 109, 134, 149
Bartak, L. 157
Baumeister, R.F. 66, 67
Begley, S. 107
Behrmann, M. 60
Belmonte, M. 26
Berg, E.A. 69
Bertone, A. 80
Bitsika, V. 103, 115, 167
Björne, P. 27, 30, 48, 54, 57, 58, 61, 69, 165–6, 173
Blackman, L. 32, 109
Blair, C. 68, 69
Blair, R.J. 53, 58, 59, 73
Blakemore, S.J. 86, 87
Bloom, B. 56, 61
Bogdashina, O. 102, 115, 152, 156
Bonnel, A. 94, 95
Bowler, D.M. 50, 58, 59, 61, 173
Bransford, J.D. 62
Brereton, A.V. 31, 156
Briskman, J. 77
Brosnan, M.J. 29
Brown, T. 68

Bryson, S.E. 105, 160
Bull, R. 71
Burack, J.A. 106, 116
Burgess, P. 66
Burgess, P.W. 66
Butera, G. 161

Caron, M.J. 95, 96
Carpenter, C. 33
Carter, A.S. 22
Casanova, M.F. 62, 95, 108, 130, 152
Cascio, C. 93, 94
Castelli, F. 54
Cesaroni, L. 129, 160
Chakrabarti, S. 31
Chamak, B. 36
Chandler-Olcott, K. 25, 41, 102, 103, 129, 148, 153
Charman, T. 49, 89
Charwaka, K. 98
Chiavarino, C.G.W. 66
Choudhury, S. 86, 87
Clark, L. 41–2
Cliff, S. 57
Coleman, M. 30, 50
Conway, C. 71
Cordess, C. 157
Craig, J. 60
Curran, J. 31, 168

Dahlgren, S.O. 49
Dakin, S. 78, 84
Dalton, K.M. 105, 110
Dawson, M. 25, 49, 74, 98, 100
Decety, J. 66
Deesing, M. 66
DeMello, L. 57
Dern, S. 72, 84, 85, 112
Dewey, J. 25
Diehl, S. 59
Dissanayake, C. 156

Doherty, M. 46
Donaldson, M. 119
Donovan, S. 62
Duncan, J. 67
Dworzynski, K. 30
Dziobek, I. 58

Einfeld, S.E. 31
Eisenmajor, R. 20
Emerson, A. 119

Findlay, J.M. 85, 86
Fireman, B. 107
Flavell, J.H. 87
Fletcher-Watson, S. 85–6
Fodor, J. 62
Foxx, R.M. 160
Frith, C.D. 45, 54
Frith, U. 26, 29, 45, 54, 58, 73, 77, 78, 79, 80–1, 84, 96, 156
Frombonne, E. 31
Frymiare, J.L. 34, 64, 165

Gallese, V. 62
Garber, M. 129, 160
Gardner, N. 37, 53, 54, 64, 85, 106, 142
Garner, I. 83–4, 86, 88
Gazzola, V. 95
Georgieva, S.S. 138
Gerland, G. 32, 53, 149
German, T.P. 56, 61
Gernsbacher, M.A. 33, 34, 64, 85, 98, 112, 143, 148, 149, 165
Gerrans, P. 48, 73
Geurts, H.M. 69
Gillberg, C. 29, 30, 50
Goldman, A. 62
Goldstein, G. 58
Goldstein, S. 49, 75, 107

Gomot, M. 26
Goodale, M.A. 60
Gottlieb 166
Grandin, T. 32, 34, 37, 53, 58,
    63, 66, 72, 110, 113
Grant, A.D. 69
Grayson, A. 119
Green, S. 87
Greenaway, R. 102
Greenberg, M. 68
Griffin, R. 87
Griffith, E.M. 74–5
Griffiths, A. 119
Groisser, D.B. 73
Grossman, J.B. 148

Hadjikhani, N. 108
Hadwin, J. 109
Hale, C.M. 58
Hamilton, D. 83–4, 86, 88
Hanafi, S.R. 86
Hancock, D.R. 86
Hancock, P.J.B. 78, 85
Happé, F. 24, 29, 40, 45, 49,
    54, 56, 61, 73, 75, 77,
    80–1, 81, 82–3, 84, 88,
    92, 96, 106, 119, 156
Harchik, A.E. 161, 162
Haywood, H.C. 161
Heaton, P. 97
Heavey, L. 54
Hermelin, B. 37, 54, 92
Herrera, G. 117, 153, 162
Hesmondhalgh, M. 56
Hietanen, J.K. 105
Hill, E.L. 40, 62, 65, 69, 70,
    73, 86
Hjelmquist, E. 49
Hobson, J.A. 60, 74, 87, 108
Hobson, R.P. 49, 62, 118
Holland, A. 33
Holliday Willey, L. 32, 74–5,
    75, 117, 129
Holmes, D. 157
Howlin, P. 49, 109, 160
Hoy, R. 53, 54, 68, 72, 103,
    109, 129
Hughes, C. 46, 93
Humphreys, G.W. 66
Humphreys, K. 60

Jackson, L. 32, 53, 54, 68, 72,
    132, 149
Johnson, C. 75, 107
Joliffe, T. 46, 100, 149
Jordan, R. 11–3
Jordan, R.R. 23, 27, 142, 150,

160, 161
Joseph, R.M. 71–2, 105
Just, M. 108

Kaland, N. 57
Kampe, K. 54
Kana, R. 130
Kanner, L. 20, 23, 31, 32, 77
Kassim, M.A. 86
Keay-Bright, W. 84
Kennett, J. 53, 58–9, 63
Kern, J.K. 20
Keysers, C. 95
Kirk, I. 73, 108, 117
Klin, A. 39, 98, 105
Klosko, J.S. 119
Kluth, P. 25, 41, 102, 103,
    114, 129, 148, 153
Koshino, H. 95, 130
Kourkoulou, A. 85, 86
Kuhl, P.K. 142
Kylliainen, A. 105

La Malfa, G. 31
Lacohee, H. 46
Lamm, C. 66
Lathe, R. 110, 156
Lawson, W. 16, 20, 32, 34, 53,
    54, 61, 64, 87, 100, 103,
    109, 112, 129, 139, 140,
    149, 156, 169, 173
Leekam, S. 46
Leekam, S.R. 85, 86, 105
Leslie, A.M. 26, 45, 46, 56, 62,
    73, 89, 109–10
Lesser, M. 16, 20, 54
Lesser, M.J. 26, 59, 106, 197
Lyons, G.L. 103, 169

Mann, T.A. 104
Marshall, K. 25
Mawhood, L. 49
McAlister, A. 53
Mehl-Madrona, L. 204
Ménard, E. 92
Mesibov, G. 31
Milne, E. 89
Milner, A.D. 60
Mineau, S. 98
Minshew, N.J. 30, 54, 57–8,
    58, 60, 68, 73, 74, 75,
    87, 105, 107, 108, 149
Mitchell, P. 46, 89
Miyake, A. 65
Moore, D.S. 57
Moreton, J. 73
Mortensen, E.L. 57

Mottron, L. 25, 40, 73, 90, 91,
    92, 93, 94, 95, 96, 98
Muggleton, J. 27, 171
Muller, U. 66
Murray, D.K.C. 16, 17, 20, 26,
    54, 59, 60, 75, 81, 87,
    102–3, 104, 106, 107,
    112, 118, 166, 197, 215
Myers, P. 214
Myin, E. 152

Newson, E. 69

O'Connor, K. 73, 108, 117
O'Connor, N. 37
O'Regan, J. 152
Orapeleng, S. 103
Ozonoff, S. 65, 86

Pammar, K. 75
Pennington, B.F. 33, 73
Perner, J. 44, 56
Pertz, I. 92
Peterson, C.C. 49, 53
Peterson, J.C. 49
Phillips, L.H. 71
Piaget, J. 119, 127
Plaisted, K. 102
Plaisted, K.C. 89, 94, 96, 100
Powell, S.D. 160, 161
Premack, D. 44
Prince-Hughes, D. 20
Pring, L. 54, 87
Prior, M. 20
Purkis, J. 53, 54, 56, 75

Reed, S.K. 120
Rees, L. 96
Riby, D.M. 78, 85
Rinehart, N.J. 33
Ring, H. 29, 105
Robins, B. 69
Robinson, E.J. 46
Rogers, S. 33
Ronald, A. 24, 75, 81, 96
Ropar, D. 89
Roth, D. 56
Roth, I. 61
Royall, D.R. 67
Russell, J. 40, 93
Rutherford, M.D. 62
Rutter, M. 49

Sainsbury, C. 103, 109
Sally, D. 62
Sandberg, A.D. 49

Sanders, J. 95
Scariano, M. 32
Schopler, E. 31
Schuster, N. 84, 112
Schwartz, J.M. 107
Schweback, A.J. 49
Scott, F. 89
Scott, L. 111–2
Shah, A. 72, 79
Shallice, T. 66, 70
Sharpley, C. 103
Shattock, P. 27
Shea, V. 31
Shore, S. 32, 53
Silberman, S. 60
Simons, J.S. 66
Sinclair, J. 19, 58
Smith, L. 57
Snowling, M.J. 135
Sparks, N. 113
Stagnitti, K. 50, 51f, 56, 57
Stone, H. 107
Stone, V.E. 48, 73
Sullivan, A. 75, 167–8
Sullivan, K. 148, 167
Swettenham, J. 49, 87, 96, 105

Tager-Flusberg, H. 50, 58,
    71–2, 105
Talay-Ongan, A. 37
Tantem, D. 157
Thomas, C.P. 60
Tonge, B.J. 31, 156
Trillingsgaard, A. 49

Van Lang, N.D.J. 79, 86
Vidyasagar, T.R. 75
Vignemont, F. 58
Vismara, L.A. 103, 169
Vogeley, K. 44, 46, 48, 55
Vohs, K.D. 66, 67
Volkmar, F. 98

Wainwright-Sharp, J.A. 160
Walker, P. 104
Webb, J. 49
Webb, S.J. 78
Wechsler, D. 79
Welsh, M.C. 73
Wheelwright, S. 46
Wicker, B. 108
Willcutt, E.G. 70
Williams, D. 32, 72, 107, 113,
    115, 166
Williams, D.L. 30, 54, 57–8,
    58, 60, 68, 73, 74, 87,
    107, 108

Wilson, B.A. 56
Wiltshire, S. 54–5
Wimmer, H. 44
Wing, L. 72, 160
Wood, K. 37
Woodruff, G. 44
Wozniak, R.H. 92

Yerys, B.E. 73
Young, J.E. 119

Zelazo, P.D. 66, 68